Supply Chain Management:

Concepts, Techniques and Practices

Enhancing Value Through Collaboration

Supply Chain Management:

Concepts, Techniques and Practices

Enhancing Value Through Collaboration

Ling Li

Old Dominion University, USA

 **World Scientific**

NEW JERSEY · LONDON · SINGAPORE · BEIJING · SHANGHAI · HONG KONG · TAIPEI · CHENNAI

Published by

World Scientific Publishing Co. Pte. Ltd.

5 Toh Tuck Link, Singapore 596224

USA office: 27 Warren Street, Suite 401-402, Hackensack, NJ 07601

UK office: 57 Shelton Street, Covent Garden, London WC2H 9HE

British Library Cataloguing-in-Publication Data
A catalogue record for this book is available from the British Library.

SUPPLY CHAIN MANAGEMENT: CONCEPTS, TECHNIQUES AND PRACTICES
Enhancing Value through Collaboration

ISBN-13 978-981-270-072-8
ISBN-10 981-270-072-2

Printed in Singapore by World Scientific Printers (S) Pte Ltd

Dedicated to the memory of my mother

Preface

This book is written for both academicians and practitioners who are interested in supply chain management in an e-business environment. It can also be used as a textbook for seniors and MBA students or for those preparing for APICS examinations. An earlier version of this book was a course pack on e-Supply chain management that I developed for MBA, EMBA, and senior undergraduate students. The course was enormously well received and led to the creation of this book.

Over the last six decades, the discipline of supply chain management has progressed from inventory, warehouse and transportation management issues to matters of strategic discussion both in the boardrooms of global enterprises as well as the offices of mid and small sized firms. In the information age, the traditional economic models bounded by regions and countries have evolved to a more globally oriented economy. The new environment enables global collaboration in creating a supply network for conducting world-wide supply chain operations. Supply chain and material management are the arteries of a nation's economy. They determine the metrics used in evaluating the level of modernization and economic power of a nation.

The driver of the modern supply chain management is information technology and the essence of the modern supply chain management is inter-organizational collaboration. In 1970 the cost of one megahertz of computing power was $7,600. By the end of the 20th century, it was 17 cents. The cost of storing one megabit of data in 1970 was $5,256. In more recent times the cost of storing one megabit is less than 17 cents[1]. Since the 1960s, technology has allowed business to create tools to ease the management of materials.

The book focuses on how to build a competitive supply chain using viable management strategies, operational models, decision making techniques, and information technology. The scope of the book is to have a core presentation on supply chain management and to include the support of new initiatives such as e-commerce, collaborative planning, forecasting, and replenishment (CPFR), datamining, knowledge management, and business intelligence. In addition, the text promotes cross-functional decisions. It fosters decision making capability and problem solving skills. By examining the cutting-edge supply chain management issues, this text captures the current trends; a list of which is presented here.

- **Broad global perspective** – the book features increased treatment of globalization and related operational issues, such as managing demand, transforming demand, transportation and logistics.
- **Expanded coverage of collaborative supply chain practices** – the book presents an expanded treatment of collaborative planning, forecasting, and replenishment in supply chain.
- **Integrative technology framework** – the book offers an integrated framework for discussing current information, technology applications across the supply chain and expanded treatment of technology within specific operations and logistics operational areas.
- **Balanced approach** – the book takes a balanced approach to illustrate both successes and failures in supply chain management cases and examples.
- **Case-based industry practice analysis** – the book provides real world cases to demonstrate various supply chain management strategies and tactics.

---

[1] Federal Reserve Bank of Dallas, (1999). "The new paradigm," 1999 Annual Report. http://www.dallasfed.org/fed/annual/1999p/ar99.pdf.

- **Spreadsheet-based quantitative problem solving methods** – the book provides solution methods to quantitative problems. Actual Excel screens are used to illustrate the use of the methods to make it easier to replicate the examples and problems, following the illustrated Excel commands.

Specifically, the book introduces supply chain design and operations. It profiles industry leaders such as the retail giant, Wal-Mart and their everyday low price strategy; the electronic innovator, Dell Inc. and its direct sell model and the apparel pioneer, The Limited, with their multiple brand strategy. The book focuses on the relationship of supply chain management to strategic thinking. Choosing a suitable strategy is a critical factor in the success of supply chain management. For example, with the right design of supply chain, Wal-Mart evolves from a local retailer to a global enterprise. K-Mart, on the other hand, lacks the right supply chain direction and filed bankruptcy protection to the US federal government in 2001.

The book has twelve chapters. Chapter 1 illustrates supply chain management theories, practices and trends. Chapter 2 provides an analysis on successful supply chain models, as well as some failed examples. Chapters 3 to 9 discuss the components of supply chain management and different decision-making methods. Chapters 10 and 11 present the impact of e-commerce and information technology on supply chain management. Chapter 12 introduces supply chain performance metrics and discusses how to achieve sustainable growth and development.

Many important issues remain to be studied in supply chain management. First, supply chain integration is a major challenge, because integration requires cohesive decision-making across the supply chain. Secondly, the supply chain is a dynamic system with its own life cycle, and supply chain relationships evolve constantly. Third, integrating data, information and knowledge in a supply chain is a practical problem. Tacit knowledge embedded in an enterprise is difficult to express and communicate. Therefore, sharing tacit knowledge in a virtual organization is an outstanding problem, which needs to be tackled.

By reading this book, readers can better understand supply chain and supply chain management, and can use the theory and methods presented in the book to solve supply chain management practical problems.

Ling Li, PhD, CFPIM
Old Dominion University
USA

Acknowledgements

It is my pleasure to acknowledge all those who have supported me and contributed to the success of the first edition of this manuscript.

I am grateful to my colleagues at Old Dominion University. Dr. Nancy Bagranoff, the Dean of College of Business and Public Administration and Dr. Li Xu are the first few to encourage me to convert a course pack to a book. I am also grateful to many colleagues and friends from whom I have learned some of the latest developments in supply chain management. In this regards, I want to thank Dr. Darryl Wilson and Dr. David Cook.

I thank Norfolk Southern Corporation for providing me with a supply chain management research grant, which enabled me to focus on this research project.

I thank Ms. Ann Moriarty for her careful editing and proofreading of this manuscript. Her excellent work has made this book a better presentation and easier to read. I also want to thank Ms. Diana McGraw for helping me prepare the indices.

My father paced me during the progress of writing this book. He deeply believes that publishing a book sets a milestone for a professor. He is very pleased to see that I have completed this project.

My husband and my son are the strongest supporters of my academic journey. My husband and I traveled together all the way along this journey. My son, being a superb student at school, filled me with joy and energy to concentrate on my writing.

Contents

PART TWO: PURCHASING, SUPPLY NETWORK, STRATEGIC SOURCING

PART FIVE: e-BUSINESS SOLUTIONS

PART SIX: SUPPLY CHAIN PERFORMANCE AND EVALUATION

Contents

PART ONE

Concepts and Strategic Issues

Chapter 1
Supply Chain Management: An Evolutionary View

Chapter 2
The Right Design of Supply Chain: Examples

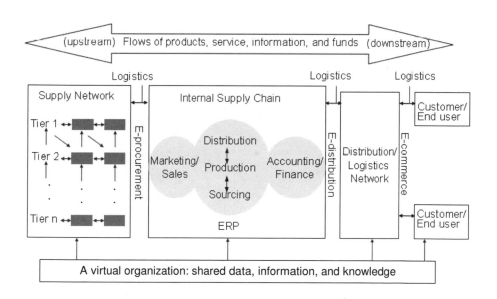

Chapter 1

Supply Chain Management:
An Evolutionary View

1.1 Overview of Supply Chain Management

A *Supply Chain* encompasses all activities in fulfilling customer demands and requests as shown in Figure 1.1. These activities are associated with the flow and transformation of goods from the raw materials stage, through to the end user, as well as the associated information and funds flows. There are four stages in a supply chain: the supply network, the internal supply chain (which are manufacturing plants), distribution systems, and the end users. Moving up and down the stages are the four flows: material flow, service flow, information flow and funds flow. E-procurement links the supply network and manufacturing plant, e-distribution links the manufacturing plant and the distribution network, and e-commerce links the distribution network and the end users.

The supply chain begins with a *need* for a computer. In this example, a customer places an order for a Dell computer through the Internet. Since Dell does not have distribution centers or distributors, this order triggers the production at Dell's manufacturing center, which is the next stage in the supply chain. Microprocessors used in the computer may come from AMD and a complementary product like a monitor may come from Sony. Dell receives such parts and components from these suppliers, who belong to the up-stream stage in the supply chain. After completing the order according to the customer's specification, Dell then sends the computer directly to the users through UPS, a third party logistics provider. This responsive supply chain is illustrated in

Figure 1.1. In this supply chain, Dell Computer is the captain of the chain; the company selects suppliers, forges partnerships with other members of the supply chain, fulfills orders from customers and follows up the business transaction with services.

Now, consider a case of purchasing a pack of Perdue chicken breast at Sam's Club. When customers buy trays of chicken breast at Sam's Club, the demand is satisfied from inventory that is stocked in a Sam's Club distribution center. Production at a Perdue Farms manufacturing facility is based on forecasted demand using historical sales data. Perdue Farms runs a vertical supply chain starting from the eggs, to the grains that feed chicks proceeding to manufacturing, packaging, and delivery. Packaging materials come from suppliers. This is an efficient supply chain and is illustrated in Figure 1.1.

These two different types of supply chain, responsive supply chain and efficient supply chain, will be discussed in detail in Section 1.4.

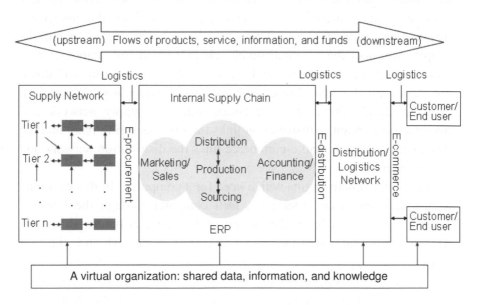

Figure 1.1. Supply chain in e-business environment

Supply Chain Management is a set of synchronized decisions and activities utilized to efficiently integrate suppliers, manufacturers, warehouses, transporters, retailers, and customers so that the right product or service is distributed at the right quantities, to the right locations, and at the right time, in order to minimize system-wide costs while satisfying customer service level requirements. The objective of Supply Chain Management (SCM) is to achieve sustainable competitive advantage.

A company's supply chain in an e-Biz environment can be very complicated. Figure 1.1 illustrates a simplified supply chain because many companies have hundreds and thousands of supplies and customers. The supply chain in Figure 1.1 includes internal supply chain functions, an upstream supplier network, and a downstream distribution network. Logistic function facilitates the physical flow of material from the raw material producer to the manufacturer, to the distributor, and finally, to the end user.

The ***internal supply chain*** of the focal manufacturing company in the middle of Figure 1.1 includes sourcing, production, and distribution. **Sourcing** or purchasing of the company is responsible for selecting suppliers, negotiating contracts, formulating purchasing process, and processing order. **Production** is responsible for transforming raw materials, parts or components to a product. **Distribution** is responsible for managing the flow of material and finished goods inventory from the manufacturer to customer. Enterprise Resource Planning systems (ERP) integrate the entire company's information system, process and store data, cut across functional areas, business units, and product lines to assist managers make business decisions. As an IT infrastructure, ERP influences the way companies manage their daily operations and facilitates the flow of information among all supply chain processes of a firm.

The ***supplier network*** on the left-hand side of Figure 1.1 consists of all organizations that provide materials or services, either directly or indirectly. For example, a computer manufacturer's supplier network includes all the firms that provide items ranging from such raw materials as plastics, computer chips, to subassemblies like hard drives and motherboards. A supplier of motherboard, for example, may have its own set of suppliers (*second-tier suppliers*) that provide inputs that are also part of the supply chain.

The ***distribution network*** on the right-hand side of Figure 1.1 is responsible for the actual movement of materials between locations. Distribution management involves the management of packaging, storing, and handling of materials at receiving docks, warehouses, and retail outlets. A major part of distribution management is transportation management, which includes the selection, and management of external carriers or internal private fleets of carriers.

E-commerce uses advanced technology to assist business transactions in a web-based environment and facilitates the transaction of information flow and fund flow. E-commerce involves business-to-business transaction (B2B) such as Covisint, business-to-customer transaction such as Amazon.com (B2C), customer-to-business transaction (C2B) such as priceline.com, and customer-to-customer transaction (C2C) such as e-Bay auction. E-commerce is conducted via a variety of electronic media. These electronic media include electronic data interchange (EDI), electronic funds transfer (EFT), bar codes, fax, automated voice mail, CD-ROM catalogs and a variety of others.

E-distribution instructs where to locate the sources of supply and advises how to access them, as well as how to move the materials to the retailers via the Internet or a web-based environment.

E-procurement is a part of E-commerce. E-procurement completely revolutionizes a manufacturing or distribution firm's supply chain, making a seamless flow of order fulfillment information from manufacturer to supplier.

Now we have characterized the nature of supply chain management, we are ready to make a few relevant points:

1. The role of supply chain management is to produce products that conform to customer requirements.
2. The objective of supply chain management is to be efficient and cost-effective through collaborative efforts across the entire system.
3. The scope of supply chain management encompasses the firm's activities from the strategic level through the tactical and operational levels since it takes into account the efficient

integration of suppliers, manufacturers, wholesalers, retailers, and end users.

1.2 Supply Chain Management in an E-Biz Environment: Virtual Integration

Virtual integration is to use technology and information to blur the traditional boundaries among suppliers, manufacturers, distributors, and end users in a supply chain. Today, the virtual corporation of various firms in a supply chain is a reality with suppliers and customer trading over the Internet in real-time to create maximum value. Virtual integration offers the advantage of tightly coordinated supply chain that has traditionally come through vertical integration. In the age of virtual organizations, managers, engineers, professional staff, and technical workers are no longer the lone custodians of the corporate knowledge base. Knowledge is shared across cultural-boundaries, time-boundaries, and space-boundaries to create strategic frontiers in global and virtual enterprises.

A seamless virtual integration of firms within a supply chain requires real-time automation of inter-organization business processes that span across trading partners. In the last decade, organizations involved in a supply chain use e-mail, faxes, and voice mail. These practices introduce delays and often require data to be re-entered multiple times. In 1997, American companies spent $862 billion, or approximately 10 percent of GNP, on supply related activities. This includes the movement of materials, storage, and control of products across the supply chain. During the late 90s of last century, productivity surged from 1.5% in earlier years to 2.5%[1]. The increase in productivity in the late 90s is a direct result of computer technology.

The traditional arm's length transaction from one stage of supply chain to the next is illustrated in Figure 1.2 (a). Organizations view their suppliers and customers as adversaries who are not to be trusted. This

---

[1] Butler, S. (2000). "The economy downshifts; the Fed tries to do what's never been done before: engineer a soft landing." U.S News and World Report, June 19, 2000.

prevents entry into successful long-term relationships. Performance is often narrowly viewed and procurement decisions are often based solely on price. Relationships are viewed in terms of a zero-sum game where there is a clear winner and a clear loser.

(a) Supply chain model: a value chain with arm's length transactions from one layer to the next

```
Supply Network ◄──► Manufacturer ◄──► Distribution Network ◄──► Customer/End user
```

(b) Dell's direct supply chain model: forge partnership with suppliers and eliminate third-party distribution

```
Supply Network ◄──► Manufacturer ◄──► Customer/End user
```

(c) Virtual integration: works faster by blurring the traditional boundaries and roles in the value chain

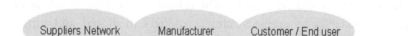

```
Suppliers Network        Manufacturer        Customer / End user
```

Figure 1.2. Supply chain in e-Biz environment

The integrated supply chain model that Dell Inc. creates is illustrated in Figure 1.2 (b). This model focuses on mutual trust and respect of supply chain members, just-in-time manufacturing, and eliminating third-party retailers. With this integrated supply chain, Dell only holds five days of inventory, and has a build cycle of two days on most systems. The integrated supply chain includes joint improvement projects, training seminars, workshops, and meetings between organizations' top management. As the degree of communication increases between customers and suppliers, higher levels of informal information sharing are witnessed.

A step ahead of integrated supply chain is virtual integration, which blurs the walls of supply chain organizations as illustrated in Figure 1.2 (c). The trend of mass-customization forces many companies to focus on their core competences, and outsource a wide range of functions including design, manufacturing, and distribution. This trend drives the need for a virtually integrated supply chain.

1.3 An Evolution: From Material Management to Supply Chain Management

Information technology is the key driving force for moving material management to supply chain management in the second half of the 20th century. In 1970, the cost of one megahertz of computing power was $7,600. By the end of the century, it was 17 cents. The cost of storing one megabit of data was $5,256 in 1970. It is less than 17 cents now[2]. Ever since the 1960s, technology has enabled business to create tools to ease the management of materials. The stages of the business model evolution are illustrated in Figure 1.3, with Bill of Materials (BOM) processor in the early 60s, Material Requirement Planning (MRP) in the 70s, Manufacturing Resource Planning (MRPII) in the 80s, Enterprise Resource Planning (ERP) in the 90s, and supply chain management (SCM) packages in the early twenty-first century. The impact in the evolution of advanced technology and computer power on materials and supply chain management is phenomenal.

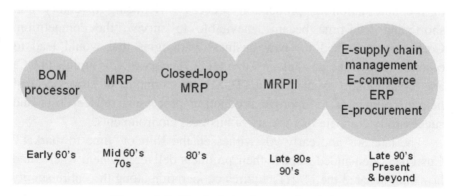

Figure 1.3. Evolution of e-supply chain

---

[2] Federal Reserve Bank of Dallas, (1999). "The new paradigm," 1999 Annual Report. http://www.dallasfed.org/fed/annual/1999p/ar99.pdf.

In the early 1960s, a BOM processor was written on a 1400 disk computer in Milwaukee. In mid 1960, the first use of the computer for planning material was introduced and was named MRP. IBM was the first to introduce MRP software to the market. The significance of MRP is that it identifies what product is required by the customer; compares the requirement to the on-hand inventory level and calculates what items need to be procured and when.

By itself, MRP does not recognize the capacity limitation. It will schedule order release even when the capacity is not available. Closed loop MRP was then introduced to include capacity requirement planning as a part of material requirement planning. Advancement of computer capacity makes the extra mathematical computations for capacity planning available and affordable.

In the Mid 80's, Manufacturing Resource Planning (MRPII) evolved out of MRP and closed loop MRP. MRPII is a method for the effective planning of all resources of a manufacturing company. MRPII closed the loop not only with the capacity planning and accounting systems but also with the financial management systems. Consequently, all the resource of a manufacturing company could be planned and controlled as the information became more accessible using MRPII.

In the 1980s, labor cost decreased and material cost increased due to the automation of production process. Reducing inventory and shortening lead-time became inevitable to survive the competition. Companies searched for new business paradigms that would lead to competitive advantage. Just in Time (JIT), Theory of Constraints (TOC) and Total Quality Management (TQM) are examples of strategies that helped companies to improve production processes, reduce costs and successfully compete in a variety of business environments.

The late 80s and early 90s witnessed the shift of 'time to market." Customers demanded to have their products delivered when, where, and how they wanted them. JIT requires cooperation along the entire supply chain with the ultimate goal of maximizing the profit of the supply chain. The beginning of JIT started along the assembly line and was not necessarily controlled by a computer but by a Kanban card using pull tags to suppliers. Sending a Kanban card or an empty container upstream along the assembly line was the signal to replenish inventory. A phone call to the supplier with an order was the trigger to deliver the next order. Companies world-wide began to embrace the philosophy of JIT and supplier partnership as a way to remain competitiveness.

The 1990s caught sight of increased globalization and the Internet. In order to improve competitiveness, companies began realize the potential of information technology to dramatically transform their business. Instead of automating old, inefficient processes, companies began to reengineer business processes using technology as the enabler. This led to the development of ERP systems that give complete visibility to the organization, integrating previously stand-alone systems. ERP became more acceptable during the mid- and late 1990s. ERP is not just MRPII with a new name. ERP is the next logical sophistication level in an evolutionary series of computer tools for material and supply chain management. ERP systems provide an integrated view of information across functions within a company and with the potential to go across companies.

In late 90s and the beginning of 21st century, electronic communications as opposed to paper transactions allow for a decrease in amount of lead-time required to replenish inventory. Cutting lead-time minimizes the risk of uncertainty in demand and decreases the probability of over or under-stocking inventory. The 90s marked the wide use of the Internet. This provided great opportunity for companies to integrate E-commerce into their business models. The primary emphasis during that period was business-to-customer (B2C). Today, the emphasis expands to include business-to-business or B2B. Back-end system integration, especially supply chain management provides greater visibility and more strategic capability for companies to improve profitability and competitiveness.

Supply chain management models emerged. A supply chain consists of all stages involved, either directly or indirectly, in fulfilling a customer request. A supply chain includes manufacturer, supplier, transporters, warehouses, retailer, third-party logistic provider, and customer. The objective of supply chain management is to maximize the overall value generated rather than profit generated in a particular supply chain.

1.4 Supply Chain Management Models

1.4.1 Competitive priorities and manufacturing strategy

The ability of a supply chain to compete based on cost, quality, time, flexibility, and new products is shaped by the strategic focus of the supply chain members. A firm's position on the competitive priorities is determined by its four long-term structural decisions: facility, capacity, technology, and vertical integration, as well as by its four infrastructural decisions: workforce, quality, production planning and control, and organization. The cumulative impact of infrastructural decisions on a firm's competitiveness is as important as long-term structural decisions.

Manufacturing strategy focuses on a set of competitive priorities such as cost, quality, time, flexibility, and new product introduction. It classifies production processes to five major types: project, job shop, batch, line, and continuous flow. "Make-to-stock", "assemble-to-order", "build-to-order" and "engineer-to-order" are a few of the manufacturing strategies used to address competitive priorities to compete on the market place.

Make-to-stock involves holding products in inventory for immediate delivery, so as to minimize customer delivery times. This is in the category of push system. Demand is forecasted and production is scheduled before demand is there.

Assemble-to-order is the strategy to handle numerous end-item configurations and is an option for mass-customization. Assemble-to-order items use standardized parts and components. They require efficient and low cost production in the fabrication process and flexibility in the assembly or configuration stage to satisfy individualized demand from customers.

Build-to-order, on the other hand, produces customized products in low volume after the manufacturer receives the orders. Build-to-order items are usually in very small volumes and require high technical competency, high product performance design, and effective due date management.

Engineer-to-order produces products that are with unique parts and drawings required by customers. Product volume is very small and typically is one-of-a-kind in a job-shop environment. The cycle time from order to delivery is usually long because of the unique customization nature. MRP planning is extremely important for engineer-to-order.

1.4.2 Efficient supply chain and responsive supply chain

One of the causes of supply chain failure is due to the lack of understanding of the nature of demand. The lack of understanding often leads mismatched supply chain design. Fisher (1997) suggested two distinctive approaches, efficient supply chain and responsive supply chain, to design a firm's supply chain.

The purpose of responsive supply chain is to react quickly to market demand. This supply chain model best suites the environment in which demand predictability is low, forecasting error is high, product life cycle is short, new product introductions are frequent, and product variety is high (Table 1.1). The responsive supply chain design matches competitive priority emphasizing on quick reaction time, development speed, fast delivery times, customization, and volume flexibility. The design features of responsive supply chains include flexible or intermediate flows, high-capacity cushions, low inventory levels, and short cycle time.

The purpose of an efficient supply chain is to coordinate the material flow and services to minimize inventories and maximize the efficiency of the manufacturers and service providers in the chain. This supply chain model best fits the environment in which demands are highly predictable, forecasting error is low, product life cycle is long, new product introductions are infrequent, product variety is minimal, production lead-time is long and order fulfillment lead-time is short. The efficient supply chain design matches competitive priority emphasizing on low-cost operations and on-time delivery. The design features of efficient supply chain include line flows, large volume production, and low-capacity cushions.

Table 1.1. Efficient supply chain and responsive supply chain

	Efficient supply chain	Responsive supply chain
Demand	Constant, based on forecasting	Fluctuate, based on customer orders
Product life cycle	Long	Short
Product variety	Low	High
Contribution margin	Low	High
Order fulfill lead time	Allowed longer fulfillment lead time	Short or based on quoted due date
Supplier	Long-term	According to product life cycle
Production	Make-to-stock	Assemble-to-order Make-to-order Build-to-order
Capacity cushion	Low	High
Inventory	Finished goods inventory	Parts, components, subassembly
Supply selection	Low cost, consistent quality, and on-time delivery	Flexibility, fast-delivery, high-performance design quality

1.4.3 Clock-speed of product, process, and organization life cycles

Fine (1999) suggests that each industry evolves at a different rate, depending in some way on its product clock-speed, process clock-speed, and organization clock-speed (Table 1.2). For example, information-entertainment industry is one of the fast-clock-speed industries. Motion pictures can have product life measured in hours. Christmas time is the best season to introduce new movies when the number of viewers is greatest. The process for information-entertainment industry changes rapidly. New processes for delivering information-entertainment products and services to our home, public centers, and offices evolve daily. CD players, DVD are just a couple of examples. Organization structure is dynamic as well. Relationship among media giants such as Time-Warner, Disney, and Viacom are negotiated, signed, and re-negotiated constantly to accommodate the changes in product and process design.

Aircraft industry is an example of slow clock-speed product industry. The Boeing Company measures its product's clock-speed in decades. Thirty years after Boeing 747 was first introduced, the profit generated from selling Boeing 747 is still flowing in. Boeing 747 produced and sold in 2000 has the same manufacturing plant as it had for the first of these aircraft.

Somewhere in the middle is automobile industry. The product does not change as fast as information-entertainment industry, nor does it as slow as aircraft industry. Passenger cars, for example, have a product life of three to five years. As for its process clock-speed, each time automaker makes a new design, it expects much of that investment to be obsolete in four to five years.

Supply chain design should reflect the nature of the product clock-speed; understanding what requirements would make it more likely for one to have an effective supply chain or vice versa. Analyzing the clock-speed of product, process and organization enables us to see with greater clarity and accuracy of the future needs from our customers.

Table 1.2. Clock-speed

	Fast Clock-speed	Medium clock-speed	Slow clock-speed
Product	< 6 mo. – 2 years	3 – 15 years	10 years or longer
Process	2 – 10 years	2 – 25 years	5 years or longer
Organization	2 – 10 years	2 – 25 years	20 years or longer

1.4.4 Pull and push processes

All processes in a supply chain fall into one of two categories: push or pull. In the push process, production of a product is authorized based on forecasting which is in advance of customer orders. In the pull process, on the other hand, the final assembly is triggered by customer orders (Figure 1.4).

In a pure push process, make-to-stock is the primary production approach as shown in the example of demand for chicken breast at Sam's Club in Figure 1.4. Demand is forecasted based on historical sales data. The need from the end users is satisfied from inventory. Production lead-time is relatively long and finished goods inventory is more than that of the pull system. The major technical sophistication that has been applied in the supply chain is Perdue Farms' vertical integration, which focuses on "We do it all for you."

In the pull approach, end users trigger the production of computers at Dell's manufacturing factory as shown in Figure 1.4. The major production strategy is make-to-order, assemble-to-order, and build-to-order. In a pull scenario, demand uncertainty is higher and cycle time is shorter than that of the push approach. Finished goods inventory is minimal. Dell is an obvious captain of the supply chain. The major technical sophistication that has been applied in the supply chain is Dell's direct model, which focuses on "Have it your way."

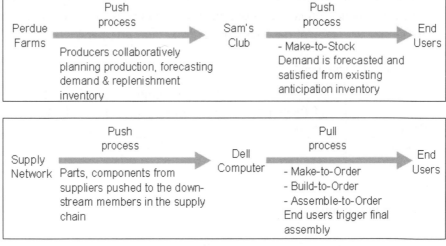

Figure 1.4. Pull vs. push process

The push/pull approach is important in designing supply chain. Demand uncertainty and variations are treated differently in these two systems. In a push system, safety stock is used to manage demand variability; while in a pull system, flexible capacity is required to meet the demand variability. Both inventory and capacity represent financial expenditure. Therefore, developing effective supply chains is crucial to achieve the cost-effective goal as well as delivering what the customer needs at the right time, right place, and in the right quantity.

1.5 Collaborative Planning, Forecasting, and Replenishment (CPFR) – An e-Biz Solution to Transforming Demand

1.5.1 The basics of CPFR

The essence of recent supply chain development is collaboration across the supply chain. Lack of collaboration in supply chain leads to inefficient production, redundant inventory stock, and inflated costs. Two examples are given to illustrate the above points[3]:

(1) It often takes a pack of cereal more than three months to be delivered from the factory warehouse to a supermarket shelf due to ineffective distribution strategy.

(2) It takes a car an average of 15 days to travel from the factory to a dealer's showroom, which usually only requires 4 to 5 days traveling time.

Many suppliers and retailers have observed the phenomenon of demand fluctuation in the upstream of the supply chain. Hau Lee describes demand fluctuation for diapers in supply chain[4]. In examining the demand for Pampers disposal diapers, Proctor & Gamble noticed that retail sales of the product were uniform; no particular day or month in

---

[3] David Simchi-Levi (2002) presentation at Conference on Optimization in Supply Chain Management and E-commerce, Gainesville, Florida.
[4] Lee, H L., Padmanabhan, V., Whang S., (1997). The bullwhip effect in supply chains. *Sloan Management Review*, 38(3), 93-103.

which the demand was significantly higher or lower than any other. The distributor's orders placed to the factory fluctuated much more than retail sales. In addition, P&G's orders to its suppliers fluctuated even more. This phenomenon of increasing variability in demand in a supply chain is referred to as the **bullwhip effect**. The bullwhip effect is essentially the artificial distortion of consumer demand figures as they are transmitted back to the suppliers from the retailer.

One way to address the bullwhip effect caused by order batching is to collaboratively plan production, forecast demand, and replenish inventory. This will lead to smaller order sizes, smoothed production volumes, and more frequent order replenishment. The result will be a smoother flow of smaller orders that the distributors and manufacturers are able to handle more efficiently.

In recently years, retailers have initiated collaborative agreements with their supply chain partners to establish on going planning, forecasting, and replenishment process. This initiative is called collaborative planning, forecasting, and replenishment issues (CPFR). The Association for Operations Management defines CPFR as follows:

"Collaboration process whereby supply chain trading partners can jointly plan key supply chain activities from production and delivery of raw materials to production and delivery of final products to end customers" - The Association for Operations Management" - *The Association for Operations Management[5]*.

The objective of CPFR is to optimize supply chain through improved demand forecasts, with the right product delivered at right time to the right location, with reduced inventories, avoidance of stock-outs, and improved customer service. The value of CPFR lies in the broad exchange of forecasting information to improve forecasting accuracy when both the buyer and seller collaborate through joint knowledge of sales, promotions, and relevant supply and demand information.

---

[5] The Association for Operations Management is formerly known as *American Production and Inventory Control Society (APICS)*.

1.5.2 Major activities of CPFR

Three major activities constitute CPFR: they are planning, forecasting, and replenishment. There are a few steps involved in each activity.

Planning: Planning starts with a contract that details the responsibilities of the companies that will collaborate with each other in providing the right products for customers. Contract terms should be negotiated first. Then a joint business plan regarding demand management, sales promotion, production quantity, timing, inventory level, will be developed.

Forecasting: First, customer demand is predicted for all the participating firms. Any differences in demand among participating firms will then be identified and resolved. Finally, a feasible sales forecast for all participating firms is developed. Modifications may be done periodically to reflect the changes in market demand.

Replenishment: First, orders for all participating firms are estimated. Any difference among participating firms are identified and resolved. Finally, an efficient production and delivery schedule is developed. Orders are fulfilled.

The idea of collaborative planning, forecasting, and replenishment was initiated at the annual Retail Systems Conference and Exposition in the mid 1990s. Later, the Voluntary Interindustry Commerce Standards (VICS) committee developed a nine-step process model as a guideline for implementing CPFR to facilitate the coordination that is needed in supply chains. This committee documents best practices for CPFR and creates guidelines for implementing CPFR. The nine steps for effectively implementing CPFR are as follows.

Step 1: Develop Collaboration Arrangement
Step 2: Create Joint Business Plan
Step 3: Create Sales Forecast
Step 4: Identify Exceptions for Sales Forecast
Step 5: Resolve/Collaborate on Exception Items
Step 6: Create Order Forecast
Step 7: Identify Exceptions for Order Forecast
Step 8: Resolve/Collaborate on Exception Items
Step 9: Order Generation.

These nine steps have guided companies to successfully implement CPFR. For example, Sears and Michelin, a French tire producer, began discussions on collaboration in 2001. Later that year they implemented a CPFR initiative followed the VICS nine steps. The mutual goal of the two companies was to improve order fill rate and reduce inventory at Sears' distribution centers and Michelin's warehouses respectively. Because of implementing CPFR, Sears distribution-center-to-store fill rate increased by 10.7 percent. The combined Michelin and Sears inventory levels were reduced by 25 percent. This practice indicates that collaboration can offer companies the opportunities to transform and radically improve their supply chain performance. Such a transformation can have dramatic benefits and create competitive advantages.

1.5.3 CPFR in practice

Companies that are able to establish collaborative supply chains will have a significant competitive edge over their competitors. Prominent companies are already beginning to lead the way. Companies such as Wal-Mart, Dell Inc., and Proctor & Gamble share point of sales data with all the other companies in their respective supply chains. The companies in these supply chains are also starting to share inventory data with each other. Sharing this kind of information provides a basis for each company to make decisions about its own activities that will yield better efficiencies and more profits for itself and for the supply chain as a whole.

Collaboration in production, forecasting, and replenishment brings a number of benefits. First, the bullwhip effect is diminished because all companies in the supply chain have access to real time sales data and share sales forecasts. This allows every member in the same supply chain to develop a better production plan, ideal inventory levels, and realistic delivery schedules. Next, everyone in the supply chain shares rise and decline in customer demand. Adjustment to the previously planned production levels is made accordingly. No retailer will lose sales revenue due to running out of inventory or lose profit due to surplus stocks. Collaboration is not easy to implement and it will take time to become more common in business.

More recently, innovative consumer goods manufacturers and retailers are forging partnership to advance the implementation of CPFR. Compaq is working with 850 of its trading partners to conduct purchasing planning over the Internet. Thomson Electronics is doing CPFR with 50 of its retailers. More trading partners have launched pilots. Canadian Tire is treading new ground with seven of its suppliers, and New Balance and Timberland are setting the pace in the shoe industry with selected retailers. Schering Plough and Johnson & Johnson are taking the lead with Eckerd Drug. Mitsubishi Motors is collaborating with its dealers to reduce customer lead-time to two weeks.

The benefits of CPFR include reduced inventory, reduced safety stock, and reduced stock outs probability. Nevertheless, it is still a challenging process to integrate a disconnected forecasting and planning process in the entire supply chain. A key issue in improving collaborative efforts revolves around the partners getting their own supply chain process in order. Companies are now recognizing the need to optimize their internal processes and have accurate data.

1.6 Issues of Supply Chain Management in a Global Setting

A month before year 2006 Christmas, I visited a shopping mall in the southern Virginia area. A majority of all their merchandise was being manufactured offshore. In the same month in Ha Noi, Viet Nam on November 19, 2006, 21 Asian-Pacific Economic Cooperation (APEC) countries had the 14th APEC Economic Leaders' Meeting. The APEC leaders acknowledged the role of comprehensive Regional Trade Agreements/Free Trade Agreements (RTAs/FTAs) in advancing trade liberalization. They also agreed RTAs/FTAs lead to greater trade liberalization and genuine reductions in trade transaction costs.

Globalization is inevitable. As we are looking five to ten years down the road, we are sure about one thing that is the continual liberalization of trade. As more and more countries get opened up to world trade, more and more companies are seeking for the most cost effective way to produce and deliver products. Companies of various sizes realize that they have to be part of the global supply chain in order to stay competitive and remain in business.

1.6.1 SCM issues in the US

In the past 20 years, the United States has been at the forefront of developing new supply chain management models, reengineering operations processes, and advancing technologies for supply chain management. Wal-Mart, Dell Inc., and HP as well as many other companies have already demonstrated their ability in managing supply chain under the electronic commerce environment.

As one of the world's largest consumer, producer, and trader, the US has a number of advantages in advancing supply chain management. First, the US citizens use the same official language, currency, and technology. Additionally, the culture is much more similar than that in the other parts of the world, although there are some variations from region to region within the country. Second, it has a well-developed transportation infrastructure. Its sea and airport facilities are adequate to handle the flow of imports and exports. As far as intra-country transportation, its freight rail system is very productive and its highway system is more than sufficient to connect all activities within the supply chain. Third, its technology is readily available to all participants in the supply chain. Convenient access to the Internet and telecommunication is a feature of U.S. supply chains. From the aspect of technology, the U.S. leads both Europe and Japan in the deployment of e-commerce systems.

1.6.2 SCM issues in Europe

In recent years, the European Union has done much to unify the continent but there are still major differences in local markets, culture, legal regulations, politics, taxation requirements, economic development, wealth, and geography. Markets vary greatly from country to country, especially now with the emergence of new democracies in Eastern Europe. Influencing these differences is the widely varying cultures from region to region. Although some standard issues in the areas of quality, health, the environment, and timeliness are emerging, consumer service values vary widely across Europe. The difference in the value system forces manufacturers to focus on customization at the local level.

Secondly, transportation infrastructure varies from country to country across Europe. The geography of a country affects accessibility, which in turn influences both transportation methods as well as distribution networks. For example, Italy chooses a more local distribution network due to its compartmentalized geography. Holland, on the other hand, tends to use a more centralized distribution network with its relatively accessible geography. These transportation and distribution issues have led some firms to establish regional stockholding distribution centers, which may reduce the need and reliance on extensive distribution networks and reduce the dependency on transportation. A considerable disadvantage of localized transportation systems in Europe is its relatively low usage of rail to transport freight. Poorly maintained infrastructure in some Eastern European countries, as well as differences in rail gauge size, technical standards, and height/width allowances between countries within Europe are the issues that slow down the development of supply chain management.

Finally, the application of current technology also varies from country to country. Unlike the U.S., the availability of reliable Internet access and current technologies is not always a given in all countries throughout Europe. The variation of Internet access from region to region has a significant impact on the ability of firms to conduct collaborative planning, forecasting and replenishment within the supply chain in order to compete on a global level.

Although the continent and its countries are fighting to overcome some inherent challenges, Europe has made some significant strides forward and has implemented innovations to overcome some of these challenges. Mobile commerce (m-commerce), vehicle tracking and dispatching, radio frequency identification (RFID) tags, silent commerce applications, and collaboration are few examples of recent development in Europe. High cell phone usage level has led to the development of mobile networks that are integrated into back end operations. Expanding on these wireless application advancements, Europe also has an increasing number of vehicle tracking and distribution systems. Nevertheless, cross-border and cross-culture issues are still the areas that need to be improved upon. The European Union has initiated to bring the whole of Europe to a single accepted standard, which may include the development of "freight corridors" via road, rail, and water to address distribution both within countries and regions as well as the continent as a whole.

1.6.3 SCM issues in Asia

Supply chain management in Asia is considered more fragmented and less competitive than those in the United States and Europe, but the gap between these regions is closing. First, the Asian market is made up of many countries varying in culture, religion, political system, language, legal system, and stages of economic development. Some of the major countries include Japan, China, India, Australia, Indonesia, South Korea, and Thailand. This list of countries presents an obvious diversity in various aspects. Culturally speaking, most Asian cultures differ greatly from Europe and the United States. As an example, Asian culture values relationships greatly, and they are established over time and past dealings. This precludes the establishment of quick business deals. The focus tends to be on the establishment of respectful relationships over time.

Second, the transportation infrastructure in many developing countries in Asia is less developed as compared to that of the US and Europe. Traditionally, rail transportation was a dominant public transportation in countries such as India, China, and Japan. Air transportation is undergoing fast development in recent years, and highway construction is advancing at a rapid pace. For example, China is aggressively developing its highway system as well as improving the efficiency of its rail freight industry. In 2000, 50,000 kilometers of new highway was added in China.

Finally, technology is also a major concern to developing efficient supply chains in Asia. There is weak availability of information technology in many developing Asian countries. Lowering production costs has been prevalent in Asia. However, the opportunity to reduce costs now lies in developing efficient logistics and distribution, which is a weak area in Asia. The use of information technology can assist greatly in this regard.

Collaboration is an area of opportunity in Asia. Currently many of the collaborative efforts have been informal. As a more formal form of collaboration develops, especially at the industry level, greater efficiency can be achieved and savings will occur. One of the main areas that need to be developed to enable this increased collaboration is information technology. Data integrity needs to be increased and information needs to be available upon request. This may require some companies to undergo a certain amount of re-engineering of their supply chains. In the near future, the outsourcing of logistics and supply chain functions will pay great dividends in the Asian market. As manufacturing companies begin to compete for a larger piece of the global market, they will need to compete on more than just low cost labor. Quality and cycle time management will be essential. To capitalize on the supply chain efficiency many small manufacturing companies, who lack the capability, have the need to turn to third party logistics providers to attain a competitive efficiency.

1.6.4 SCM issues in Latin America

Latin American countries can offer U.S.-based firms an opportunity to expand their list of suppliers and cut down on costs. The NAFTA agreements give the US access to Mexico's low labor market. However, the differences in currency, transportation, infrastructure, political systems, and laws are just some of the hurdles facing businesses looking to take advantage of the opportunity in Latin America.

Technology is also a major concern to developing efficient supply chains in Latin America. While computers are common in Mexico and other Latin American countries, high-tech communications aren't as reliable as they are in the U.S. Fewer people are networked via the Internet than those in the US, which makes it difficult to automate supply chains and reliably monitor inventory as it passes from one link to another. In the rural area, technology is old or even not available.

Because of Latin America's technology disparities, a company looking to connect with suppliers there will either have to invest in a mixed infrastructure involving electronic data interchange (EDI), Web, phone and fax systems or link up with third-party logistics providers that offer the necessary interfaces. For example, Ryder transports 3,000 different parts from Latin America for an automotive manufacturer that assembles trucks in Indiana. To keep track of inventories, Ryder uses a mixed radio, cell phone and EDI communications system. Each Sunday, Ryder gets e-mail with the plant's requirements. Half of the parts makers are either online or have EDI capabilities; the other half requires phone or fax-based transactions. The company had to build a considerable infrastructure to facilitate various communication devises.

1.7 Summary

1.7.1 Supply chain management challenges

Supply chain integration is difficult for two primary reasons: first, the supply chain is an integrated system that requires cohesive decisions to optimize the system profit and value. In practice, different facilities in the supply chain may have different, conflicting objectives. Second, the supply chain is a dynamic system, which has its own life cycle and continually evolves. For example, customer demand and supplier capabilities change over time, as do supply chain relationships.

A number of important challenges exist for supply chain managers. For example, supply chain design and strategic collaboration are quite difficult because of the dynamics and the conflicting objectives employed by different facilities and partners. Inventory control is another tough issue. What is the effect of inventory on system performance? Why should a supply chain member hold inventory? Distribution network configuration involves management's making decisions regarding warehouse locations and capacities; determining production levels for each product at each plant; and set transportation flows between facilities to minimize total production, inventory, and transportation costs and satisfy service level requirements.

The sharing of data, information, and knowledge is a challenge of virtually integrating a supply chain. It must be noted that a large extent of corporate technical knowledge is difficult to articulate and tacitly resides in the minds of knowledge workers. To what extent can emerging information technologies help explicate complex tacit knowledge so that they can be shared across dispersed or virtual organizational environments?

1.7.2 Road map for supply chain management

This text is about managing supply chain through collaboration and is divided into six major parts: "Concepts and Strategic Issues," "Purchasing, Supply Network, and Strategic Sourcing," "Demand Transformation in Supply Chain," "Distribution Network and Transportation," "e-Business Solutions," and "Supply Chain Management Performance and Evaluation." The flow of topics reflects the theme of how supply chain management can provide a sound basis for market competitiveness and sustainable growth through collaboration.

Figure 1.5 shows a road map that spans across departmental and organizational boundaries of a supply chain.

Once it is clear about the concept of supply chain management, the discussion is extended to how to create supply network and build strategic partners, how to transform customer's demand to goods, and how to deliver the right products to the right customers at the right time and right place.

Since the recent driver in the evolution in supply chain management is information technology, the text covers cutting-edge e-solutions that trigger many of the current initiatives in supply chain management. In the last part, the focus is placed on evaluating effective supply chain performance, which is interfaced with every supply chain stage.

After the initial wave of e-business, many companies realize that beneath the Internet application is sourcing structure and physical distribution. Supply chain management is concerned with more than just movement of materials from raw material producers to manufacturers, and finally to the end users. The goal of supply chain management is to create value for the supply chain members with an emphasis on the end users. The mechanism to realize value-added activities in supply chain is collaborative planning, forecasting, and replenishment among the supply chain members.

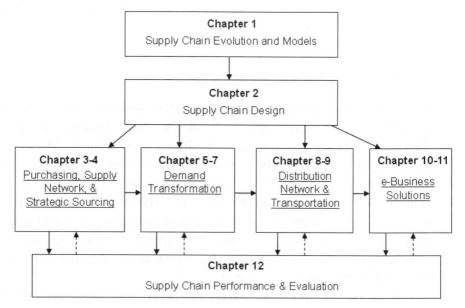

* Dash Lines Are Feedbacks for Supply Chain Evolution and Continuous Improvement

Figure 1.5. Structure of the book

References

Boalow, J. (2000). "Transformation of Economy Real." *Houston Chronicle*, July 16, 2000.

Butler, S. (2000). "The economy downshifts; the Fed tries to do what's never been done before: engineer a soft landing." U.S. News and World Report, June 19, 2000.

Chopra, S. and P. Meindl (2001). Supply Chain Management: Strategy, Planning, and Operations. Upper Saddle River, NJ: Prentice Hall.

Deans, P. C. and K. R. Karwan, Eds. (1994). Information Technology and Leadtime Management in International Manufacturing Operations. Global Information Systems and Technology: Focus on the Organization and Its Functional Areas. London, Idea Group Publishing.

Findlay, Charles. "Europe's Unique Supply Chain Opportunities, Challenges, and Innovations." *ASCET,* Vol. 4, May 16, 2002.

Ferrer, James. "European Supply Chain Management Characteristics and Challenges." *ASCET,* Vol. 5, July 26, 2003.

Fine, C.H. (1999) Clockspeed. Reading, MA: Perseus Books.

Fisher, M. L. (1997). "What is the right supply chain for your product?" *Harvard Business Review* (March-April 1997), p.105-116.

Handfield, R. B. and J. Ernest L. Nichols (2002). Supply Chain Redesign. Upper Saddle River, NJ: Prentice Hall.

Krajewski, L. J., Rotzman, L. P. (2002). Operations Management. Upper Saddle River, NJ, Prentice Hall.

Lee, H. (1997). "Information distortion in a Supply Chain: The Bullwhip Effect." *Management Science*, 43, 4.

Magretta, J. (1998). "The power of virtual integration: An interview with Dell computer's Michael Dell." *Harvard Business Review*, March-April 1998.

Ptak, C. A. (2000) ERP: Tools, Techniques, and Application for Integrating Supply Chain. New York: The St. Lucie Press.

Simchi-Levi, D., P. Kaminsky, et al. (2003). Designing and Managing the Supply Chain, 2nd edition. New York: McGraw-Hill.

Steermann, H (2003) "A practical look at CPFR: the Sears - Michelin experience." *Supply Chain Management Review*, July/ august 2003, pp. 46-53.

VICS, 2000 VICS, 2000. CPFR Guidelines. Voluntary Inter-industry Commerce Standards, available at http://www.cpfr.org.

http//:www.optimizemag.com/issue/002/custorner4.htm: Domeika, Bill and Crawford, Fred. Focusing on success, December 2001.

http//:www.optimizemag.com/issue/006/management2.htm: The New Darwinism, April 2002.

Chapter 2

The Right Design of Supply Chain: Examples

2.1 Design the Right Supply Chain

Today, supply chain managers are overwhelmed with a range of leading-edge supply chain strategies and new business initiatives. However, not all these initiatives and strategies are appropriate for all businesses. Supply chain managers need to understand the constraints of the supply of their products and the uncertainties of demand from customers before trying to match these constraints and uncertainties with the right supply chain strategies. A framework for analyzing supply chain practices is proposed in Figure 2.1 based on the constraints of various industry environments.

Figure 2.1 integrates the concept of efficient supply chain and responsive supply chain view, the clock-speed view, and the level of supplier's collaboration we discussed in Chapter 1. In designing supply chain in an e-Biz environment, companies have to integrate various aspects of competitive priority, the nature of the product, and the complexity of the manufacturing process in order to be successful. When designing a supply chain, some fundamental principles of value chain should be exploited to respond quickly to the dynamic business environment. As such, supply chain design needs to be fine-tuned constantly to match the evolving industry paradigm.

When new product introductions are frequent and product variety is high, the responsive supply chain option is more attractive as it reacts quickly to market demand. When product life cycle is long, demand is relatively stable, and demand volume is high, efficient supply chain is

31

more appropriate.   Both responsive supply chain and efficient supply chain can be applied to fast, medium and slow clock speed products.

A product clock-speed can be fast, medium, or slow. A product life cycle and its manufacturing process life cycle determine the production volume, the choice of supply chain collaboration level, and the type of supply chain design.

The level of collaboration in a supply chain is closely associated with the product clock-speed. The collaboration spectrum on the left-hand side in Figure 2.1 indicates, on one end, virtual companies in that they outsource much of their business activities through the market place. At the other end of the spectrum, vertical integration companies manage almost everything in-house from raw material production to the distribution channel and to the final users.   In the middle of the collaborative spectrum is strategic alliances and joint venture. At this level, companies share benefits, risks, and responsibilities.   A number of supply chain models are introduced in the following section.

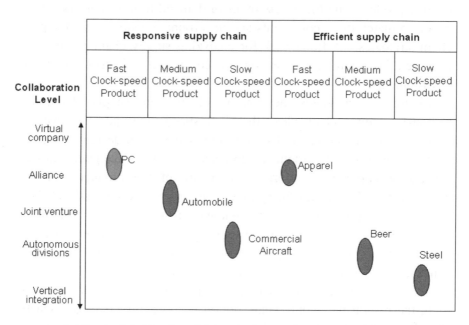

Figure 2.1. Product life cycle and supply chain design

2.2 Responsive Supply Chain in Manufacturing Industry

2.2.1 Responsive supply chain and fast clock-speed product – Personal computer

The PC industry is a fast clock-speed industry in that the industry faces short product life cycles. The product is generally made in a make-to-order production environment. Facing this business environment, PC producers adopt the responsive supply chain strategy to reduce order cycle, production cycle, and procurement cycle. Let us consider Dell Computer as an example.

Dell Computer designs, manufactures, and markets a wide range of systems that include desktops, notebooks, workstations, and network servers. Dell also markets software and peripherals as well as service and support programs. Centered on two key elements: a direct business model and intense customer focus, Dell strives to eliminate retailers and other resellers so as to reduce product delivery cycle time and cost. Dell sells computer systems and related services directly to customers in the global market through the Internet and call centers.

To reduce order cycle, Dell uses the Internet and call centers to promote its direct order model (Figure 2.2). The traditional PC supply chain has distribution network as an additional link in the supply chain. Customers can order PCs directly from Dell and configure computers to meet their needs. The orders are directly routed to the manufacturing floor. From there the PCs are built, tested and sent to the customer all within 5-7 days after the customers placed orders. Dell's direct model allows for better understanding of customers needs.

To reduce its procurement cycle time, Dell shifts from a traditionally fashioned assembly line to cellular manufacturing techniques and established strategic alliances with its key suppliers. It forges partnerships with reputable suppliers rather than integrating backward into parts and components manufacturing. Since new parts and components are introduced so fast that inventory is obsolete in a matter of months or even quicker, Dell only holds 10-day inventory. Meanwhile, Dell supplies its inventory data and production needs to its suppliers at least once a day. Collaboration with suppliers is close enough to allow Dell to operate with only a few hours of inventory for some parts and a few days of inventory for other components. Dell's direct model capitalizes the benefits of e-commerce.

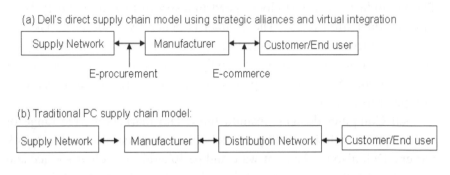

Figure 2.2. Supply chains for Dell and traditional PC makers

2.2.2 Responsive supply chain and medium clock-speed product – Automobile industry

The auto industry is a medium clock-speed industry. New models are introduced every four to six years and the variety of configurations is numerous. Cars are made in an assemble-to-order fashion. The challenge in this production environment is to manage hundreds and thousands of suppliers and react quickly to the market needs (Figure 2.3).

General Motors is the world's largest industrial corporation and a full-line vehicle manufacturer. It operates in 30 countries and employs more than 330,000 people. GM has approximately 27% of the auto market. In 2001 alone, GM sold more than 8.5 million cars and truck in more than 200 countries. GM's products include Chevrolet, Pontiac, Buick, Oldsmobile, Cadillac, GMC, Saturn, Hummer, Saab, Opel, Vauxhall and Holden. Being the world's largest industrial corporation, an effective supply chain system is very important to GM to earn a competitive edge. GM forges joint ventures with its suppliers and strategically coordinates sourcing plans with its suppliers to ensure a smooth flow of material at a minimum cost.

In order to guarantee a steady supply of aluminum that is used in everything from wheel covers to power trains, General Motors signed with Alcan Aluminum a 10-year, multi-billion-dollar agreement to buy aluminum at predictable prices. GM also has a joint venture with Alcan Aluminum to co-develop new automotive applications. In a similar manner, GM agreed to buy more than $1 billion worth of recycled aluminum to be used in a variety of engines and other vehicle components. Under this novel 13-year contract, IMCO Recycling will build a $22 million plant in Milwaukee, Michigan, and GM will buy all of the recycled specification aluminum alloys from that plant.

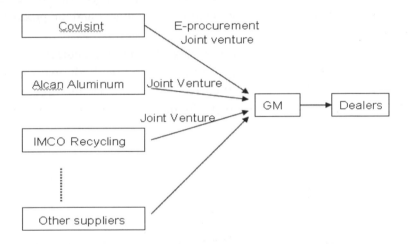

Figure 2.3. GM's supply chain using joint venture and strategic alliances

Doing business with over 80,000 different suppliers, GM created an automotive parts tracking system in order to find fast and efficient ways to track material flow in its supply chain. The system helps reduce time spent on information lookup and manual information transcription. With this system, dealerships know exactly where their products are located and how long it will take to arrive. Most importantly, it informs the dealership of what is in stock and what they need to re-order.

GM realizes the importance of long-term forecasting, leveling production and reducing excess finished goods inventory. With increased advances in technology, GM implements the JIT system which incorporates EDI, supplier relations, cost reduction analysis, and scheduling of workers. The philosophy of JIT allows MG to be more responsive to market needs.

2.2.3 Responsive supply chain and slow clock-speed product – Commercial aircraft

Commercial aircraft is a slow clock-speed product manufactured in a make-to-order production environment. The product technology lasts for 10-20 years and the manufacturing process technology lasts for 20-30 years. It is in a build-to-order production environment and the product is highly customized.

Boeing Company is the world's largest aircraft manufacturer with hundreds and thousands of suppliers. It relies on both internal and external suppliers for 5 to 6 million parts and components (Figure 2.4). The goal is to put the right parts in the right airplane in the right sequence.

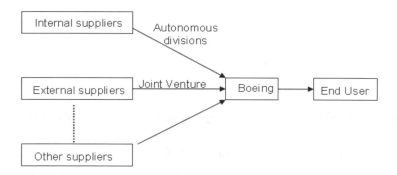

Figure 2.4. Supply chains for commercial aircraft

Boeing has experienced unreliable suppliers and delay in order arrivals. The unreliable suppliers and delivery schedules forced Boeing to shut down two of its major assembly lines for a month in 1997 that resulted in a big loss. Today, Boeing is proactively restructuring its supply chain and production systems to make sure such problems never happen again. Phasing out its World War II-era technologies, Boeing is heavily investing in new production systems that include Baan's ERP system, CimLink's factory floor control system, i2 Technologies' forecasting system, and Trilogy's product configuration system.

Instead of making customer made airplanes, Boeing is moving toward a small batch production environment in which it starts building planes before an order is placed.   The new system reduced cycle time dramatically. Customers will no longer have to wait 36 months from the time they order a plane to the time it is finally delivered. Boeing Commercial Airplanes is aiming to deliver commercial aircraft in eight to 12 months.

Boeing forges joint ventures and partnerships with suppliers from their large-account customer's native countries. Both Japanese airline and Chinese airlines are large Boeing customers for commercial aircrafts. Boeing established "working together" relationships with the People's Republic of China. Several Chinese factories produce major assemblies and parts for Boeing airplanes. There are also joint ventures for component manufacturing, airplane modification and repair.

Since commercial aircraft is a slow clock-speed product, the supply chain is fairly stable.   A number of Japanese companies such as Mitsubishi Heavy Industries (MHI), Kawasaki Heavy Industries (KHI) and Fuji Heavy Industries (FHI) have supplied Boeing for more than 30 years.

2.3 Efficient Supply Chain in Manufacturing Industry

2.3.1 Efficient supply chain and fast clock-speed product – Apparel industry

The apparel industry produces large batch, fast clock-speed garments. As such, an efficient supply chain model echoes throughout the apparel industry as a critical strategy for success. The fact that the apparel industry continues to experience relentless deflation is an indication of the complexities in supply chain management.   Today, a popular business model applied in the apparel industry is to keep design and color selection at the company's headquarters or home country and to outsource labor intensive production offshore.

The Limited Brands is one of the companies that are fully aware of the importance of supply chain management. In 1963, the Limited opened one women's apparel store in Columbus, Ohio. Since then, it has grown to more than 5,000 retail out-lets, plus catalog and online commerce, with seven retail brands: Victoria's Secret, Express, Bath & Body Works, the Limited, the White Barn Candle Co, Aura Science, and Henri Bendel. To reflect its multiple product lines, The Limited is renamed as Limited Brands. To reflect the nature of the fast-clock industry, the Limited cuts the length of its supply chain by dropping the distribution network in its supply chain (Figure 2.5).

To transfer from the traditional make-to-stock production strategy to the build-to-order and replenish-to-sale business model, The Limited Brands has developed enhanced relationships with their suppliers. For example, The Limited established relationship with Li & Fung Co., a fabric and garment supplier in Hong Kong, who in turns works to identify local materials they are able to obtain on short lead time. Orders for colors and fabrics can be changed much more readily as a result of the cultivated supplier network. Retailers can go online to change the color, size and style of their garment orders as the items are being made.

(a) The Limited supply chain model using strategic alliances

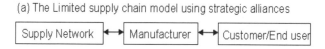

(b) Traditional apparel industry supply chain model:

Figure 2.5. Supply chains for apparel industry

One of the vital links in a supply chain is customer order forecast and demand management. This link serves as a prelude to apparel retailers' production planning, capacity management, and order fulfillment. The Limited tries to accurately predict customer's needs with the delayed differentiation method which is a recent trend in apparel industry. The Limited asks its manufacturers to reserve a certain amount of production capacity so as to delay the key decisions on sizes, colors, volume, shipping dates, and destinations. Traditionally, the lead time was six months, but this strategy delays production almost to the point of shipping. It fine-tunes the forecast process to the point of demand planning.

Each Limited company's brand has a vivid personality that serves as a retail fashion icon in their respective category. For example, when you think of fashion-forward you picture Express, and when you think of lingerie you picture Victoria's Secret. There isn't much time to ponder options or return next weekend with a friend for a second look of the Limited product. By then, there'll be a whole new set of collections on the floor - and most of today's fashions will be gone.

2.3.2 Efficient supply chain and medium clock-speed product – Beer industry

The beer industry is a medium clock-speed process industry. Due to its volume production with internal vertical integration, efficient supply chain is a good match. Beer production is planned in batches. The product technology clock-speed is about 3-10 years, organization clock-speed is about 3-25 years, and the manufacturing process technology is about 3-25 years.

In the prepared food industry, the producer has already incurred more than 85% of the production cost before demand takes place. Beer is a unique blend of malt extract, barley, hops, rice and water. Consequently, great care must be taken to create and maintain the quality of the finished product. If any of the product spoils or does not meet quality standard, a total loss is felt as it is discarded.

Anheuser-Busch is the world's largest brewer. It has been brewing beer for a hundred and fifty years using an old-world brewing method with today's technology. It operates 14 breweries, 12 in the United States, and two overseas. Anheuser-Busch has capitalized its reputation for consistent, perceived quality, and has expanded that reputation internationally through forging partnership with Corona Beer in Mexico and the Tsingdao Beer in China.

In order to produce the right amount of beer at the right time, Anheuser-Busch controls the majority of its supply chain including agricultural supply, brewing, and distribution (Figure 2.6). It outsources transportation function to third party providers. By owning the supply chain, vital information is easily exchanged allowing for a smoother production and delivery flow.

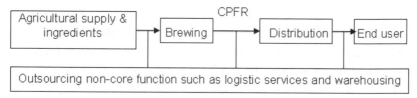

Figure 2.6. Supply chains for Anheuser-Busch

Anheuser-Busch has one of the strongest distribution systems in the beer industry. Distribution is key in getting the product to the consumer as soon as possible, because beer is better the fresher it is. Anheuser-Busch implemented the Wholesaler Support Center project in 1998. The low volume products are pooled and then shipped to one of the 44 wholesaler centers. This arrangement leads to better inventory control and reduces safety stock.

Anheuser-Busch outsources its transportation program to third party logistic providers to boost the efficiency of its distribution network. Outsourcing a non-core labor-intensive function prevents Anheuser-Busch from requiring a resident team on payroll. The savings on administration, labor, and overhead reduce overall cost and enable Anheuser-Busch to maintain a good profit margin.

2.3.3 Efficient supply chain and slow clock-speed product – Steel industry

The steel industry is a slow-clock industry. Steel products have been used extensively for thousands years and its production process remains fairly stable. The capital intensive steel plant is estimated to have a life cycle of 20-30 years. As such efficient supply chain is a well-accepted business model for the steel industry.

Nippon Steel Corporation is the world largest integrated steelmaker. It produces steel bars, sheets, special steel, pipes and other steel products. It is a highly vertical integrated company (Figure 2.7).

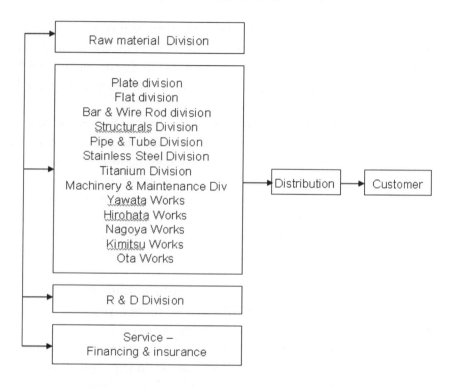

Figure 2.7. Supply chains for Nippon Steel Corporation's
Source: www.nsc.co.jp

Nippon Steel engages in everything from raw material supply to the distribution of finished products. It manufactures steel plates, sheets, pipes, and tubes, as well as specialty, processed, and fabricated steel products. The company's operations include engineering, construction, chemicals, nonferrous metals, ceramics, electronics, information and communications, and urban development. As vertically integrated company, Nippon Steel extends to energy, finance, and insurance services.

2.4 Service Industry

2.4.1 The book industry – Amazon.com

Amazon.com is a new business model in the book industry with a market capitalization of more than $20 billion. It sells books, music, and other items over the Internet. Amazon.com is based in Seattle and started by filling all orders using books purchased from a distributor in response to customer orders (Figure 2.8).

One reason that Amazon.com has flourished is because it has no physical stores for customers to stop at. It is able to take advantage of e-commerce technology via the Internet. According to Jeff Bezos, CEO of Amazon.com, "The foundation for e-Commerce is technology, as opposed to the foundation for retail commerce, which is real estate. As real estate gets more and more expensive, technology gets cheaper and cheaper. Amazon takes full advantage of the Internet along with its effective inventory management policies that saves them a lot of money."

This inventory management policy enables Amazon to turn its inventory over every two weeks, which is 26 times a year. The average inventory turns of the bookstore industry is about 2.6 times a year. Amason.com differs from traditional bookstore in that they purchase directly from publishers and stock books in the anticipation of customer orders. Amazon.com only stocks best-selling books, though it still gets other titles from distributors. It uses the U.S. Postal Service and other package carriers like the United Parcel Service (UPS) and FedEx to send books to customers.

Configuring distribution centers is a key supply chain linkage of the bookstore industry. Amazon.com consolidated its distribution centers by closing down two of its seven warehouses and reconfigured the internal layout of the remaining five warehouses to make it easier to locate, sort, and ship customer orders. Currently, they have five distribution centers strategically located across the US to provide customer orders in a timely manner.

Amazon forms its unique sourcing strategy. It partners with the Ingram Book Group, which ships single book orders directly to Amazon's customer when Amazon does not have the book in stock. In return, Amazon pays Ingram for any orders it has fulfilled. In a different partnership with Toys "R" Us, Borders and Target, Amazon handles inventory and shipping duties in return for fees and a percentage of sales, and these partners pay inventory handling cost and assume all the risks of excess inventory.

(a) Amazon.com supply chain

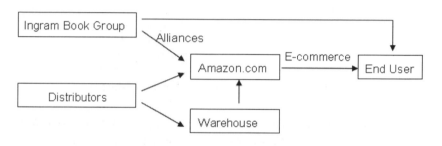

(b) Traditional bookstore supply chain

Figure 2.8. Supply chains for Amazon and traditional bookstore

2.4.2 The retail industry – Wal-Mart

Wal-Mart is a retail chain built on providing unparalleled consumer value through everyday-low-price (EDLP) strategy. Retail is the sale of goods in small quantities directly to the consumer. Therefore, Wal-Mart essentially represents the interface between the consumer and the manufacturer.

Wal-Mart has become a benchmark for creating a responsive supply-chain network capable of rapidly recognizing changes in customer demand and communicating these changes to the supplier. The level of response accelerates inventory turnover (Figure 2.9).

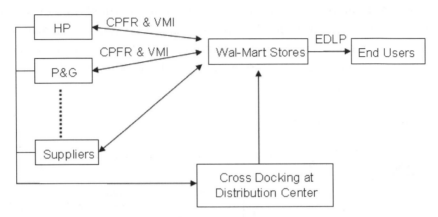

Figure 2.9. Supply chain for Wal-Mart

Inventory management is a major strategic point of Wal-Mart's supply-chain system. Wal-Mart has adopted the vendor managed inventory (VMI) approach to track their inventory replenishment. According to the company's inventory module, product supply is placed in a position of satisfying the retailer's specifications.

Wal-Mart is the captain of its supply chain. It requires every supplier to submit a supplier proposal to describe its targeted customers, future market demand, impact on related products currently sold at Wal-Mart, and potential market share growth if Wal-Mart sells the product. Additionally, the potential suppliers are required to demonstrate financial stability, insurance policy, lead-time and timely shipping capabilities, quality testing, industry knowledge and integrity, and basic technology such as UPC labeling. Suppliers should also be willing to join Wal-Mart's Retail Link, EDI system, and Transportation Link, to establish and maintain efficient supply management. Wal-Mart is recognized for its best practice in the retail industry.

2.5 Synchronizing Supply Chain

2.5.1 Link manufacturer to retailer – HP and Wal-Mart

Wal-Mart is one of Hewlett-Packard's fastest growing consumer accounts. In the middle of 1990s Wal-Mart almost discontinued selling computer products due to low profit margin. HP initiated a new marketing strategy to help Wal-Mart sell PC products. In 1999, the week after Thanksgiving, Wal-Mart sold a few hundred truckloads of HP Pavilion PCs in an eight-hour period, coupled with HP scanners, printers, and ink cartridges.

Since 1996 HP and Wal-Mart have jointly managed inventory at Wal-Mart stores. HP involves in determining stocking levels for Wal-Mart stores and warehouses, predicting weekly demand at each store, and estimating HP production lead-time. Sales of HP printers and inventory turns at Wal-Mart increased 3 times over a 9-month period. Product availability in stores improved from less than 80% to more than 95%. Based on the success of retailer-manufacturer's alliances, Wal-Mart has asked HP to manage inventory for their entire electronic products category. Savings generated through high inventory turnovers enable HP to reduce price for Wal-Mart; and Wal-Mart is able to offer EDLP to its customers[1].

2.5.2 Linking suppliers to manufacturers – Covisint

Covisint is an Internet-based business-to-business exchange hub and is one of the most important developments that support business processes between manufacturers and their supply network as shown in Figure 2.10. Covisint connects the auto industry in a virtual environment and collaborates with large powerful industry leaders to sponsor vertical industry e-marketplaces.

---

[1] HP Invent (2003) "Case studies & white papers: Wal-Mart". www.hp.com/country/us/eng/welsome.html.

Covisint is a central hub where original equipment manufacturers (OEMs) and Suppliers of all sizes come together to do business in a single business environment using the same tools and the same user interface, with one user ID and password. Covisint has three major objectives: (i) promotes collaborative product development by harnessing the Internet's communications prowess; (ii) streamlines procurement process for the auto companies by setting up market mechanisms such as auctions; and (iii) streamlines the operations of the auto industry's supply chains. As networks of buyers and suppliers interact in the virtual space, the members of Covisint, such as General Motors, Ford, DaimlerChrysler, Nissan and Renault, hope that the auto industry's business processes will become more efficient and customer-friendly[2].

GM invested in many information technologies to improve their core competencies. Using Covisint portal, GM is able to streamline the supply chain process with only one entry. Additionally, GM requests its suppliers to use the web-based exchange for all transactions regarding materials and parts so as to reduce the overall transactional costs.

Covisint offers different features. For example, Covisint Fulfillment is a web-based direct material fulfillment service for the auto industry. It provides quicker responses to problems with real time visibility of actual supply and demand.

The ultimate goal of Covisint is to optimize supply chain performance by exchanging all supply chain information through this web-enabled vehicle. With Covisint, suppliers have access to real time data so that they can optimize their own supply chains to serve the Covisint trading partners better. Some of the information exchanged is inventory levels, usage history and demand patterns, forecasts, in-transit inventories and other important information. Covisint speeds up decision making, eliminates waste, and reduces cost.

---

[2] e-biz Chronicle.com.

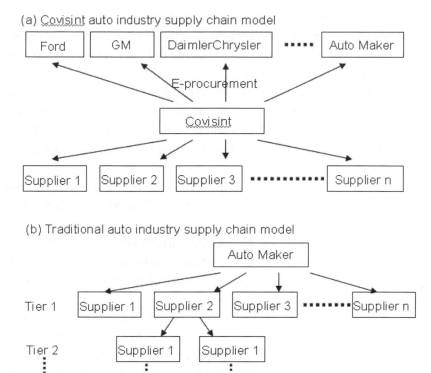

Figure 2.10. Covisint supply chain & traditional auto maker supply chain

2.6 Lessons to Learn

2.6.1 Retail industry – K-Mart

K-Mart was once a leader in the US retail industry. Since its creation in 1962, Kmart's main strategy was to offer quality products at lower prices. As a discount department store, Kmart relies on reaching out to customers through expanding the number of its stores in the United States and the overseas markets in Canada, Puerto Rico, Czech Republic, Slovakia, Mexico, and Singapore. Currently, it has more than 2,100 stores in the US. The market segment it targets is low- to middle-income class with an average annual income of $40,000. Kmart's business strategy: place, price, promotion, products, service, inventory management and technology investment did not evolve with the changing supply chain paradigm.

Place. Many Kmart stores are older than those of its competitors and located in less-than attractive urban areas. This makes the stores less appealing to shoppers. It also makes it hard for trucks to deliver merchandise efficiently, which makes it difficult to achieve economies of scale.

Price. Low price is supposed to be its competitive strength. But Kmart was not able to match the prowess of Wal-Mart's "Every Day Low Price".

Promotion. Kmart kept the promotions-driven business model, which basically relies on special sales to attract customers to stores. This approach along with a less developed supply chain management system led to high drops in demand for products[3].

Product. Kmart signed exclusive deals with highly recognized brands like Martha Stewart, Jaclyn Smith and Sesame Street. To achieve growth through diversification, K-mart acquired Builders Square, Borders Group, Sports Authority, and 22% of Office Max. An exclusive Disney line has been added to its children's clothing in 2001. Historical data have not been adequately used to determine which products ought to be dropped. Consequently, items offered at the K-mart stores keep broadening. As a result, Kmart returned to the Bluelight.com to promote its back inventory.

Service. Kmart did not emphasize the importance of service with an assumption of being a discount store. But service does have an effect on shopper satisfaction and loyalty.

Inventory. Kmart inventory management was not effective. It has had a hard time matching the merchandise pushed through its distribution system with the items it was promoting through sales. There was no rational link between local prices and local demand. The low price for promotion led to early depletion of inventories before season ends.

---

[3] Steve Konicki, *"Now in Bankruptcy, Kmart Struggled with Supply Chain"*. InformationWeek, Jan 28, 2002.

Kmart's inventory control system didn't provide an easy way to view the data or help to provide the right information for decision-making on time. In 2000, Kmart's inventory turnover rate was 3.6 times, while Wal-Mart had 7.3 turnovers and Target 6.3 turnovers.

Information Systems. Kmart continues to upgrade the technological infrastructure and information systems used in its stores, distribution centers and headquarters. When it developed a supply chain execution expert (EXE) system for organizing the warehouse management system, Kmart chose to modify the existing system rather than adopt the best of the breed. This technology decision means pallets in a warehouse sometimes wait for 24 hours before they're logged into a central tracking system.

Kmart considers low cost as its major competitive priority based on the assumption that lowering prices can increase demand for its products. However, much of these strategies did not allow Kmart to maintain its position as a leader among the discount retailers. A critical question has been asked by many: "What has led the company to such a decline?" Charles Conaway, the former CEO of Kmart, answered: "I believe the supply chain is really the Achilles heel of Kmart. Just fixing the supply chain could really turbo-charge Kmart".

2.6.2 PC industry – IBM

IBM's experience of developing personal computer through virtual integration is a useful example of supply chain design. When IBM first introduced personal computer, it was a fully vertically integrated computer manufacturer. It produced microprocessor, operating system, application software, and accessories. It also controlled its own distribution channel and retail outlets. Meanwhile, IBM was facing a three-dimensional design challenge: creating a new product, developing a new manufacturing process to produce the new product, and develop a supply chain to supply parts and components for the newly developed product.

To speed up its new product introduction to market and keep cost low, IBM chose a modular product design and outsourced its major components. In the early 80's, IBM outsourced its microprocessors to

Intel and its operating system to Microsoft. IBM was able to deliver its first product to market in 15 months. By 2000, the microprocessor has survived 10 generations, 8088, 286, 386, 486, Pentium, Pentium-Pro, Pentium II, Pentium III, and Pentium IV. IBM has since been distanced in the PC industry by its two hand picked suppliers. The two key components that IBM outsourced are the ones customers care most about: the power of a PC's processing speed and the architecture of the operating system.

IBM designed its PC with an open architecture that could use widely available components. The open architecture attracted many highly motivated third-parties who were able to develop hardware accessories and software applications and later assembled IBM compatible computers. By forging a virtual supply chain for hardware, software, and distribution, IBM reduced investment in developing PC and was able to launch an attack on Apple Computer, a fast growing computer company in the early 80s. By 1984, IBM owned 26% of the PC market, and by 1985, IBM owned 41% of PC business[4].

It seemed to many people in the 1980s that the business model IBM created for delivering PC might be an approach for business in the future. By 1995, IBM's PC market share was down to only 7.3%. IBM has been surpassed by many of its third-party suppliers and competitors. The decision IBM made to form a supply chain with Intel and Microsoft costs IBM its leadership position in the PC industry. The painful lesson is "when designing your supply chain, whatever your industry, be aware of Intel Inside[5]."

2.7 Summary

Based on a number of best practices introduced in this chapter, we may conclude that the driver of supply chain is globalization, the enabler is technology, the mechanism is collaboration, the way supply chain does

---

[4] Chesbrough, H.W. and Teece, D.J. (2002), Organizing for Innovation: When is Virtual Virtuous? *Harvard Business Review*, August 2002, 5-11.
[5] Fine, C.H. (1999) <u>Clockspeed</u>. Reading, MA: Perseus Books.

business is process management, and the objective is revenue management and customer service.

Both Dell and Wal-Mart are the captains of their respective supply chains. Dell's supply chain excellence lies at the core of its consumer-direct model, which is based on build-to-order manufacturing, effective supplier management, just-in-time processes, and using technology to integrate with customers and suppliers. Wal-Mart's supply chain excellence lies at its everyday-low-price strategy realized through consistently wringing greater efficiency from its supply chain, cutting-edge technology application, and innovative distribution and inventory policy.

Supply chain models are the key to success in today's global market. Therefore, how a supply chain is formed, where the plants and warehouses are located, what degree of flexibility each supply chain has, and what capacity each plant needs to maintain are the issues considered during the process of designing a supply chain. Supply chains are not static. As such, supply chain design needs to be fine tuned constantly to match evolving industry dynamics and changing business paradigm.

Questions for Pondering

1. Today, Dell purchases its microprocessors from Intel and its operating system from the market place just like IBM did in early 80's. Why is Dell a successful example in supply chain management while IBM is not? If you were able to travel back to early 1980's and had the opportunity to be the CEO of IBM, what would you do differently?
2. What supply chain decisions make the difference between Wal-Mart, Target, and K-mart?
3. What advantages does selling books and music via the Internet provide over a traditional bookstore? Are there any disadvantages to selling books and music via the Internet?
4. For what products does the e-commerce supply chain channel offer the greatest advantage? What characterizes these products?

References

Atkinson, H. and Mongelluzzo, B. (2002) "King of the Jungle: Mass Retailers Dictate Terms for Suppliers and Transportation Providers, but Inventories Still Offer Huge Potential for Savings." JoC Week, Feb 4, 2002, Vol. 3, Issue 5, p. 9-11.

e-biz Chronicle.com, May 1, 2001.

Fine, C.H. (1999) Clockspeed. Reading, MA: Perseus Books.

Kestelyn, J. (2000) "Delivering the Goods." *Intelligent Enterprise Magazine*, March 2000, Vol. 3, No.1.

Kinsey, J. (2000) "A Faster, Leaner, Supply Chain: New Uses of Information Technology." *American Journal of Agricultural Economics*, Nov. 15, 2000, Vol. 82, Issue 5, p. 1123.

Lebhar-Friedman, Inc. (2001). "Vendor Partnerships Enhance Product Quality and Pipeline Efficiency. (Wal-Mart's Relations with Suppliers). DSN Retailing Today, (June 2001), p. 14.

Magretta, J. (1998). "The Power of Virtual Integration: An interview with Dell computer's Michael Dell." *Harvard Business Review*, March-April 1998.

Narendra Mulani, Lee, H. (2002). New Business Models for Supply Chain Excellence, (5/15/2002) *ASCET*, Vol. 4, www.ascet.com.

Neef, Dale (2001). e-Procurement: Form Strategy to Implementation. One Lake Street, Upper Saddle River, NJ: Prentice Hall PTR.

Nippon Steel Tries SRM by Editorial Staff, www.isourceonline.com.

Reeve, J.M. and Srinivasan, M.M. (2005). "Which supply chain design is right for you?" *Supply Chain Management Review*, May/June 2005, 50-57.

Stein, T. and Sweat, J. (1998) "Six companies are using supply chains to transform the way they do business." *Killer Supply Chains*, November 9, 1998.

Troy, M. (2001) "Behind-the-Scenes Efficiency Keeps Growth Curve on Course." *DSN Retailing Today*, Vol. 40, Issue 11, p. 80.

Welch, D. (2000) E-Marketplace: Covisint, *Business Week On-line*, June 5, 2000.

www.anheuser-busch.com.

www.covisint.com.

www.dell.com.
www.gm.comlcompany/corp info/profiles/.
www.limited.com.
www.nsc.co.jp.
www.supplysolution.com/newsroorm/news_press0l_1024.htm.

PART TWO

Purchasing, Supply Network, and Strategic Sourcing

Chapter 3
Purchasing and e-Procurement

Chapter 4
Supplier Relations and Strategic Sourcing

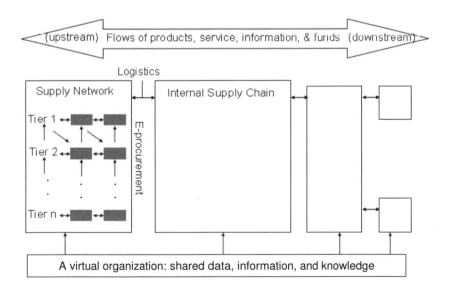

Chapter 3

Purchasing and e-Procurement

3.1 The Role of Purchasing

3.1.1 Introduction to purchasing

The role of purchasing is to obtain raw material, components, parts, as well as information that are needed for the production of goods or providing services. The purchasing process includes many aspects, such as request for quotation (RFQ), supplier market analysis, supplier selection, contract negotiations, and purchase plan implementation.

The purchase function plays a liaison role between various departments within an organization and numerous suppliers outside the company. The purchase goal is to develop and implement a purchasing plan that supports the company's daily operation and the overall strategic plan.

It is estimated that the purchased material cost accounts for 60% of the total product cost in the manufacture sector. In the retail and wholesale environments, the cost of a purchased commodity can be as high as 90%. According to the US Census Bureau 2002 manufacturing research report, the cost of purchased raw material, parts and components exceeds the amount of the value-added portion during the manufacturing process. Therefore, effectively managing purchasing and sourcing can enhance a firm's competitive advantages.

For a long time, purchasing was regarded as a supporting function in an organization. Today, in the age of supply chain management, the purchasing function plays an important role in implementing a company's overall business strategy. Important aspects of supply chain management include outsourcing, searching for better quality products, and emphasizing lean and profitable production. The introduction of the Internet technology, e-commerce, on-line auction, and vendor-managed inventory has significantly influenced the purchasing relationship between the buyer and supplier.

Before 1980s, it was common to have purchasing and logistics functions housed in the same department. As the role of purchasing becomes increasingly important in supply chain management, purchasing and logistics functions are separated. For example, in the 1970s and 1980s, purchasing and logistics were actually in the same department at Procter & Gamble. Then in the late 1980s and early 1990s, the two functions were separated. The task responsibilities were re-established by the late 1990s. In general, logistics tend to be operational; so managing the flow of the goods is its main task. The purchasing or sourcing personnel, on the other hand, are more attuned. They make certain supplier selection to reflect a company's goal in terms of cost control, longer-term production capacity, product quality, and other pertinent objectives.

Purchasing usually can be divided into two categories: commercial purchasing and industry purchasing. Wholesalers engage in commercial purchasing, which enables the retail sales process. The commercial purchase takes advantage of large quantity discount, then, breaks down the large quantity to small volumes for retail sales. This process provides material management services to retailers and end users. Industry purchasing, on the other hand, buys raw material, components, parts, etc. for the purpose of manufacturing products. Industry purchasing may also include acquiring indirect materials for the purpose of maintenance, repair and operation (MRO).

This chapter focuses on purchasing and e-Procurement. Supplier market analysis, supplier selection, and outsourcing are discussed in Chapter 4, Collaborative Relations and Strategic Sourcing.

3.1.2 Evolution of purchasing and supply chain management

The evolution of purchasing and supply chain management can be categorized into seven periods according to National Association of Purchasing Management[1], and Monczka, Trent, and Handfield (2005)[2]. Based on these two sources, the evolution of purchasing and supply chain management is illustrated in Table 3.1.

The history of purchasing can be traced back to 19th century. One of the first books that mentioned the purchasing function is *"On the Economy of Machinery and Manufacturers"* by Charles Babbag[3] in 1832. In the book, the purchasing function is discussed. The growth of the early years occurred after 1850. Railroad companies first recognized the purchasing function as an independent department. By 1866, the Pennsylvania Railroad in the US gave the purchasing function department status under the title of Supplying Department. The head purchaser reported directly to the president of the company. Since the chief purchaser played an important role in the company's overall business, he was granted the top managerial status[4].

In the purchasing procedure refining years (1900-1914), the industrial purchasing function came into view. Qualified purchasing agents and material specifications were discussed in industrial magazines. *The book on Buying* was published in 1905 to introduce the principles of buying. Nevertheless, purchasing was regarded as a clerical job.

During the war years (1919-1945), the importance of the purchasing function increased due to the need of obtaining materials and supplies for military missions. Additionally during this time, Ford Motors introduced mass production. Purchasing became an important component of the large scale manufacturing production.

During the quiet years (late 1940s – mid-1960s), purchasing function became more refined and the number of trained purchasing professionals

---

[1] www.napm-centraltexas.org/History/ISM_History.htm.
[2] Monczka, R. Trent, R. and Handfield, R. 2005. "Purchasing and Supply Chain Management," 3rd edition, p.20-24.
[3] Charles Babbage, "On the Economy of Machinery and Manufacturers." 1832. London: Charles Knight Publishing.
[4] H. Fearon, "History of Purchasing," *Journal of Purchasing*, February 1968, p. 44-50.

Table 3.1. History of purchasing

Period	Evolution Stage
The Early Years (Early 1800s – 1900)	After the industry revolution, mass production made purchasing a necessary function of organizations. Railroad companies in the US gave 'purchasing', department status for the first time.
The Purchasing Procedure Refining Years (1900 - 1914)	Purchasing procedures and ideas were refined and published. However, purchasing was considered a clerical task.
The War Years WWI - WWII (1914 - 1945)	The importance of purchasing function was increased due to the need to obtain war materials and supplies. Additionally, mass production initiated by Ford Motor made purchasing an important function.
The Quiet Years (Late 40's - mid-1960s)	Purchasing function became better refined as the number of trained professionals increased.
The Age of Materials Management (Mid-1960s – early 1980s)	MRP was introduced in the late 1960s. The purchasing function became more managerial-oriented. MRP evolved to MRPII to include more than the factory production and material needs. During the 1980s JIT production methods were popularized, which emphasized supplier relationship. Purchasing evolves to procurement during this time.
The Age of Globalization and e-Commerce (Late 1980s - 2000)	The advancement of technology and the Internet changed the way purchasing operates. B2B, B2C, and C2B became new business transaction models. Supply network was expanded to the global market. Mom and papa stores were replaced by super retail stores such as Home Depot and Wal-Mart.
The Age of Integrated SCM (2000 & beyond)	Increasing integration with supply networks and information technology. Process reengineering, which is influenced by advanced technology, becomes strategically important.

increased. The main responsibility associated with purchasing included records management, purchase order implementation, and vendor selection and interaction.

The age of materials management (mid 1960s – early 1980s) ushers the concept of materials management. In the late 1960s, George Plossl and John Orlicky introduced MRP. Later, MRP evolved to MRPII to include financial and other resources. Meanwhile, JIT production methods were popularized, which had an emphasis on supplier relationship. The purchasing function became a more tactical than operational activity and evolved from pure purchasing to procurement. Procurement includes a wide range of activities including purchasing, development of service requirements, supplier quality management, and market analyses.

The age of globalization and e-Commerce (Late 1980s -2000) is a period in which purchasing became more integrated into the overall corporate strategy. The 1990s continued to move purchasing into the computer age. Requisitions were computerized and purchase orders were electronically delivered daily. E-commerce narrows down the physical distance between countries and regions. Mom and papa stores were replaced by super retail stores such as Home Depot and Wal-Mart, which further transformed purchasing to procurement. As a result, global sourcing became a common practice.

The age of integrated supply chain management (2000 and beyond) witnesses even more changes. Small supply stores and manual typewriters are becoming history. Purchasing is experiencing increased integration with supply networks and information technology. The purchasing field evolves from a tactical function to being a part of strategic supply management team. In addition to purchasing and procurement activities, strategic purchasing is involved in long-term acquisition plan development, continuous improvement, corporate strategy formulation, and supplier development.

The results of over 150 years evolution in purchasing include formalization of purchasing departments, professional growth of purchasing and procurement personnel, involvement in cross-functional teams internally, and supply chain creation with trading partners externally.

3.1.3 Commodity types and purchasing strategy

The purchasing strategy is determined according to the nature of various commodities. The objectives for an effective purchasing strategy for each major commodity include defining a strategic vision for the commodity which supports overall business objectives, developing a sourcing strategy for each commodity based on assessments of the commodity profile, and total costs of acquisition and possession. There are four kinds of commodity characteristics: non-critical commodity, leveraged commodity, key commodity, and strategic commodity. The commodity map illustrated in Figure 3.1 is a two dimensional matrix. One dimension reflects the impact of the commodity usage on business and the other the complexity of supply sources. When formulating commodity-sourcing strategy, the overall business strategy ought to be considered and supply market should be analyzed. Sourcing strategy should be in line with the company's overall business strategy. Figure 3.1 provides an example of utilizing the commodity map.

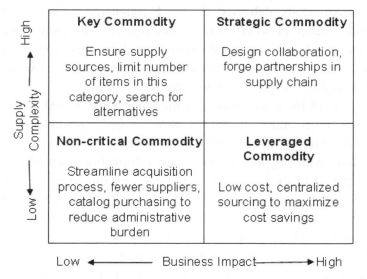

Figure 3.1. Commodity characteristics and purchasing strategy

Key commodity in Figure 3.1 has low impact on business and high supply challenge. This type of product has complex manufacturing processes. There are a few alternative products and qualified suppliers. The objective of managing this type of commodity is to minimize the number of items in this category. Purchase strategy includes long-term contract, the whole supply chain management, and new supplier development.

Strategic commodity has high impact on business and supply challenge. Strategic commodity has complex product design specifications and tends to have an important impact on a firm's profitability. Product quality is very important. The objective of this type of commodity is to create product differentiation. There are very few qualified suppliers. Purchasing strategy includes long-term agreement, product design collaboration, seamless supply chain processes between the trading partners. Additionally, a contingency plan is also necessary for this type of commodity.

Leveraged commodity has high impact on business and low supply challenge. This type of product generally has high volume expenditures such as maintenance, repair, and operating (MRO) items. The supply source is rich. Alternative suppliers are available. Purchasing strategy includes competitive bidding, centralized procurement to achieve volume discount, and value-added service package from suppliers.

Non-critical commodity has low impact on business and low supply challenge. This type of commodity has low value and usage volume is low. There are many existing supply sources on the market. Sourcing strategy includes simplifying acquisition process to achieve efficiency and cost reduction. Long-term contract, vendor managed inventory, and catalog purchasing can be considered.

3.1.4 Centralized purchasing vs. decentralized purchasing

Centralized purchasing and decentralized purchasing is a choice many companies have to make because very few companies employ a pure centralized purchasing strategy or a pure decentralized purchasing strategy. Both centralized and decentralized sourcing approaches have advantages and disadvantages. Furthermore, sourcing decisions have implication for the control of supply chain and impact on firm's overall performance.

Centralized purchasing consolidates the entire company's purchasing needs. A Purchasing department identifies potential suppliers, negotiates contracts and implements the purchasing plan. The advantages of centralized purchase include greater purchasing specialization, buyer's influence, and quantity discount due to large volume purchase. Increased purchasing quantity created by combining orders also means obtaining better service, ensuring long-term supply sources, and developing new supplier networks. The large quantity centralized purchasing tends to have a fewer orders. The disadvantages of centralized purchasing include losing control at the department or division level. Lead-time associated with centralized purchasing is longer than the decentralized purchasing approach. In general, centralized purchasing is a choice for leveraged commodity as mentioned in Figure 3.1.

Decentralized purchasing gives the local business unit more power to choose the best fit of suppliers and can effectively use local resources. The advantages of decentralized purchasing include better understanding of user's needs and product specifications, easier communication and coordination as well as, shorter sourcing lead-time. The shortcomings of decentralized purchasing include the loss of quantity discount and whole truckload freight rate. The decentralized sourcing approach can be a choice for key commodity as mentioned in Figure 3.1.

Considering the advantages and disadvantages of centralized and decentralized purchasing, a hybrid purchasing system that integrates both centralized and decentralized purchasing is ideal for organizations that have different divisions and business units. The hybrid approach can take advantage of both centralized and decentralized purchasing needs. For example, firms can employ the centralized sourcing approach to purchase large quantity items such as spot and leveraged commodities, and utilize decentralized sourcing approach to purchase key and strategic commodities.

Example Problem 3.1

A university bookstore sells textbooks, magazines, greeting cards, gums, university reminiscent items such as mugs, hats, T-shirts, reference books, etc. Using the purchasing metrics discussed in Figure 3.2 to determine sourcing strategy and partnership relationship for commodity items.

Solution

To a university bookstore, textbooks are the strategic items as illustrated in Figure 3.2. Publishers and bookstores usually forge strategic partnership. Publisher's representatives keep close contact with professors and the university bookstore to promote new books and learn educational needs at the university. Extensive services are provided to ensure that the right textbooks are provided at the right time in the right quantities.

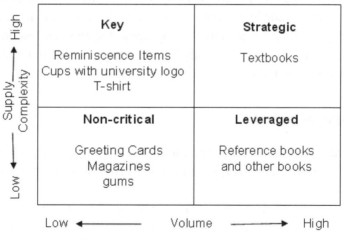

Figure 3.2. University bookstore

Reference books such as dictionaries and GMAT study guides are the leveraged items to a university bookstore. Centralized purchasing is a common sourcing strategy for this type of commodity. Contract is usually negotiated at the corporate level to achieve large volume quantity discount and better service.

University mugs and T-shirts are reminiscent items. Since these items have special requirements, decentralized sourcing approach can be taken. Reminiscent items can be outsourced to local vendors who have specific techniques or provide accommodating services that the bookstore is looking for.

Magazines, gums, and chocolate are non-critical commodities to a university bookstore. The supplier relationship is arm's-length oriented, that means when transaction is completed, the relationship ends.

3.2 Purchasing Procedure

3.2.1 Supplier market analysis

Supplier market analysis provides important information for purchasing decisions. For example, the number of available suppliers, the supplier's technical capability, the supplier's geographic location, and so on. After conducting supply market analysis, the buyer will have a better understanding about the market.

3.2.2 Types of request

There are a few approaches to solicit offers from potential suppliers: Request for Quotation (RFQ), Request for Proposal (RFP), and Request for Bid (RFB).

RFQ is applied when the buyer is able to articulate the need. For example, when purchasing working gloves, the buyer is able to specify the quality of the material and sizes. As the buyer receives the quotations from various suppliers, he will decide with whom he is going to do business.

RFP is applied when the buyer has complicated requirements and is looking for technical expertise. Negotiating for price, quality, delivery schedule, and service are appropriate activities. For example, when purchasing a maintenance package, the buyer may specify various maintenance schedules for each different functional area and negotiate for price and service standards.

RFB is similar to RFP in terms of looking for specific packages. RFB is appropriate when the buyer is looking for competitive bids for the lowest price (or other specifications), and the lowest offer is accepted without negotiation. Other issues need to be considered include whether it is a sealed offer, or if there is opportunity for negotiation after the bid is submitted.

3.2.3 Purchase plan implementation

The purchasing process includes passing the material requirement information of the user to the purchaser, then from the purchaser to the supplier. After the purchasing information is passed on to the appropriate supplier, the materials purchased are delivered to the user and the invoice is sent to the accounting department. Meanwhile, quality and quantity of the purchased items is verified and checked. In general, there are six steps involved in the purchasing process as illustrated in Figure 3.3.

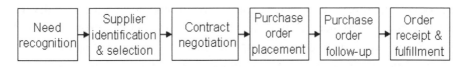

Figure 3.3. Purchasing process

Step 1 <u>Recognition of Need</u> – Purchase starts from the recognition of need from an individual or a department of the company. The request may include the kind of material, quantity, delivery time, as well as quality standards.

Step 2 <u>Supplier Identification and Selection</u> – Supplier selection is extremely important to a company. After the user communicates the need to the purchaser, the purchaser will conduct an analysis on the price trend, supplier availability, and market condition. In general, cost is one of the important competitive factors. Other factors considered include material quality, on-time delivery, service, and so on. Section 4.2 provides detailed discussion on supplier selection.

Step 3 <u>Contract Negotiations</u> – Before negotiating a purchasing contract, the purchasing personnel divide the items they want to purchase into various categories using commodity characteristics map (described in 3.1.3) or ABC analysis method. For example, Category A items usually account for 20% of the usage and 80% of the total purchasing value. Category B items account for about 30% of item usage and 15% of the total purchasing value. Category C usually account for 50% of the usage and 5% of the total purchasing value. As such, the purchaser can sign a long-term contract with suppliers for category C items and negotiate for quantity discount. For category B items, order one item at a time using centralized purchasing approach. The usage of category A goods is very low so the department that has initiated the need can directly contact the supplier to ensure that specifications are clearly communicated to the supplier.

Step 4 <u>Purchase Order Placement</u> – The buyer issues the purchase order after the buyer and supplier have signed the purchasing contract. The purchase order form includes information such as the purchased product, quantity, unit price, total cost, company address, delivery arrangement, payment provision, free on board (FOB) provision, and other relevant issues. Once the supplier receives the order form from the buyer, the purchase order form becomes an effective legal document.

Step 5 <u>Purchase Order Follow-up</u> – The purchaser should keep track of the order status after the supplier receives the order form and make sure that the order is promptly fulfilled. If there is any change in quantity and delivery date from the user side, the purchaser should contact the supplier immediately.

Step 6 <u>Order Receipt and Fulfillment</u> – When the buyer receives the order, the quantity and quality should be verified and checked. If the quantity or quality does not match the description on the purchase order, the errors should be corrected immediately.

3.3 E-procurement

3.3.1 The role of technology in purchasing

Business-to-business electronic commerce describes a broad array of applications that enable an enterprise or business to form electronic relationships with their distributors, resellers, supplier, and other partners. Business-to-business (B2B) electronic commerce implies that that both buyer and supplier are business entities, while business-to-customer (B2C) electronic commerce implies that the buyers are individuals.

E-procurement applies web-based technology to streamline order processing and enhance purchasing administrative functions. However, e-procurement is more than just making purchases online. A properly implemented e-procurement system links organizations and their business processes with suppliers while managing all interactions between them. This includes making bids, quoting prices, sending emails to participants, and communicating electronically with suppliers and customers. Typically, e-procurement web sites allow qualified and registered users to look for buyers or sellers of goods and services. Depending on the approach, buyers or sellers may specify prices or invite bids.

The benefits of an e-procurement system include: availability of relevant information, well organized data, standardized transaction processes, improved contract compliance, less inventory, and reduced material and process costs. The benefits of e-procurement to a buying company mean more choices of suppliers, easier access to the seller's product list, faster ordering, lower transaction costs, less paper work, and increased efficiency. The benefits of e-procurement to a seller include increased sales volume, reduced operating costs, more collaboration between the buyer and seller, better communication with customers, and improved performance.

There are some shortcomings associated with e-procurement. The downside includes system-to-system integration and compatibility, initial investment in hardware and software, system maintenance, information security, data accuracy, and reengineering the procurement process.

3.3.2 Vertical and horizontal partnerships

Supply chain partners can be categorized to two groups, vertical partners and horizontal partners. Vertical partners have complementary, non-overlapping skills and are relatively equal to their contribution to the value-add efforts. Horizontal partners, on the other hand, usually have overlapping capabilities.

Table 3.2 shows the direction of partnerships. A horizontal partner is a partner at the same echelon[5]. Partner's skills and expertise may overlap. For example, two distributors forge partnership in order to offer better geographic coverage. In this case, the distributors' expertise overlaps.

Vertical partnership does not have overlap capability. An example is Limited Brands' partnership with its fabric and garment supplier, Li & Fung in Hong Kong. Limited Brands provides point-of-sale information to Li & Fung. Li & Fung, a company in the upstream of the supply chain, delivers the shipments to Limited Brands' stores. Vertical partnership reflects the trend toward integration in many supply chains.

Table 3.2. Direction of partnerships

Direction	Description
Horizontal	Partners are at the same echelon in the supply chain.
Vertical	Partners are at different echelons of the supply chain.
Hybrid	Expansion of capability occurs both horizontally and vertically.

The hybrid partnership integrates both horizontal and vertical partnership practices.

3.3.3 One or many relationships

One or many relationships reflect relative strength of each partner and the number of partners available for collaborating. Table 3.3 uses the

---

[5] J. B. Ayers, *Handbook of Supply Chain Management,* 2001, p. 131.

data management terms to show the partnership relationship[6]. In column one, company is identified and the available suppliers/choices are indicated in the second column.

Many to Many. In this scenario, a company has many partner candidates from which to choose. None of the partners is currently a dominant company. The apparel industry fits this category. There are many companies specialized in apparel production, such as Levi, the Limited Brands and many clothing are available.

Table 3.3. One or many relationships

Supply Relationship	Description
Many to many	A single company has many partner candidates from which to choose. Neither partner is currently a dominant company.
One to many	Characterized by large companies with many available suppliers.
Many to one	A company with low market share competes with many companies for the business of the strong partner.
One to one	This is a peer relationship with dominant partners on each side. There is little choice for partner selection.

One to Many and Many to One. In the commercial airline industry, Airbus is a "one to many" company. It has many suppliers. On the other hand, a supplier to Airbus is a "many to one" company". A "one to many" company has a lot of power in sourcing, while a "many to one" company would have a tough time to compete for orders.

One-to-One. A One-to-One relationship is not very popular in the market place; it presents a risk to business should anything unexpected happen. For example, Deere & Co. is one of the world's major providers of agricultural equipment. It has manufacturing facilities and offices in

---

[6] J. B. Ayers, *Handbook of Supply Chain Management,* 2001.

160 countries. Excelsior is one of very few manufacturers of tractor attachments. Deere purchases tractor attachments from Excelsior. Deere's business accounts for 95% of Excelsior's revenue. On the other hand, Excelsior owns the design of the attachments that it builds for Deere[7]. When Deere wanted Excelsior to invest in a new manufacturing process, Excelsior was hesitant to do so because of the investment cost. If the two companies broke their relationship, the cost would be enormous to both. Deere would have a difficult time to find a replacement, and Excelsior would lose its business.

3.3.4 e-Marketplace

E-marketplace or e-hub displays supplier's goods or services on the Internet in the same way a catalog did in a hard copy or printed form. By using e-marketplace companies are able to identify new suppliers, negotiate for services, and streamline their supply chains.

3.3.5 Supplier-oriented marketplace

The most common B2B model is the supplier-oriented marketplace. In this model, both individual customers and business buyers use the same supplier-provided marketplace. Thus, suppliers are able to focus on their most lucrative trading partners and contracts.

Companies like Dell Inc., Intel, Cisco, and IBM have successfully implemented the supplier-oriented business model. It is reported that Dell Inc. sold 90 percent of its computers to business buyers, and Cisco sold $1 billion worth of routers, switches, and other network interconnection devices in 1998 mainly to business customers or industry buyers through their Internet e-marketplace.

The supplier-oriented business model is successful as long as the e-marketplace has a sound reputation and loyal customers. This model is not always efficient for the large and repetitive business buyer, because the large buyer's information is stored on the suppliers' servers. Under

---

[7] Howard Forman, "Supplier development at Deere & Company." Penn State University, 2001 Case Writing Workshop.

the supplier-oriented marketplace platform, the buyer's procurement department has to manually enter the order information into its own corporate information system. Searching e-stores and e-malls to find suppliers and comparing suppliers and products is time consuming and can be costly to companies who purchase thousands of products on the Internet.

Another application of the supplier-oriented marketplace is proprietary auction sites like computer reseller Ingram Micro[8]. These sites are accessible only to existing customers. The sites are designed to forge good business relationships between the company and its regular buyers. Sale of surplus goods is easily facilitated on this kind of e-marketplace site, promotion of such enables business customers to realize deep discounts.

3.3.6 Buyer-oriented marketplace

Big buyers often wish to open their own marketplaces where they invite potential suppliers to bid on the announced Request for Quote (RFQ). For example, Wal-Mart's e-Marketplace invites proposals from potential vendors. In this case, the buyer's procurement department needs to define the scope of products to buy and invite vendors to bid.

As more companies move to this model, it will become increasingly difficult to trace all buyer-oriented web sites. This situation can be improved by providing online directories that list the open RFQs. Another way to address this problem is via the deployment of software agents that can reduce the human burden in the bidding process.

3.3.7 Intermediary-oriented marketplace

An intermediary-oriented platform features an electronic intermediary company that runs a marketplace where business buyers and sellers can meet. This concept is similar to the intermediary-based e-stores and e-malls.

---

[8] www.ingram.com.

An example of an intermediary-oriented marketplaces is Covisint, the automotive trade consortium formed by GM, Ford, Daimler-Chrysler, Renault, and Nissan. In the airline industry, Boeing's PART (part analysis and requirements tracking) serves as an intermediary marketplace. Boeing's PART links over 500 airlines with 300 key suppliers of Boeing's maintenance parts. Customers of PART place orders online and the orders can be shipped on the same day or next day. The paperless e-procurement transaction is fulfilled at a significantly lower cost than paper purchasing orders, faxes, and telephone calls.

An auction on the Internet creates an intermediary-oriented marketplace. Online auction started in 1995. A host site such as e-Bay acts like a broker; it offers services for sellers to post their goods for sale and allows buyers to bid on those items. Most auctions open with a starting bid, which is the lowest price the seller is willing to accept. Detailed information for each item is posted to the site. Bidders look at the descriptions and then start the bidding by sending an e-mail or filling out an election form. The bidding, which may last several days, is shown on a page at the host's web site and is continuously updated to show the current high bids.

3.3.8 Disintermediation and reintermediation

To disinter mediate is to reduce one or more steps in a supply chain by cutting out one or more intermediaries. For example, Dell Computer is well known for selling computers and other PC related electronic appliances online to businesses and individual customers. Through its application of the Direct Model, Dell Computer cuts out the retail function from its supply chain.

To reintermediate is to introduce a new intermediary to the supply chain. For example, to inject a fee-for-transaction website into a supply chain is to introduce a new intermediary. The web-based travel agency, Travelocity.com, consolidates and filters information on hotels, resort areas, airline flights, car rental, local attractions, etc. Customers can arrange their entire trips on-line. In this case, Travelocity.com serves as a new intermediary to the tourism supply chain.

Another example of reintermediary is the introduction of a third party escrow service to the value chain of online auction. Customers who conducted auctions online complained that the items they received were materially different from the seller's representation. When Amazon promoted its auction service, it ensured customers by offering a guarantee; promising satisfaction or their money back on items valued at $250 or less. A third party escrow service is recommended for items that are more valuable. The escrow service provider is a new party in the on-line auction supply chain.

3.4 Green Purchasing

Rapid environmental deterioration over the last few decades has dramatically increased corporate awareness of environmental responsibility. A growing number of companies, such as Du Pont, Coca-Cola, PepsiCo, Procter & Gamble, and H.J. Heinz, are developing environmentally "green" products[9].

Formulation of a green purchasing strategy is challenging because green purchasing may result in increased material cost and fewer qualified suppliers. A survey conducted in the US on the issue of green purchasing[9] identified three strategies that could be used to reduce the sources of upstream waste. The three strategies are (i) reducing the purchased volume of items that are difficult to dispose of or are harmful to the ecosystem; (ii) reducing the use of hazardous virgin materials by purchasing a higher percentage of recycled or reused content; and (iii) requiring that suppliers minimize unnecessary packaging and use more biodegradable or returnable packaging

Recycling and reuse are important components of green purchasing strategies and waste management programs. Recycling is the most popular method to reduce waste. Recycled commodities include soft drink cans, newspaper, cardboard, aluminum, plastics, and ferrous metal. To effectively implementing recycling strategy, buying firms need to specify their recycling policy involving collection, separation, storage,

---

[9] Hokey Min & William P Galle. *International Journal of Purchasing and Materials Management.* 33(3), 10-18.

transportation, reprocessing, and remanufacturing. Purchasing professionals should identify items that are recyclable, figure out how recyclables are sorted, and trace where recyclables are sold back or remanufactured.

Reuse is different from recycle. Reuse may result in "non-durable" products or parts unreusable. As such, reuse seems to be restricted to commodities that are more durable, such as pallets, cardboards, and paper.

Current green purchasing strategies seem to be reactive in that they try to avoid violations of environmental statues, rather than embedding environmental goals within the long-term corporate policy. The linkage between green purchasing and supplier quality assurance is still weak.

3.5 Total Cost of Ownership Analysis in Purchasing

'Total cost of ownership' is a financial estimate designed to help business managers assess direct and indirect costs related to the purchase of any capital investment, such as computer or other devices. A total cost assessment provides a comprehensive statement which reflects not only the initial purchase cost but all aspects in the further use and maintenance of the equipment, device, or system considered. This includes repairs, maintenance, upgrades, service and support, networking, security, user training, and software licensing, among other expenses[10].

Total cost of ownership (TCO) analysis originated with the Gartner Group in 1987. Since then, the concept has been broadly applied. For example, the total cost of an automobile includes the cost of purchasing a vehicle, insurance, gas consumption, maintenance, and finally its resale value. A comparative cost analysis that studies various car models helps consumers choose a car to fit their needs and budget.

Total cost of ownership studies can serve as the basis to make decisions such as a make-or-buy decision, supplier selection, and buy-or-lease decision. To determine TCO, all the important cost drivers should be identified, especially some hidden costs, such as administrative

---

[10] http://en.wikipedia.org/wiki/Total_cost_of_ownership.

costs, upgrade costs, technical support costs, end-user operation costs, and so on.

Example Problem 3.2: Total cost ownership

A buyer receives bids from two suppliers for a specially designed motor for its latest production. Use the information given below to determine which supplier should be chosen. Cost of working capital is 10% per year. Assume there are 360 days in a year.

	Supplier A	Supplier B
Motor purchase price	$1,000/unit	$1,200/unit
Terms	2/10, net 30	1/15, net 30
Number of motors needed	20	20
Weight per motor	55lb.	58lb.
Transportation cost	$5/ton-mile	$4.5/ton-mile
Distance	200 miles	150 miles
Installation fee	$3,000	no charge

Notes: per ton-mile = 2,000 lbs per mile

Solution

Table 3.4 presents the results. Cash discount terms from supplier 1 means the supplier will give 2% off if the buyer pays the bill within 10 days after he receives the invoice. Additionally, the buyer will gain 10 day's interest if he pays the bill on the 10th day. Supplier 1 charges $3,000 for installation and supplier 2 does not charge installation fee. According to the cost analysis, the buyer will purchase motors from Supplier 1, who offers a lower total cost package than that of supplier 2.

3.6 Enhancing Value through e-Procurement

E-procurement has added value to supply chain management in recent years. Since 1996, General Electric Lighting forged strategic

Table 3.4.

Item	Cost	Supplier 1
Motor Purchase Price	20*$1000	20,000
Cash Discount	$20,000*[(10%*(10/360))+2%]	(456)
Transportation Cost	200mile * ((20*55)/2000) * $5.00	550
Installation Cost		3,000
		$23,094
		Supplier 2
Motor Purchase Price	20*$1200	24,000
Cash Discount	$24,000*[(10%*(15/360))+1%]	(340)
Transportation Cost	150mile * ((20*58)/2000) * $4.50	522
Installation Cost		0
		$24,182

partnerships with its suppliers and piloted its Trading Partner Network (TPN) to conduct online procurement[11]. Requisitions are sent electronically to the sourcing department from internal customers; then Requests for Quotations (RFQ) packages are sent out electronically to would-be-respondents. The Internet provides the sourcing department access to suppliers around the world. The system is capable of automatically attaching accurate drawings to the electronic requisition forms. Suppliers are notified within two hours of the time the sourcing department begins the process via e-mail, fax, or EDI that a RFQ is on its way. Suppliers are given a seven-day window for bid preparation and for sending that bid back to GE Lighting. The bid is routed to the proper evaluator, and a contract can be awarded the same day.

General Electric Lighting purchased over $1 billion in goods and services over the Internet during 1997. The estimated annual savings through streamlining the procurement process is about 500 - 700 million dollars. The benefits of e-Procurement gained by GE and its suppliers, include:

---

[11] http://tpn.geis.com.

1. Labor involved in the procurement process has declined 30 percent. At the same time, material costs have declined 5 to 20% due to an increased ability to reach a wider supplier base.
2. Of the staff involved in the procurement process, 60% have been redeployed. The sourcing department has at least 6 to 8 more days a month to concentrate on strategic activities. Days that were previously utilized performing manual processing activities.
3. It used to take 18 to 23 days to identify suppliers, prepare a request for bid, negotiate a price, and award a contract to a supplier. Today, it takes 9 to 11 days.
4. With the transactions handled electronically from beginning to end, invoices are automatically reconciled with purchase orders, reflecting any modifications that occurred along the way.
5. GE procurement departments across the world now share information about their best suppliers. In February 1997 alone, GE Lighting found seven new suppliers through the Internet, including one that charged 20 percent less than the second lowest bid.

The benefits of strategic partnership have extended beyond the confines of GE. Suppliers also gained benefits. Exposure to other units of GE helped GE's suppliers by introducing them to other potential customers.

3.7 Purchasing Performance Metrics

Establishing key performance indicators for purchasing helps to benchmark purchasing activities with the firm's overall goal, identify gaps, and make continuous improvements. In general, purchasing performance metrics can be classified into two categories, efficient and effectiveness.

3.7.1 Efficiency metrics of purchasing

Efficient metrics try to describe how efficient the purchasing process is. The required information needed for analyzing various industries.

However, the emphasis is on total dollar volume of purchases and total dollars spent for department operating expenses[12].

(i) Purchase dollar as a percent of sales dollars.

(ii) Purchase operating expenses as a percentage of purchase dollars.

(iii) Purchase operating expenses as a percentage of total sales dollar.

(iv) Purchase operating expenses per purchasing employee.

Comparing the results of the above, with the previous period's results and the industry average provides some insight on the efficiency of the purchasing function

When examining purchasing costs and prices, external market and economic conditions should be considered. The purchasing price should be compared with (i) standard costs that are applied by accounting methods; (ii) quoted market price; and (iii) target costs as determined by market index price (reflecting changes for the material and commodities). However, these numbers do not provide information on purchasing function effectiveness.

3.7.2 Effective metrics of purchasing

Effective metrics try to explain how well purchasing is done. These measures include quality of the items purchased, on-time delivery, customer satisfaction, faster time-to-market, contribution to the firm's overall profit, increased sales, etc.

Some inventory investment measures can be used as surrogate measures to measure purchasing performance. Measures such as days of supply, ratio of inventory dollar investment to sales dollar volume, and numbers of inventory turnovers are meaningful indicators to evaluate purchasing in the management of a supply chain.

Purchasing and supplier collaborative activities provide useful information to measure purchasing. These measures can be percentage on-time deliveries, percentage of cost reduction, number of change orders issued, number of requisitions received and processed, employee workload and productivity, reduction in the number of out-of-stock cases and cycle service levels.

---

[12] CAPS Research, www.capsresearch.org, August 2004.

Effective measures require examining the relationships from both the buyer and seller sides. If purchasing is to contribute to the competitiveness of the firm, it must focus on quality, flexibility, cost, service, cycle time, and on-time delivery.

3.8 Summary

In this chapter, we have discussed the evolution of purchasing and the emergence of e-Procurement. Traditionally, purchasing was considered as a clerical function, and did not contribute significantly to a firm's overall business strategy. However, in the last decades, the purchasing function has evolved into an integral part of supply chain management and adds significant value to a firm's overall performance, as well as that of the supply chain itself.

The commodity and purchasing strategies described in this chapter can be applied to analyze the characteristics of various commodities and be used to develop appropriate sourcing strategies. The Total Cost of Ownership model, on the other hand, considers the total cost of purchasing and takes into consideration other qualitative and quantitative factors.

Questions for Pondering

1. Relate the objective of purchasing to (i) a large fast-food restaurant chain, (2) a hospital emergency room, and (3) a government division. What are the strategic, leveraged, key, and non-critical items?
2. Discuss the challenges faced by a supply manager working in (i) a highly centralized organization structure and (ii) a highly decentralized organization structure?
3. The Wal-Mart retail chain purchases hundreds and thousands items from suppliers and enjoys great purchasing power. The Limited Brands, on the other hand, owns Mast Industries, which produces fashion items, sold in the Limited stores. Compare and contrast the

purchasing and sourcing strategy of the two retail giants. Why do they employ different purchasing and sourcing strategies?

5. Explain how and when equipment purchasing might be strategic?

6. Describe your own experience of purchasing on-line. What factors make you favor on-line purchasing? Moreover, what factors hinder you from buying on-line? Or Why do you hesitate to buy on line?

7. Find three e-Procurement examples on the Internet. Describe the objectives, implementation mechanisms, and the performance outcome of the three examples.

8. Based on the Commodity Map presented in Figure 3.1, give an example to each quadrant, and discuss the commodity characteristics and purchasing strategy

Problems

1. Given the information below, use total analysis to determine which supplier is more cost-effective. Cost of working capital is 12% per year. Assume there are 360 days in a year.

	Supplier A	Supplier B	Supplier C
Equipment purchase price	$65,100/unit	$71,200/unit	$68,500/unit
Terms	2/10, net 30	1/15, net 30	3/10, net 20
Number of motors needed	10	10	10
Weight per motor	150 lbs.	130 lbs.	170 lbs.
Transportation cost	$10/ton-mile	$9/ton-mile	$12/ton-mile
Distance	200 miles	150 miles	120 miles
Installation fee	$2,000	no charge	$1,500

Notes: per ton-mile = 2,000 lbs per mile

2. Table 3.5 presents various costs associated with four car models. Conduct a Four-Year Total Cost Analysis based on cost information given in Table 3.5. Suppose the user purchases the car with cash and

drives 10,000 miles a year. Cost of working capital is 10% per year. Assume there are 360 days in a year.

a. Which car should the user purchase?
b. Identify other hidden factors that might be important to the user in choosing a car?
c. Reconsider the choice of the car including costs in Table 3.5 and the hidden factors.

Table 3.5.

	Honda Accord LX	Toyota Camry LE	BMW 525 Xi	Mercedes Benz E350
Price	$20,825	$20,500	$45,395	50,825
Maintenance	3 yrs / 45000 miles	3 yrs / 36000 miles	48 mon. / 50000 miles	48 mon. / 50000 miles
Gas / mile City/highway	24/34	28/36	20/30	19/27
Resale value after 4 yr.	$10,000	$10,000	$30,000	$32,000
Color Choice	6 colors	8 colors	11 colors	15 colors
Wheelbase in inches	107.9	109.3	113.7	112.4

References

APICS, 1998. *Dictionary*, 9th edition. Falls Church, VA.
Ayers, J.B. 2001. *Handbook of Supply Chain Management*, New York: The St. Lucie Press.
Chen, I.J. and Paulraj, A. (2004) Understanding supply chain management: critical research and a theoretical framework. *International Journal of Production Research*. 42(1), 131-163.
Chesbrough, H.W. and Teece, D.J. 1996. "Organizing for innovation: When is virtual virtuous?" *Harvard Business Review*, p. 6.

Chopra, S. and Meindl, P. 2002. *Supply Chain Management*. New Jersey: Prentice Hall.

Leenders, M.R., Johnson, P.F., Flynn, A.E., Fearon, H.E. 2006. *Purchasing and Supply Management*. New York: McGraw-Hill/Irwin.

Monczka, R. Trent, R. and Handfield, R. 2005. *Purchasing and Supply Chain Management*, 3rd edition. Ohio: South Western.

Neef, D. 2001. *e-Procurement: From strategy to Implementation*. New Jersey: Prentice Hall.

O'Brien, Kevin "Value-Chain Report -- Strategic Sourcing." Retrieved on February 17, 2006 from http://www.industryweek.com.

"Purchasing Activity Analysis." Retrieved on February 17, 2006 from http://www.strategicpurchasingservices.com.

Schneider, Gary P. 2004. *"Electronic Commerce: The Second Wave."* 5th edition. Canada: Thomson Course Technology.

Chapter 4

Supplier Relations and Strategic Sourcing

4.1 The Basics of Supplier Relations

No matter how big and powerful a company, it will have some suppliers and partners as an integral part of its business. In this sense, supply chain relationships are perhaps the most difficult aspect of supply chain management. The term supply chain implies that a firm is seeking outside suppliers or partners to better accomplish its operations and fulfill customer orders. Well-established partnerships can offer significant opportunities in most supply chains to quicken the pace of new product development and production. On contrary, poorly executed supplier relationships can have negative impact on the company and the supply chain as well.

4.1.1 Types of supply relations

While companies are interested in decentralizing, downsizing, and forging alliances to develop and produce products or deliver services, the decision of outsourcing or establishing virtual integration with suppliers should be based on the nature of product a company produces and its production system. When a product can be developed without relying on suppliers, vertical integration and autonomous divisions are good choices. However, when a product can be produced only in conjunction with related suppliers and complementary parts and components, alliances and virtual integration will be a better choice.

As a company moves toward self-sustained centralization and relies less on suppliers, its ability to coordinate activities and settle conflicts increases, at the same time, its incentive to take risk decreases. Whereas, when a company chooses to outsource most of its operations, its ability to manage market competition increases. Table 3.1 presents six possible supplier relationships. Vertical integration, autonomous division, arm's length relationship, joint venture, strategic alliances, and virtual integration are the ways that a product can be produced or service be delivered.

Vertical Integration: the degree to which a firm has decided to directly control multiple value-add stages from raw material production to the sale of the product to the ultimate consumers. The more steps in the sequence, the greater the vertical integration. A manufacturer that decides to begin producing parts and components that it normally purchases is said to be backward integrated. Likewise, a manufacturer that decides to take over distribution and perhaps sales to the ultimate consumer is considered forward integrated[1]. Perdue Farms that we discussed in Chapter 1 is an example of vertical integration company.

Autonomous Divisions: between the vertically integrated corporation and the joint venture is the autonomous division. Product can be manufactured independently from parts and components produced within the division of a large corporation. Nippon Steel Corporation, the world's largest integrated steelmaker, discussed in Chapter 2 is an example of autonomous divisions.

Arm's length: Arm's length is a transaction relationship. The seller usually offers standardized products to a wide range of customers. Negotiation focuses on low price. When a transaction completes, the relationship ends.

Joint Venture: Joint venture is an agreement between two or more firms to share risks in equity capital in order to achieve a specific business objective[1]. Boeing has joint venture relationships with its large-account customer's native countries. For example, Japanese companies, such as Mitsubishi Heavy Industries (MHI), Kawasaki Heavy Industries (KHI) and Fuji Heavy Industries (FHI) have supplied Boeing for more than 30 years.

---

[1] APICS, Dictionary, p. 47.

Strategic Alliances: Strategic alliance is a long-term, goal-oriented partnership between two companies who share both risks and rewards. For example, instead of pushing for a price cut, Toyota builds strategic alliances with suppliers and focuses on a value-based supply relationship. By doing this, Toyota has been a top selling automaker in the market place.

Virtual Integration: Virtual companies coordinate much of their business through the marketplace, where free agents come together to buy and sell one another's goods and services. Thus, virtual companies can harness the power of market forces to develop, manufacture, market, distribute, and support their offerings in ways that fully integrated companies cannot duplicate[2]. Dell Inc.'s direct model is an example of virtual integration.

Table 4.1. Types of supply relationships

Supply Relations	**Organizational Structure**	**Commitment**
Vertical Integration	Centralized organization	Directly owns multiple value-add stages within the company
Autonomous Division	Moderately Centralized	Between vertically integrated corporation and joint venture
Arm's length	No joint commitment and operations between the seller and buyer	When the transaction completes, relationship ends
Joint Venture	Certain level of commitment	Agreement to share risks in equity capital
Strategic Partnership	Moderately Decentralized	Long-term relationships, sharing both risks and rewards
Virtual Integration	Decentralized organization	Coordinate much of the business through the marketplace

---

[2] Chesbrough and Teece, 1996.

4.1.2 Strategic sourcing

Strategic sourcing goes beyond just purchasing and e-procurement. Strategic sourcing plays a proactive role in implementing a firm's overall goals and business objectives. The long-term focus is to establish cooperative supplier relationships to match a firm's competitive stance. Sourcing performance is measured in terms of contributions to the firm's overall success.

Strategic partners involved in strategic sourcing usually have a high degree of understanding between trading partners with respect to each other's goals and business practices. There is a high degree of confidence and willingness between the trading firms, and an agreement on matters of benefits and risk.   Strategic partners have a high degree of compatibility of activities, resources, and goals. The communication process between strategic partners tends to be timely and credible. Activities are smoothly coordinated between the partners.

Strategic sourcing affects every function of an organization. Firms need to think about their relationships with their suppliers and reconsider their entire supply chain from suppliers to customers. The complicated nature of strategic sourcing causes companies to rethink what materials and services to purchase, outsource, or produce in-house. Once these decisions are made, computer systems needed to accommodate sourcing activities can be selected accordingly.

Strategic sourcing has also been popularized in the service industry. For example, Alabama Power has made alliances with some of its key suppliers, including those that give the utility priority when it needs material. They established a coalition group called the Mutual Emergency Material Solutions (MEMS).   Members of MEMS collaborate during emergencies and share information on material sources.

4.1.3 Supply base development

The supply base refers to a list of suppliers a firm uses to purchase materials, services, or information. Many organizations have come to realize the importance of having a supplier base that they can rely on to provide materials and services that meet the design specifications, to consistently offer competitive prices, and to deliver products on time. This supplier base relies on strategic partnerships. The partners are not only willing to go the extra mile for each other, but also are truthful about quality, prices, promises, and due dates. This relationship forges loyalty among the partners and creates financial success in the supply chain.

Many companies have come to realize that if they purchase a large quantity from a smaller supplier base, it will enable them to achieve volume discounts, reduce administration costs, and cooperate on product development. There is some reported evidence of the advantages of supply base reduction. For example, world-class manufacturers in the automotive sector have reduced their supplier base typically by 50% and have moved to single-sourcing and one supplier per part in the mid 1990s[3]. In 1980s, Xerox reduced its supply base by 90% to consolidate volume into one or fewer suppliers.

Toyota is well-known for its supplier base management. Unlike some large manufacturers who put pressure for cost cutting disproportionately onto suppliers' shoulders, Toyota concentrates on a value-based supplier base management to build and maintain a collaborative supplier strategy. By doing this, Toyota is more competitive in the market place.

Aimed at cost and quality control at the process level, Toyota recognizes that fulfilling the enterprise potential of Toyota Production System requires a substantial cultural shift toward supplier collaboration and continuous improvement. For instance, Toyota's $800 million facility in Texas assembles the full-sized Tundra. Supplier proximity was a concern that was solved by incorporating an on-site supplier park that accommodates 21 suppliers[4]. Toyota has demonstrated a commitment to strengthening its suppliers. When Visteon and Delphi were separated from Ford and GM, Toyota continues its commitment of close collaboration with the two companies, including increasing its equity position in suppliers.

---

[3] Asmus, David and John Griffin, "Harnessing the Power of Your Suppliers," The McKinsey Quarterly, No. 3 (1993), pp. 63-78.
[4] John Teresko, learn from Toyota again. IndustryWeek.com, February 1, 2006 http://www.industryweek.com/PrintArticle.aspx?ArticleID=11301.

Cultivating a successful supplier base requires a firm to have a good understanding of its core competence and conduct a baseline analysis of its business. After the core competence has been identified, a firm is able to determine what should be outsourced and what should be produced in-house. Then, an analysis of business activities can be conducted to determine the baseline cost and performance. For example, Starwood Hotels & Resorts Worldwide is a leader in the hospitality industry. Its competitive success is to attract and retain guests. After analyzing its core competency, Starwood Hotels & Resorts Worldwide realizes that IT infrastructure is not its core business. Therefore, Starwood turned to HP to form a partnership. The two companies pooled resources and expertise to build a new global reservation system that is managed by HP. Because of collaboration, Starwood experiences a substantial savings on operating costs and increased agility. It even re-designs, deploys, and manages the new reservation system, based on HP servers. Anticipated to handle millions of guest transactions each year, the new solution will roll out in all of Starwood's distribution channels, including its world-class global customer contact centers, its Web sites and 750 hotels worldwide[5].

Setting a realistic objective for partnering is an important step in managing a supplier base. The objective of the McDonald's restaurants and Coca-Cola partnership is to improve their market presence. McDonald's is Coca-Cola's largest customer, and Coca-Cola is McDonald's' largest supplier of beverages. When McDonald's opened new restaurants in India, Coca-Cola India created ice tea and cold coffee exclusively for McDonald's under the brand umbrella of 'Georgia Gold'[6]. Coca-Cola India R&D developed the equipment. The Georgia Gold brand is the first vending solution in ice tea and cold coffee that Coca-Cola developed for McDonald's across the system worldwide. This brand has been in the Japanese market for over two decades and enjoys the highest share in the Japanese ready-to-drink coffee market. In India, the Georgia Gold Roast and Ground premium hot coffee was launched in

---

[5] Susan Twombly, "HP wins in strategic outsourcing," November 2004, www.hp.com.
[6] McDonald's, Coca Cola ready ice tea & cold coffee, http://www.indiantelevision.com/mam/headlines/y2k4/may/maymam100.htm.

India exclusively with McDonald's in July 2002, and has been termed a success.

McDonald's seeks to leverage the diversity within its supplier community through growing its existing supplier base, as well as developing new supplier relationships. The more diverse Macdonald's customers become, the more important it is to have diverse suppliers group in order to channel wealth back into those respective communities.

McDonald's buys from dedicated suppliers. J.R. Simplot, McDonald's leading potato producer, is an excellent example of this. When J.R. Simplot developed a better process to freeze potatoes, McDonald's rewarded the company with a better contract and share the technology with the rest of their suppliers. This practice creates sustainable partnership that improves both products and financial status[7].

4.2 Supplier Selection

Supplier selection involves the responsibility of various functional areas of an organization. The procurement manager needs to team up with engineers, production manager, marketing manager, and shop floor supervisors for selecting suppliers.

The selection process is usually based on well-established criteria such as price, quality, delivery promise, and service. Nevertheless, sometimes, qualitative criteria such as communication convenience and the quality of relationship are considered more important than price. Therefore, a balanced approach should be taken when considering suppliers.

4.2.1 Value analysis

Value analysis in supply chain is to systematically analyze the entire business process to improve the product and service performance through cost reduction, quality improvement, and customer service enhancement.

---

[7] http://www.mcdonalds.com.

Value analysis addresses issues that are related to a firm's or a supply chain's strategic goals. Issues raised include:
- What is the core and non-core supply chain activity?
- What is the role of a certain function in the supply chain?
- Does the function add value to the manufacturing or service process?
- Can the process be simplified?
- If yes, what tasks can be reduced or outsourced?
- Can a certain component be produced more efficiently?
- Can a lower-cost standard component be identified to substitute the one that are used now?

Value analysis is a continuous improvement process of a supply chain and aims at improving supply chain performance.

Value analysis can focus on either internal supply chain or external supply chain management. The level of supplier involvement in value analysis may vary from making minor material alteration ideas to providing major process reengineering suggestions. For example, Motorola includes suppliers in the early development stages of new product development. The buyer and suppliers jointly find solutions to design issues, product development speed, material problems, and manufacturing processes. Through information sharing, both the buyer and suppliers are able to forecast demand more accurately, develop production plans more effectively, and replenish materials more efficiently.

The '20-80 Rule' is a convenient approach used by industries to determine sourcing and procurement. The rule states that about 80 percent of what a businesses purchases represent 20 percent of the total purchase value and about 20 percent of items accounts for 80 percent of the purchase value. Large usage volume, low value items can be procured using centralized purchasing contract to negotiate for price discount, on time delivery, and better services. High value, low usage items should be purchased at the division level. Therefore, the user can communicate the specific requirement directly to the suppliers.

4.2.2 Techniques: Decision model for supplier selection

4.2.2.1 Preference matrix

Very often, multiple criteria are used to evaluate a supplier. In this case, the multiple performance attributes need be converted to a single score to compare a few suppliers. Preference matrix is the method of choice used to convert multiple criteria to a single measure.

A preference matrix is a table that can be used to rate a supplier according to several performance attributes. The performance attributes can be scored on any scale, such as from 1 to 7, one is the poorest and seven the best. Each performance attribute is weighted according to its perceived importance. The total of the weights usually sum up to 100. The total weighted score is obtained by multiplying the weight by the score for each performance attribute. The following is an example.

Example Problem 4.1

Mac, Inc. is seeking an IT service provider. The following is the rating for three vendors that Mac has contacted. Performance attributes are rated from 1 to 5, one being the poorest and 5 being the best. Additionally, the weight for the manager determines each attribute based

	Column A	Column B		Column C		Column D	
Performance Attribute	Weight	Vendor 1		Vendor 2		Vendor 3	
		Score	A*B	Score	A*C	Score	A*D
Quality	20	3	60	3	60	5	100
Flexibility	30	5	150	3	90	2	60
Supply chain cost	20	2	40	1	20	5	100
Asset utilization	10	5	50	5	50	4	40
Responsiveness	20	5	100	3	60	2	40
Total Weighted Score	100		400		280		340

on historical experience. Which one should Mac choose as its IT supplier? Use preference matrix method to solve the problem.

Solution

Column A presents the weight for each attribute. The sum of all weights equals 100. For example, the quality score for Vendor 1 is 3 and the weight for quality is 20. Vendor 1's weighted score for quality is 3*20 = 60. Continue this computation for all the vendors. Finally, sum up the weighted scores by each vendor.

The total weighted score for Vendor 1 is 400, which is the highest among the three. Therefore, vendor 1 is selected as the supplier for Mac, Inc.

The advantage of this method is that it can be applied to compare qualitative attributes of suppliers.

4.2.2.2 Make-or-buy decision

Breakeven analysis is a convenient method to determine when outsourcing of a component or function should be considered. The breakeven point is a point at which total revenue equals total costs. The computation formula is as follows.

$$Q = \frac{F}{p-c}$$

Total cost $= F + cQ$
Total revenue $= pQ$

Where:
p = unit price
c = unit variable cost
F = Annual fixed cost
Q = Annual production or sales volume

Example Problem 4.2

July Cox, the owner of Cox Products, is evaluating whether to outsource a new innovation to a supplier or make the product in-house. After an analysis of the production cost, she estimates that the annual fixed cost is $75,000, unit variable cost which includes material and labor costs is $20, and the product sells for $35 per unit. Should July Cox outsource the new innovation?

Solution

$$Q = \frac{F}{p-c} = \frac{75000}{35-20} = 5,000 \text{ units}$$

Total cost = 75,000 + 20(5,000) = $175,000
Total revenue = 35(5,000) = $175,000

The breakeven point is 5,000 units, which is the breakeven quantity at which total cost equals total revenue. If Cox Products can sell 5,000 units or more, the new innovation can be made in-house. However, if Cox's annual sales volume is less than 5,000 units, it should consider outsourcing.

4.2.2.3 Decision tree

Decision tree is a schematic model of alternatives available to the decision maker, along with their possible consequences. A simple decision tree model is shown in Figure 4.1. The meaning of the model notations is as follows.

- Square node: representing decisions points and the branches representing alternatives.
- Round node: representing event. The probabilities for all branches leaving a round node must sum to 1.0.
- The conditional payoff: is the payoff for each possible alternative. Payoff is shown at the end of each combination.

After drawing the decision tree according to the given information, the problem is solved from right to left, calculating expected payoff for each node.

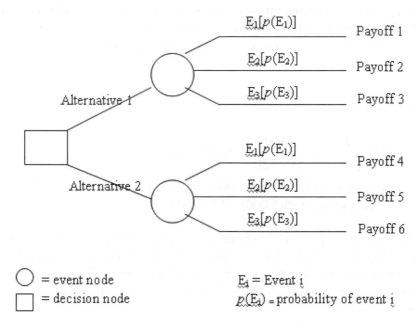

Figure 4.1. A decision tree model

Example Problem 4.3: Supplier Selection

The general manager of Tower Light needs to decide whether to hire one supplier or two. If one supplier is hired and demand proves to be excessive, the second supplier can be hired later. If the second supplier is hired later, some sales will be lost because the lead time for producing the special lights is five months.

The cost of hiring two suppliers at the same time would be lower because the fee was charged only once by the hiring consult firm. The probability of low demand is estimated to be 30% and high demand is 70%.

Hiring two suppliers at the beginning: The net present value of hiring two suppliers together is $180,000 if demand is low and $360,000 if demand is high.

Hiring one supplier at the beginning, the manager will consider the scenarios associated with high and low demand as illustrated follows.

If demand is low: one supplier is hired, the net present value is 240,000.

If demand is high: the manager has three options.
(i)   Doing nothing has a net present value of $240,000;
(ii) Hiring the second supplier, payoff is $280,000;
(iii) Subcontracting, payoff is $320,000.

a. Draw a decision tree for this problem.
b. Should the company hire one or two suppliers initially? What is the expected payoff for this alternative?

Solution

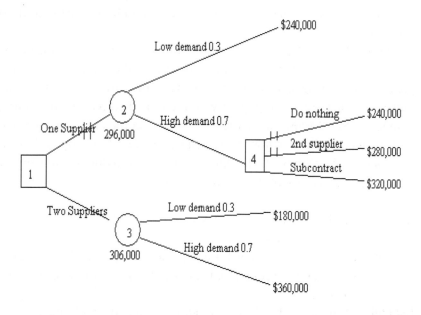

Figure 4.2.

Decision Node 4: Compare three options, 'doing nothing' and 'hiring 2nd supplier yields lower expected return. Therefore, prune the options of doing nothing and 2nd supplier because 'subcontract' has a higher net present value.

Event Node 2: $(240,000*0.3 + 320,000*0.7) = 296,000$
Event Node 3: $(180,000*0.3 + 360,000*0.7) = 306,000$

Decision Node 1: Comparing the result from Event Nodes 2 and 3, we should hire two suppliers initially. The expected net present value is $306,000

4.2.3 Supply certificate – ISO series

The most popular supply certificate is ISO 9000 series. ISO 9000 is a set of international standards on quality management and quality assurance that was first established in 1978. It was most recently revised in 2001. Many companies around world require their suppliers to be ISO 9000 certified to ensure that the product they purchase meets a unified standard.

ISO 9000 standards require firms to document their quality control systems at every step (incoming raw materials, product design, in-process monitoring and so forth) so that they will be able to identify those areas that are causing quality problems and correct them at a timely manner. ISO 14000 standards assessing a company's environmental performance in three major areas: management systems, operations, and environmental systems. Companies are required to document everything that affects the quality of goods and services.

ISO 9000: Helps companies determine which standard of ISO 9001, 9002, and 9003 applies.
ISO 9001: Outlines guidelines for companies that engaged in design, development, production, installation, and servicing of products or service.
ISO 9002: Similar to 9001, but excludes design and development components.

ISO 9003: Covers companies engaged in final inspection and testing
ISO 9004: The guidelines for applying the elements of the Quality
         Management System
ISO 10011: Quality system auditing guide
ISO 10013: Quality manual development guide
ISO 14000: A set of international standards for assessing a company's
         environmental performance

When an organization feels that its quality system is good enough, it may ask an accredited registrar or other third party audit team for pre-assessment. The final audit begins with a review of the company's quality manual, which the accredited registrar or third party audit team typically uses as its guide. The audit team checks to see that the documented quality system meets the requirement of ISO 9000 and that the organization is practicing what is documented. When the registrar is satisfied with the favorable recommendation of the audit team, it grants registration and issues a registration document to the company.

4.2.4 Trust and commitment

Supply chain is built on a foundation of trust and commitment. Trust is conveyed through faith, reliance, belief or confidence in the supply partners and is viewed as willingness to forego opportunistic behavior. Trust has various forms, such as calculative trust, relational trust, cognitive trust, inter-organizational trust, etc. Calculative trust has a significant impact on buyer-supplier relationships and supply chain performance. Relational trust does not have a formal contract and can be an efficient governance mechanism that reduces transaction costs by minimizing searching, contracting, and monitoring, and enforcement of costs over the long term. Inter-organizational trust can enhance supplier performance, lower costs of negotiation, and reduce conflict.

Commitment, on the other hand, implies that the trading partners are willing to devote resources to sustaining partnership relationship. Committed partners dedicate resources to sustaining and furthering the goals of the supply chain. With commitment, supply chain partners become integrated into their major customers' processes and more tied to their goals.

4.3 Outsourcing

Outsourcing is to let an outside contractor produce a certain part or component, or provide certain services, which they may specialize in, such as software development.

Business process outsourcing (BPO), on the other hand, involves more than letting a partner produce parts and components. A BPO service provider brings a different perspective, knowledge, experience and technology to the existing function and will work with the firm to reengineer its process into an improved or new process. Business process outsourcing is an outcome-based result, not just a pure cost reduction issue. The new process will interact or be integrated into the company in a way that can bring value to the customers.

4.3.1 Creating outsourcing vision

When an organization outsources its business applications or its IT infrastructure, it uses outsourcing to reshape the way it does its business and hopes to achieve better business performance. An outsourcing initiative that aims at business transformation will offer the greatest opportunities for radical improvement through rethinking critical management processes.

However, outsourcing is not driven by the same vision in all businesses. The pursuit of value through outsourcing is taking two significantly different paths:

(i) Organizational strategic transformation.

(ii) Production efficiency.

Industry on the strategic transformational path typically approaches outsourcing as a tool to implement a strategic agenda. For example, Cisco Systems outsources its entire logistics function to UPS Logistics. UPS Logistics coordinates Cisco's manufacturing interfaces, inbound and outbound shipments, and customer's order fulfillment. In this case, the outsourcing initiative is more complex and more mature, and both parties are expecting high potential value.

On the contrary, business on the production efficiency path primarily views business applications and IT infrastructure outsourcing as a tool for achieving cost reduction and increasing productivity. For example, Anheuser-Busch outsources its logistics program to third party logistic providers thereby boosting the efficiency of their distribution network. Outsourcing a non-core labor-intensive function prevents Anheuser-Busch from requiring a resident team on payroll. The savings on administration, labor, and overhead cost enables Anheuser-Busch to maintain a good profit margin.

Businesses are outsourcing for a broad range of reasons, such as the need to provide existing and additional services, lack of available expertise to produce certain products, and operating expense reduction. Whatever the reasons, outsourcing is not just to reduce cost, but also to deliver increased value.

4.3.2 Model for implementing outsourcing

To be successful in implementing outsource tasks, a mechanism should be created to facilitate all the steps involved. Figure 4.3 illustrates a four-step sourcing model: (i) the motivation for outsourcing; (ii) compatibility of the organizational characteristics of buying and selling companies; (iii) outsourcing implementation components; and (iv) outsourcing outcome measurement. The model suggested here is adapted from Lamber's partnership model[8].

The outsourcing motivation is the first step, which examines the compelling reasons to outsource business functions or products. For example, the reason for outsourcing is to focus on core competence, cost reduction, new product introduction, etc. The two different outsourcing paths, organizational strategic transformation or production efficiency, should be determined.

---

[8] Doouglas M. Lambert, Margaret A. Emmelhainz and John T. Gardner, "Developing and implementing partnerships." *The International Journal of Logistics Management*, Vol 7, No. 2 (1996), p.3.

The second step is compatibility of the organizational characteristics that are the supportive factors of the two companies involved in outsourcing. Supportive factors include but not limited to corporate compatibility, managerial philosophy, benefits and risk sharing, close proximity, and shared customers. If the corporate environment does not support the partnership relationship, the potential benefits of outsourcing or partnership will be reduced. The strength, weakness, opportunity, and risk (SWOT) model can be applied here to determine the compatibility of partners.

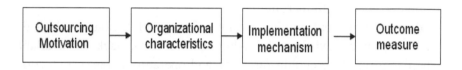

Figure 4.3. Outsourcing model

The third step is implementation mechanism, which consists of managerial activities, and procedures that are applied to create and sustain the outsourcing relationship. Planning, operational control, communication, risk and reward sharing, and contract negotiation are all components of the implementation mechanism.

The final step is the outcome measure that is to assess the result of outsourcing. The metrics of outsourcing can be returns on investment, asset utilization, inventory turns, inventory holding costs, customer satisfactory level, etc.

This model can be used to assess a potential outsourcing project, as well as diagnose an existing outsourcing relationship. The dynamics of a supply chain change overtime. Therefore, the outsourcing projects should be evaluated accordingly. Through re-assessing the outsourcing motivation, organizational characteristics, and implementation mechanism, the buyers and sellers can determine if the supply chain is strong enough to stay market competition, identify the weak link of the supply chain, and strengthen the relationship.

Example 4.4: University Bookstore

Consider the university bookstore case in Chapter 3. The sourcing model in Figure 4.3 can be applied to analyze the strategic item, textbooks, in that case. To the bookstore, the motivation of the partnership with publishers is to ensure that all the textbooks will be available before school starts and the book chosen best reflects the course curriculum. To the publisher, the motivation of partnering with the bookstore and professors is to ensure that its textbooks are current and meet the market needs. Besides, the publisher would like to sustain and expand its market.

The organizational characteristics of the bookstore and the publisher should be compatible. The publisher should have commitment to publishing textbooks that meet university teaching needs and provide services to the university bookstore to support the partnership relationship.

The implementation process includes contract negotiation between the university bookstore and the publisher. Additionally, demand forecast, production planning, transportation and delivery, operational control, and timely communication between the bookstore and the publisher need to be coordinated.

The result of the partnership or outsourcing should be measured using appropriate metrics. Items such as return on investment, asset utilization, inventory turns, inventory holding costs, customer satisfactory level, safety stock level, the number of rush orders, or shortage of required textbooks are all examples of outcome measurements.

4.3.3 Outsourcing benefits and risks

Outsourcing is a process by which two parties make commitment to a common task or goal. Benefits derived from outsourcing include lower purchase costs, production flexibility, less complicated staff management, reduced procurement overhead, improved contract terms, and a win-win approach to share reward.

As outsourcing has become more popular in recent years, most supply chains are getting more complex than they were a decade ago.

Consequently, the more parts, components, services, function, and processes a company outsources to its suppliers, the less visibility and control of the problems it has. Furthermore, potential problems are not only hidden in the supply chain, but are not easy to fix when the company does identify them.

Conflicting goals are a risk the supply chain faces. For example, the risk management strategies a company intends to implement in order to avoid vulnerability often conflict with strategies designed to improve supply chain excellence by the other company. For example, a North America healthcare and consumer product manufacturer had 10 distribution centers in the US. However, when it built a massive centralized distribution center in Atlanta to improve supply chain efficiency, it gradually arranged to have about 80% of its sales funnel through this facility. This strategy was successful until a hurricane struck the facility, ripped the roof off, and cut the power. A contingent risk management plan of stocking two week's extra inventory was suggested by a 3PL consultant, but was not well considered [9]. The reason is that the contingent plan proposed by 3PL is obvious in conflict with the manufacturer's idea of cost saving.

Supplier stability is another risk that virtually all supply chain managers must address. Buyers should have knowledge of what they are buying, from whom they are buying, as well as the suppliers' financial status such as their profitability, growth, financial strength, their management effectiveness, their production capabilities, and backup supply plans.

Sourcing from Low Cost Countries is getting popular. The retailer giant, Wal-Mart purchases hundreds and thousands of products from vendors in low cost countries. There are potential sourcing risks associate with Low Cost Country Sourcing program. These risks include leadtime management, quality problems, security issues, supply disruption, political environment, and some hidden costs.

---

[9] *Source*: Chris Holt, UPS Consulting, Vice President.

4.4 Third Party Logistics and Fourth Party Logistics

Third Party Logistics (3PLs) is the term used to describe the outsourcing of logistics management, which include providing basic service or value-added service. An example of basic services is to rent storage space to a client. An example of value-added services is renting storage space plus managing inventory for a client. 3PL is asset-intensive. In a price sensitive market, 'return-on-investment' and 'financial performance' is major concerns.

Forth Party Logistics (4PLs) is an integrator that assembles the resources, capabilities, and technology of the service provider and its client to design, develop, and implement comprehensive supply chain solutions[10]. The 4PL has emerged into the service vacuum created by 3PLs and is refined based on the idea of 3PL. The evolution of 3PL to 4PL is to move from the mass service market segment to the professional service market segment. 4PL is far less asset based than 3PL and focuses more on coordination. A 4PL provider is a technological service provider who owns computer systems and intellectual capital. 4PLs combine process, technology and human capital to manage process or reengineering process for clients. A 4PL will even manage 3PLs that a customer is using.

4.4.1 Third party logistics practices

Creation of a 3PL presents a way for a commodity-service logistics provider to move into higher margin with bundled services. In 1996 3PLs purchased about $25 billion worth of logistics services on behalf of their clients in the US[11]. Drawing on its core business, whether it be forwarding, trucking or warehousing, they moved into providing other services for customers. Initially, candidates for outsourcing were companies that either needed to reduce their assets or play catch-up with a competitor. Today a 3PL client may be a large company that sees an advantage in trimming non-core functions. Progressive companies are

---

[10] http://en.wikipedia.org/wiki/4PL.
[11] *Distribution* April 1996.

much more likely to outsource their warehousing, transportation functions because they are not good at or cannot manage these functions profitably.

Today with worldwide supply sources and markets, outsourcing some of the logistics functions becomes a common practice of many companies. Businesses are much more likely to demand a single vendor to support their massive operations on a global basis. For example, the on-line bookseller, Amazon.com, uses the U.S. Postal Service and other package carriers like the United Parcel Service (UPS) and FedEx as 3PL logistic providers to ship books to customers.

4.4.2 Fourth party logistics practices

A 4PL provider can present for customers to take control of their supply chains. They can structure the relationship and the process in a way that best meets the requirements of the customer. The business model of 4PL created by UPS Logistics for Cisco Systems is a good example[12]. The partnership between UPS Logistics and Cisco Systems started as 3PL project and evolved into 4PL that coordinates manufacturing interfaces, inbound and outbound shipments, and customers order fulfillment.

For inbound shipments, UPS provide value-added professional service. When UPS Logistics receives the notification of product shipment from Cisco plants and contract manufacturers all over the world, it will pick up the products within 24 hours. Meanwhile, UPS Logistics arranges aircraft to send the shipments to the European logistics center, which is owned and operated by UPS.

For outbound shipments, UPS Logistics provides more tailored services. When a new shipment is to be transported to a customer, UPS information systems generates a solution which not only is based on optimized algorithm of pricing, time-in-transit and service level, but also based on a postal code level. The system then provides a RFQ (request for quotation) to identify the most appropriate carrier from an approved list. Throughout the process, the order status is registered in UPS's

---

[12] Remko I. can Hoek, "UPS Logistics and to move toward 4PL – or not?" Cranfield School of Management, UK.

information system as well as Cisco's information system, so Cisco is able to communicate the order fulfillment status to its customers. Additionally, UPS consolidates shipments with common destinations to minimize the number of shipments and reduce congestion at the loading dock.

4.5 Enhancing Value through Supplier Relations and Strategic Sourcing

Strategic partnership and outsourcing not only enhance the value of supply chain through collaboration but also create a viable virtual business organization. The benefits of strategic outsourcing include core competence enhancement, personnel cost savings, production capabilities balance, flexibility improvement, fast time-to-market cycle, less information system costs, less technical obsolescence risk, reengineer processes, converting fixed costs into variable costs, and many other benefits.

Increased focus on core business processes lead to creation of 3PL logistics and 4PL logistics. 3PL and 4PL help to reduce distribution costs, effectively utilize capital, shorten product life cycles, and improve customer service. The result is better position the supply chain for future growth.

Supply chain competition is becoming increasingly defined by supply chain capability. In particular, the upstream supply chain, which includes the suppliers and supplier network, has been recognized for supply chain cost-saving potential.

As time passes, business competition becomes increasingly global. Advanced technology combined with a general breaking down of trade barriers between global trading regions have moved business toward one dynamic global market. The global orientation makes outsourcing, 3PL and 4PL even more desirable. For a long time, rising costs simply were passed downstream in the supply chain and ultimately were borne by the end user. Today, end users expect prices to decline each year, even if energy costs, material costs, and other overhead costs rise. Therefore, outsourcing business functions to low cost countries becomes a common practice. Businesses must reduce costs, year after year, or profitability will decline.

4.6 Sourcing Performance Metrics

Sourcing performance is measured in terms of contributions to the firm's overall success. Traditionally, performance measurement focuses on cost. Now quality, flexibility and delivery reliability are all important performance indicators. The following are a number of sourcing performance metrics that can be considered.

- Reducing purchasing cycle time
- Reducing purchasing cost
- Enhancing budgetary control
- Eliminating clerical errors
- Increasing buyer productivity
- Lowering prices through product standardization
- Lowering prices through centralized buying
- Improving information management
- Improving the payment process

4.7 Summary

In this chapter, we discussed the types of supply chain relationships, strategic partnership relationship, and outsourcing. Effective supplier management starts with the selection of the most appropriate suppliers, using criteria such as providing high quality parts, aggressive pricing, and reliable delivery. Criteria used to rating the suppliers can be varied according to the need of the company that is seeking for a supplier.

The outsourcing implementation model described in this chapter ensures that the partnership is forged with visions, and implemented with appropriate measures. Additionally, a number of decision models introduced in this chapter provide quantitative tool for evaluating potential suppliers.

Questions for Pondering

1. Why single sourcing has become attractive to companies? Do you see any risks associated with single sourcing?
2. Use outsourcing implementation model in 4.3.2 to analyze (i) automobile makers sourcing strategy; and (ii) a business of your choice.
3. Select a commodity that you believe might be strategically important to a company and develop a sourcing strategy.
4. Compare and contrast the benefits and risks of 3PL and 4PL logistics.
5. Provide a list of companies that use 3PL logistic services, based on your reading of recent articles in the newspapers, magazines, and professional journals.
6. Provide a list of companies that use 4PL logistic services, based on your reading of recent articles in the newspapers, magazines, and professional journals.
7. Develop a survey questionnaire that can be used to evaluate suppliers, define, and discuss the characteristics of an effective supplier survey.
8. Explain backward vertical integration. What are the advantages and disadvantages of outsourcing compared to backward vertical integration?

Problems

1. The Eastshore Company is screening three suppliers for subcontracts. Only one supplier will be used. The following estimates have been made for five performance criteria that management believes to be important.

Performance Criteria	Rating		
	Supplier A	Supplier B	Supplier C
Product quality	6	8	3
Schedule flexibility	7	3	9
Unit cost	4	7	5
Responsiveness	10	4	6
Delivery reliability	2	10	5

a. Calculate a total weighted score for each alternative. Use a preference matrix and assume equal weights for each performance criterion. Which supply is best?

b. Suppose that unit cost is given twice the weight assigned to each of the remaining criteria (the total weight is still 100). Does this modification affect the ranking of the three potential suppliers?

2. (Decision tree) Analyze the decision tree presented below. What is the expected payoff for the best alternative? You need to sign the missing probability first.

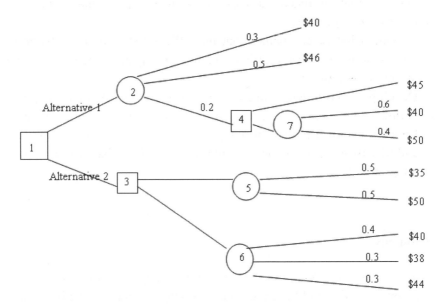

3. (Supplier selection using financial analysis)

Electro, a manufacturer of electronic components, is trying to select a single supplier for the raw materials that go into its main product, the triple-lock, a new component for the cellular phone. Two companies can provide the necessary materials: EXUL and ARC.

EXUL has a very solid reputation for its products and charges a higher price due to their reliability of supply and delivery. EXUL dedicates plant capacity to each customer, and therefore, supply is assured. This allows EXUL to charge $1.30 for the raw materials used in each triple-lock.

ARC is a small raw material supplier that has limited capacity. It charges only $1.10 for a unit's worth of raw materials. However, it does not have enough capacity to supply all its customers all the time. This means that orders to ARC are not guaranteed. In a year of high demand for raw materials, ARC will have 105,000 units available for Electro. In low demand years, all products will be delivered. Assume there is a high demand for both years.

If Electro does not get raw materials from its suppliers, it needs to buy them on from subcontractors. A subcontractor's price for single lot purchases (such as Electro would need) is $2.00 for the raw material used in a unit.

Electro sold 120,000 triple-locks this year. Next year, the demand has a 75 percent chance of rising 20 percent over this year's demand and a 25 percent chance of falling 10 percent. Electro uses a discount rate of 20 percent. Electro wants to use only one company as its supplier

    a. Which supplier should Electro choose?
    b. What other information would you like to have to make this decision?

4. (Base on problem 3) The manager of Electro has received an offer in which flexibility of demand can be accommodated. The information is given below:

- Electro can have the flexibility of using 90,000 to 140,000 units of triple-lock at price of $1.20
- An extra upfront payment of $10,000
- Minimum of 90,000 units each year must be ordered, i.e. 90,000@$1.20 = $108,000. If Electro orders less than 90,000 units, the minimum change will be $108,000 annually.
- If the demand exceeds 140,000 units, Electro has to use subcontractors. Other pertinent information is the same as in Part 1.

The manager wants you to analyze the fixed contract and flexible contract and make a recommendation to him.

References

Alonso, A., Donenberg, D., Gamba, D. and Vely, D. under the supervision of Professor Sunil Chopra, 1996. "Third Party Logistics: Current Issues and World Wide Web Resources," Kellogg Graduate School of Management, Northwestern University.

APICS, 1998. *Dictionary*, 9th edition. Falls Church, VA.

Ayers, J. B. 2001. *Handbook of Supply Chain Management,* New York: The St. Lucie Press.

Chen, I.J. and Paulraj, A. (2004). Understanding supply chain management: critical research and a theoretical framework. *International Journal of Production Research.* 42(1), 131-163.

Chesbrough, H.W. and Teece, D.J. 1996. "Organizing for innovation: When is virtual virtuous?" *Harvard Business Review*, p. 6.

Chopra, S. and Meindl, P. 2002. *Supply Chain Management.* New Jersey: Prentice Hall.

Neef, D. 2001. *e-Procurement: From Strategy to Implementation.* New Jersey: Prentice Hall.

Fitzgerald, K.R. (2005). Big savings, but lots of risk, *Supply Chain Management Review.* 9(9), 16-20.

Lambert, D. 2006. *Supply Chain Management: Process, Partnerships, Performance.* 2nd edition, Sarasota, Florida: SCMI.

Lemke, F., Goffin, K., Szwejczewski, M., Pfeiffer, R., Lohmuller, B. (2000). Supplier base management: Experiences from the UK and Germany: *International Journal of Logistics Management.* 11(2), 45-59.

"Outsourcing in government is growing and getting more sophisticated, finds new research." *eGovernment News*, 20 May 2003.

Supplement 4.1

Discount Cash Flow Analysis

Supply chain design decisions usually remain in place for an extended period of time. Therefore, they should be evaluated as a sequence of cash flows over that period. Discount cash flow analysis evaluates the present value of any stream of future cash flows. It is also referred to as the rate of return or opportunity cost of capital.

Present value of a stream of cash flow is what that stream is worth in today's dollars.

$$\text{Discount Factor} = \frac{1}{(1+k)}$$

$$\text{Net Present Value} = C_0 + \sum_{t=1}^{T}\left(\frac{1}{(1+k)}\right)^t C_t$$

Where:

k = rate of return

t = time period

C_t = cash flow for time period t

Example Problem

a. Interest rate is 5%. If you invest $100 today, how much do you have in a year?

Solution: $100 * (1+0.05) = \$105$

b. Interest rate is 5%. If you want to have $105 next year, how much should you invest today?

Solutions: Present value $\dfrac{105}{(1+0.05)} = \$100$

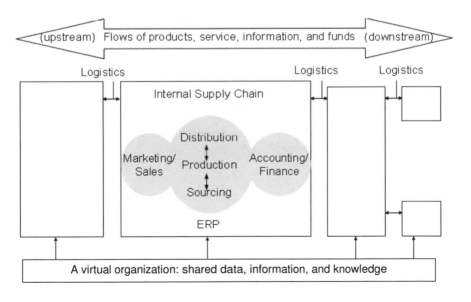

Chapter 5

Demand Management:
Customer Order Forecast

5.1 Demand Management through Collaborative Forecasting

Demand management is an attempt to influence the timing and quantity of customer needs of products. Demand management includes forecasting demand, order processing, and order fulfillment. Additionally, when demand is low, the supply chain manager may launch a promotion to stimulate demand. When the demand is higher than the production capacity level, the management may increase delivery lead-time and price. Sales promotion may also be applied to increase market share, introduce new products, and shift the timing of demand to ease the pressure on production capacity. Demand management can be effective when there are some coordinating efforts throughout the supply chain.

Coordinating planning and forecasting in a supply chain requires good estimates of customer demand. These estimates are typically in the form of forecast and predictions. For certain type of planning problems, such as inventory control and economical purchasing, forecasting costs and lead-time may be needed as well. This chapter examines how companies manage the linkage of their production with their customers' needs using demand management measures and forecasting procedures.

Collaborative forecasting in a supply chain is to collect and reconcile the information from diverse sources inside and outside the company; to come up with a single unified statement of demand for the company and the entire supply chain. In Chapter One, we mentioned material flow, service low, information low, and fund flow are the four flows move up and down the supply chain. As such, forecasting is to use historical demand information flow to predict material flow and fund flow. Consequently, many companies focus on enabling a collaborative planning, forecasting and replenishment supply-chain model to balance demand and supply capacity, to manage customer demand with strategic business partners, and to share information and plans with these same partners. Collaborative forecasting works to solve two of the greatest challenges faced by supply chain managers:

(1) Stock outs of strategic or leverage products that lead to lost sales; and

(2) Excessive safety stock and wrong inventory that tie up monetary capital.

The first challenge relates to customer service level and revenue management and the second challenge affects the overall cost of supply chain. In order to prevent excess inventory, forecasts of future demand must be as accurate as possible. Although customers are not able to tell precisely the products they need in the future, collaborative forecasting can improve productivity and profitability throughout the supply chain.

5.1.1 Forecast characteristics

Customer order forecast and demand management are vital links in a supply chain. Demand forecast serves as a prelude to production planning, capacity planning, and inventory management. Although, there are different forecast procedures we can apply to project future demand, a few forecast characteristics are common to all forecast methods.

First, forecast will never be accurate because it uses historical data to project future demand. For example, green tea was not a popular soft drink in the US market. Due to consumers' healthy diet concerns, the demand for green tea is increasing faster than the demand for other soft drinks in recent years.

Second, forecast time horizon affects the accuracy level of forecasts. In general, long-term forecasts are less accurate than short-term forecasts. Just like weather forecasting, it is more accurate to forecast tomorrow's weather than the weather of a month from today.

Third, forecast for a family of product is more accurate than for an individual Stock Keeping Unit (SKU) item. For example, the data for soft drink can be stable even when data for diet Pepsi is unstable.

Fourth, greater distortion of demand information is observed when a firm is farther away from the end user in a supply chain than a firm is closer to the end user. For example, the demand for Procter & Gamble Pampers diaper is stable at the retail stores. However, the distributors' orders to P&G fluctuate much more than the retailer sales. Furthermore, P&G's orders to its suppliers, such as 3M, swings even greater than the distributor's orders. Consequently, greater distortion of Pampers diaper demand information has been observed at 3M than at the retail stores.

5.1.2 Forecast in efficient supply chain vs. responsive supply chain

In an efficient supply chain (as oppose to responsive supply chain that is discussed in Chapter 1) customer demand is stable, forecasting error is low, product life cycle is long, new product introductions are less frequent, and product variety is limited. In this case, proactively manage customer demand will be the choice of the supply chain manager. As illustrated in Figure 5.1, time series forecasting methods are pre-dominant procedures applied to predict future demand when demand uncertainty is low. The need from the end users is usually satisfied from inventory. For example, the demand for Perdue chickens is stable with an upward trend over years. Therefore, Perdue Farms forecasts the quantity of eggs it needs for chicks and pushes the product all the way down the supply chain to the end users. When there are unexpected incidents such as bird flu, promotion and coupons are proactive demand management approaches to increase sales.

Responsive supply chain, on the other hand, is to react quickly to uncertain demand. In this case, demand predictability is low, forecasting error is high, product life cycle is short, new product introductions are frequent, and product variety is high. To meet customer demand, the supply chain will forecast on system flexibility and capacity cushions. If both demand variability and sales volume are high, forecast may focus on parts and components. The users will pull the production of the final product. For example, since every computer will need microchips, the variation of chips is low. Dell Inc. uses a push system to forecast its needs for computer chips. At the same time, Dell Inc. predicts the capacity cushion it requires to support direct orders from end users, which is a pull production system. The need for parts and component inventory is forecasted based on historical data, but final assembly is pulled by customer orders. The interface of push and pull system is at the stage before assembly starts.

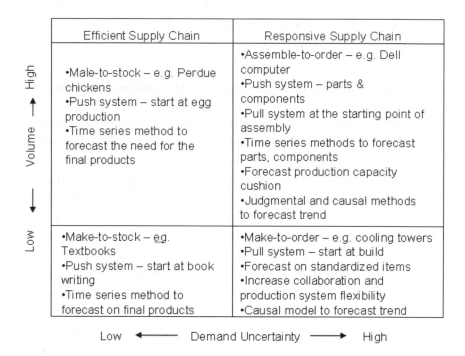

Figure 5.1. Forecast methods for efficient and responsive supply chain

5.1.3 A better method: Collaborative forecasting in supply chain

Let us consider a supplier and inventory scenario. Culex is a manufacturer of cooling towers and 3G is its supplier of gearbox.

Suppose Culex Industries uses G32 gearboxes in the production of cooling towers. On average, Culex builds 20 cooling tower units each month. Because G32 gearbox is critical to Culex's production, its supplier, 3G, normally keeps 40 G32 gearboxes in stock.

However, in early March, Culex's managers decided they needed to build 80 cooling units in April to meet the high demand before summer starts. Since 3G Distribution always has an ample supply of gearbox in stock, so it does not occur to Culex's buyer to notify 3G of the increased need for production occurring in four weeks.

At the beginning of April, Culex starts production of cooling towers. After completing 40 units, they stopped production because there were no more gearboxes. Culex's production manager strongly expressed his unhappiness at the buyer. The buyer in turn was frustrated at 3G. As a result, Culex experienced capacity imbalance and extra production costs. 3G gave excuses to meet the unusual demand and offered to increase its G32 gearbox inventory from 40 to 80 units. As such, 3G has an unhappy customer and carries additional stock that will increase 3G's inventory holding costs.

This situation happened due to the seasonal demand of cooling system, promotion plan of the manufacturer, and poor communication between the trading partners. If Culex and 3G implemented CPFR system, Culex would have notified 3G of the increased need for the gearboxes as soon as it made April production plan. 3G would have ordered more gearboxes for summer promotion. From Culex example, we are able to draw the following remarks:

(i) Understanding and communicating the type of data needed for forecast between the trading partners.

(ii) Determining forecast procedure that is appropriate for the nature of the products.

(iii) Synchronizing forecasts between different trading partners of the supply chain.

In recently years, supply chain coordination becomes a popular way to manage demand. Collaborative forecasting comprises of estimating customer demand for all the participating firms, identifying and resolving any differences in demand among participating firms, and developing a feasible sales forecast. For example, in the spring of 2001, Sears and

Michelin (a French company) began discussions on collaboration. Later that year, they implemented a collaborative planning, forecasting and replenishment information system. The mutual goal of the two companies was to improve order fill rate and reduce inventory at Sears' distribution centers and Michelin's warehouses respectively. Because of implementing CPFR systems and better forecasts, Sears' distribution-centers-to-store, fill rate increased by 10.7 percent. The combined Michelin and Sears inventory levels were reduced by 25 percent. This practice indicates that equipped with advanced information technology, coordination and collective decisions can offer companies the opportunities to transform and improve their supply chain performance radically. Such a transformation can have dramatic benefits and create competitive advantages[1].

5.2 Components of Demand Forecast

5.2.1 Patterns of demand

(1) Spatial demand versus temporal demand

Spatial demand addresses the place or where the demand takes place. Spatial location of demand is needed to plan warehouse locations; balance inventory levels across the supply chain network and geographically allocate transportation resources.

Temporal demand addresses the time or **when** the demand takes place. Timing is one of the most important outcomes of forecasting. Demand variation associated with time is a result of growth or decline in sales rates, seasonality in the demand pattern, and general fluctuations caused by a multitude of factors. Most short-term forecasting is often dealt with time series.

---

[1] Steermann, H (2003). "A practical look at CPFR: the Sears - Michelin experience." *Supply Chain Management Review*, July/August 2003, pp. 46-53.

(2) Regular versus lumpy demand

Demand pattern can be decomposed to trend, seasonal, and random components. Major demand patterns are shown in Figure 5.2. Observe the four patterns clock-wise, we can tell that

(i) Indicates a level or random demand pattern with no trend or seasonal elements

(ii) Shows a random demand pattern with an increasing trend but no seasonal element. In general, trend can be either up or down and may be linear or non-linear

(iii) Plots a random demand pattern with seasonal elements. Values of a series move up or down on a periodic basis which can be related to the calendar; and

(iv) Shows a cyclical demand pattern. The value of a series moves through long term upward and downward swings, which are not related to the calendar year.

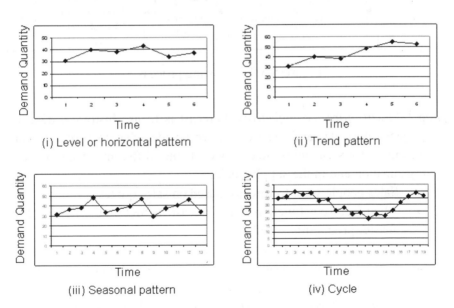

Figure 5.2. Demand patterns

(3) Independent versus dependent demand

Independent demand is forecasted. For example, the number of tables a furniture store will sell is forecasted. Dependent demand is derived. For example, the number of legs and tabletops the manufacturer needs to produce is derived from the number of tables the manufacturer needs to make.

5.2.2 Forecast process

Regardless what product to forecast and which method to employ, there are some common steps in the forecast process as illustrated in Figure 5.3.

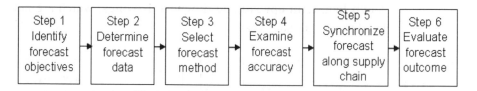

Figure 5.3. Forecasting process

Step 1 *Identify forecast objectives.* Forecast is to use historical data to project future demand. Therefore, we decide what to forecast. For example, forecast units may vary at the different levels of an organization and in the supply chain:
- Sales people want to forecast based on sales quotes.
- Manufacturing function may forecast in SKU units needed for master production schedule.
- Financial function may forecast in sales dollars to prepare budget.
- Distribution and transportation may forecast in product family to achieve full truckload quantity.

Step 2 *Determine forecasting variables and data.* Data used in forecast should be determined first. For example, demand and shipments are two different types of data. If there is a shortage of certain products, a portion of demand will not be satisfied. As a result, a customer may find a substitute product, or simply fill the order from a competitor. Therefore, actual demand can be higher than shipments. Forecast data may include:

- Demand - overall market demand for a certain product
- Supply - amount of product available
- Product character - product features that affect demand
- Market competition - market competition from producers of similar products
- Historical data, sales projections, promotion plans, etc
- Market share data, trade inventory, and market research

Step 3 *Select forecast method.* In general, forecast methods can be grouped into two categories qualitative and quantitative methods.

(i) *Qualitative forecasting method.* This method is known as judgmental forecast. Forecast is based on educated guess or expert experience. Such method may be useful when a firm tries to predict demand for a new product, which does not have historical information.

(ii) *Quantitative methods.* Quantitative methods are based on mathematical models. Most often used methods are time series and causal model.

    (a) *Time series.* Time Series is a set of numbers, which are observed on a regular, recurring basis. Historical observations are known; future values must be forecasted. Forecast can be generated based on patterns in the data. For example, grocery stores can forecast demand for milk based on the pattern of historical data.

    (b) *Causal method.* Causal forecasting method assumes that demand data is correlated with some environmental factors. For example, sales volume is associated with product price. As such, promotion sales and coupons can be used to increase sales volume.

A forecast model, which has been tuned to fit a historical data set, may not necessarily forecast future demand accurately. A complicated model can fit the old data well, but it will probably work poorly with new demand.

If time series or regression method is chosen, software can be used. There are numerous stand-alone forecast software available[2].

Step 4 *Examine forecast accuracy.* Accuracy is a measure of how closely a forecast aligns with observations of the series. Bias is a persistent tendency of a forecast to over-predict or under-predict demand. Bias is therefore a kind of pattern, which suggests that the procedure being used is inappropriate.

Once the forecast is conducted, the forecast outcome is evaluated by the managers along the supply chain to ensure that the forecasted demand is acceptable. If the demand is seasonal, a method that incorporates seasonality should be selected. Meanwhile, top-down forecasting approach can be used to aggregately forecast a family of product first, and then specify each SKU item. Another way is bottom-up forecasting, which forecasts each SKU product first, then aggregate a family of products.

Step 5 *Synchronize forecast results.* Different functions in an organization prepare their own forecasts to reflect their focus. Marketing focuses on trends occurring in the marketplace, finance emphasize on budgeting, and sales forecast based on sales quotas While in theory all these forecasts would roll up the same number, this is rarely the case. Therefore, a few forecasts can be prepared, one for production planning, one for marketing and sales, and another for accounting and finance. It is important that forecasts are synchronized collectively to reduce forecast variation and plan for production flexibility.

Roth products, a division of Abbott Laboratories found that the forecasting needs of the entire company could be met with three forecasts, one for marketing, one for production, and one for finance[3].

Step 6 *Evaluate forecast outcome.* Forecast results should be evaluated periodically to refine the forecast and to determine the best

---

[2] Elikai, Fara, Rvija Badaranathi and Vince Howe (2002). "A review of 52 forecasting software packages." Journal of Business Forecasting and Systems, Vol. 21, no. 2, p. 19-27.

[3] Helms, M. M., Ettkin, L.P., and Chapman, S. (2000). "Supply chain forecasting – Collaborative forecasting supports supply chain management." *Business Process Management Journal*, 6(5), 302.

component to forecast in a supply chain[4]. For example, Sport Obmeyer continuously refines its forecast procedure. In addition to forecasting finished goods demand, it forecasts the need for production capacity, so that it can reserve its supplier's capacity for making products in a later date.

5.3 Determine Forecasting Methods

There are many forecasting models in common use. These models include time series, causal model, simulation, and qualitative methods. The selection of the model depends on the nature of the demand observation and the type of industry. For example, demand for diapers is constant, so moving average method can be a choice. On the other hand, allergy medicine, sun block lotion, and Christmas items are seasonal products. Consequently, a seasonal method should be considered.

When there is no historical information for new products, fashion products, or high tech products, judgmental approach and expert experience are the appropriate approaches.

The time series methods are often chosen for short term forecasting with a time horizon of three months to one year. In this book, we focus on time series techniques.

5.3.1 Moving average

Moving average is an arithmetic average of a certain number of the most recent observations. As each new observation is added, the oldest observation is dropped. The value of the number of periods to be included for the average reflects responsiveness versus stability.

$$F_{t+1} = (\Sigma L_t) / n \tag{5.1}$$

Where: n = number of periods to be included for computing average
L_t = observation for period t

---

[4] Fisher, M.L., Hammond, J.H., Obermeyer, W.R., and Raman, A. (1994). "Making supply meet demand in an uncertain world." *Harvard Business Review*. May-June 1994, 83-93.

Example Problem 5.1: Moving Average

Demand for napkins is given in the table below. Use moving average number of period (**n**) = 4 to predict the demand for December 2004.

Solution to example Problem 5.1

2004	Sales	Forecast
June	97	
July	112	
Aug.	98	
Sept.	96	
Oct.	102	100.8
Nov.	94	102
Dec.		97.5

Use the first four months' data to predict the fifth month's demand by averaging the demands from June through September. The forecast for October is 100.8. December's forecast is computed by averaging the demands from August through November. So, forecast for December is 97.5.

In general, the fewer number of periods of historical data used to predict future demand, the better the forecast reflects the recent demand trend. On the contrary, the more number of periods of historical data used, the greater weight to past demand the forecast gives.

5.3.2 Weighted moving average

In the moving average problem, each demand observation is weighted equally. For example, for a 4-period problem, each observation is weighted 0.25. Sometimes, analysts want to give certain observations more weight to reflect the real situation. This is called weighted moving average. The formula for the weighted moving average is as follows:

$$F_{t+1} = \Sigma W_t * L_t \qquad\qquad (5.2)$$

Where: W_t = weight for period t; the sum of all the weights is 100%.
$\qquad L_t$ = observation for period t.

Example Problem 5.2: Weighted Moving Average

John wants to forecast sales of floor detergent for April using a 4-period weighted moving average method. The sales information of January through March is given in the table below.

Solution to example Problem 5.2

Month	Sales	Weight	Sales*weight	Forecast
Jan.	650	0.50	325	
Feb.	600	0.25	150	
March	700	0.25	175	
April				650
Total		1.00		

The forecast for April is 650.

5.3.3 Exponential smoothing

Exponential smoothing is a weighted moving average forecast technique that allows weights to be used for forecasting. There are three components to know before making a forecast.

(i) Actual demand for time period t

(ii) Forecast for time period t.

(iii) A smoothing coefficient.

The exponential smoothing model is:

$$F_{t+1} = F_t + \alpha(D_t - F_t) \tag{5.3}$$

Where: D_t = sales volume for month t

F_t = forecast for month t.

α = smoothing coefficient.

The following is the key issues of exponential smoothing method.

1. The value of α is between 0 and 1 ($0 <= \alpha <= 1$)

2. A value of α close to 1 produces a forecast that reacts more quickly to changes in the data.

3. The term $(D_t - F_t)$ is the difference between actual demand and forecast in this period and is known as forecast error. If we use a large α value, the model is more responsive to the recent discrepancy.
4. What is a good α value? It all depends on the pattern of the data.
    - Large α values emphasize recent levels of demand and result in forecasts more responsive to changes in the underlying average.
    - Small α values treat past demand more uniformly and result in more stable forecasts.

Example Problem 5.3: Exponential Smoothing

The forecast for July is 56. If alpha (α) is 0.2, calculate the forecast for August through January next year?

Month	Sales	Forecast
July	56	56
August	67	56
September	62	58.2
October	58	59
November	65	58.8
December	60	60
January		60

Apply formula (5.3):

$F_{Aug} = F_{July} + \alpha(D_{July} - F_{July}) = (56) + .2(56\text{-}56) = 56$

$F_{Sept} = F_{Aug} + \alpha(D_{Aug} - F_{Aug}) = (56) + .2(67\text{-}56) = 58.2$

Repeat the above steps to complete the forecast for January. The forecasted demand for January is 60.

5.3.4 Double exponential smoothing for trended data

The following model demonstrates a way to manage linear trend. The procedure separates the average from the trend in the data and develops an estimate for each component. To complete double exponential smoothing for trended data forecast, we need to use three formulas.

$$L_t = \alpha D_t + (1 - \alpha) (L_{t-1} + T_{t-1}) \tag{5.4}$$
$$T_t = \beta (L_t - L_{t-1}) + (1 - \beta) T_{t-1} \tag{5.5}$$
$$F_{t+1} = L_t + T_t \tag{5.6}$$

Where: L_t = average demand, also known as level demand

T_t = trend

α is the weight for average demand

β is the weight for trend.

The following is a couple of issues related to double exponential smoothing method.

1. Both the values of α and β are between 0 and 1.
2. A value of α or β close to 1 is responsive to the changes in the data but nervous; a value of α or β close to 0 generates forecast that is stable and calm. Appropriate α or β values are usually determined through trial and error.

Example Problem 5.4: Double Exponential Smoothing for Trended Data

The average demand for July is 300 and trend is 150. If alpha (α) is 0.6 and beta (β) is 0.6, calculate the forecast for August through January next year.

Solution to Problem 5.4

Since the value for level and trend are given for July, so forecast for August is:

$$F_{Aug} = L_{July} + T_{July} = 300 + 150 = 450$$

Start from forecast for September, we need to apply the formulas 5.4-5.6:

$$L_{Aug} = \alpha D_{Aug} + (1 - \alpha) (L_{July} + T_{July})$$
$$= 0.6 (400) + (1-0.6) (300 + 150) = 420$$
$$T_{Aug} = \beta (L_{Aug} - L_{July}) + (1 - \beta) T_{July}$$
$$= 0.6 (420 - 300) + (1-0.6) (150) = 132$$
$$F_{Sept} = L_{Aug} + T_{Aug} = 420 + 132 = 552$$

Month	Demand	Level	Trend	Forecast
July	310	300	150	
Aug.	400	420	132	450.0
Sept.	380	448.8	70.1	552.0
Oct.	485	498.6	57.9	518.9
Nov.	550	552.6	55.6	556.4
Dec.	535	564.3	29.2	608.1
Jan.				593.5

Repeat the above steps to complete forecast for January. The projected demand for January is 593.5.

5.3.5 Multiplicative seasonal method for seasonal data

Most products have seasonal demand pattern. For example, demand for sun block lotion is higher in summer than that of other seasons. Multiplicative Seasonal Method is one of the methods we can use to estimate seasonal demand. The procedure of Multiplicative Seasonal Method is as follows:

(1) Calculate the average demand and total demand for each year.
(2) Divide the actual demand of each period by the average demand of that year to get a seasonal index.
(3) Calculate the average seasonal indices for each period.
(4) Estimate the demand for next year.
(5) Multiply the seasonal index of a period by the estimated average sales in that year to get forecasted sales for the given period in a future year.

Example Problem 5.5: Multiplicative Seasonal Method

The following is the quarterly sales of sun block lotion for 2003, 2004, and 2005. The manager wants to forecast the quarterly sales of sun block lotion for 2006.

Quarter	2003	2004	2005
1	114	212	250
2	384	418	458
3	312	388	436
4	222	218	264

Solution to example Problem 5.5

The following table gives the answer using steps (1), (2) and (3) of Multiplicative Seasonal Method.

	2003		2004		2005		Avg.
Quarter	sales	Index	sales	Index	sales	Index	Index
1	114	0.44	212	0.69	250	0.71	0.61
2	384	1.49	418	1.35	458	1.30	1.38
3	312	1.21	388	1.26	436	1.24	1.23
4	222	0.86	218	0.71	264	0.75	0.77
Avg.	258		309		352		
Total	1032		1236		1408		

Step (1). Annual sales for 2003: (114 + 384 + 312 + 222) = 1032
Average quarterly sales for 2003: (114+384+312+222) / 4 =258
Step (2). Seasonal index for quarter 1 of 2003: 114 / 258 = 0.44
Step (3). Average seasonal index for Quarter 1: (0.44 + 0.69 + 0.71) / 3 = 0.61
Step (4). Estimated sales for 2003 (there are different ways to project future sales. The following is only one of the ways to project future demand).
　(i) The average increase of demand from 2003 to 2004 and from 2004 to 2005 is: (1236-1032) + (1408 -1236) / 2 = 188.
　(ii) The estimated annual demand for 2006 is the total sales for 2005 plus average increase of the previous two years: 1408 + 188 = 1596.
　(iii) The average quarterly demand for 2006: 1596 / 4 = 399.
Step (5). Forecasted quarterly demand for 2006 (See the table below).
Forecast demand for quarter 1, 2006 is: 399*0.61 = 244. Repeat the same procedure for every quarter in 2006.

2006	Average		2006
Quarter	Demand	Index	Forecasted Demand
1	399	0.61	244
2	399	1.38	551
3	399	1.23	493
4	399	0.77	308
Total			1596

5.4 Reduce Forecast Variability

5.4.1 Sources of variability

There are two sources of demand variability. One is identifiable variability and the other is random variability

The identifiable demand variability, such as anticipation for higher toys sales during the Christmas season, can be managed and reduced. For example, Toys-R-Us builds anticipation inventory in advance to satisfy high demand during the holiday season. At the same time, Toys-R-Us proactively manages demand through promotion sales in October to shift demand to a less busy season. In doing this, inventory can be reduced and production capacity can be better balanced.

The random demand or supply variability, such as oil production disruption due to hurricane, cannot be avoided. Therefore, the only method we have is to reduce random variability.

To reduce demand and supply variability, we need to understand where the variability comes from. The following are a few examples of sources of variability.

- Demand uncertainty in time, quantity, and location. It is difficult to precisely predict what customers want to buy, when they buy, and what they buy.
- Supply uncertainty in quantity, time, and quality. There is no guarantee that suppliers will deliver the product in the right quantity, at the right time, and in right quality.
- External factors such as promotions that trig high demand level.
- Sales promotion at the end of season can lead to high demand.

- Market competition such as new products or substitutable products can cause demand variation.
- Inconsistent forecast measurement units can create variability. For example, production department forecasts in SKU units, sales department forecasts in number of orders, and finance department forecasts in dollar value. The outcome of forecast can be very different.

Demand variability is a common phenomenon and there is no way to eliminate it. Therefore, we should be able to measure the variability and determine the acceptable variability and unacceptable variability. Section 5.4.2 discusses variability measures.

5.4.2 Measure variability

Variability from both demand and supply is constant in a supply chain. So, do not cover the variability. Measure it, minimize it or eliminate it.

We discussed a few forecast models in section 5.3. Different forecast models generate different forecast results. So the question is: "which forecast approach is a better one?" Usually managers tend to select a model that has a smaller forecast error. The following is a number of methods we can apply to measure forecast variability.

- Forecast error (e_t) is the difference between the actual demand for period t and forecasted demand for period t.

$$e_t = D_t - F_t \tag{5.7}$$

- Mean Absolute Deviation (MAD). A common measure of forecast error is mean absolute deviation (MAD). MAD is easy to compute and interpret. It measures accuracy of the forecast model.

$$MAD = \frac{\sum_{t=1}^{n} |e_t|}{n} \tag{5.8}$$

- Mean Squared Error (MSE).

$$MSE = \frac{\sum_{t=1}^{n} e_t^2}{n} \tag{5.9}$$

- Mean Percentage Error (MPE).

$$MPE = \frac{\sum_{t=1}^{n} \frac{e_t}{D_t} * 100}{n} \qquad (5.10)$$

5.4.2.1 Measure bias and accuracy

Example Problem 5.6: Forecasting Error Measurement

The following is 6-month demand and forecast of Klee, Inc. Determine forecast error and variability.

Solution to example Problem 5.6

Period	D_t	F_t	e_t	$|e_t|$	e_t^2	$e_t\%$	$|e_t\%|$
1	623	620	3	3	9	0.48%	0.48%
2	512	660	-148	148	21904	-28.91%	28.91%
3	624	620	4	4	16	0.64%	0.64%
4	590	660	-70	70	4900	-11.86%	11.86%
5	695	620	75	75	5625	10.79%	10.79%
6	723	660	63	63	3969	8.71%	8.71%
Total			68	208	14,494	7.6%	31.4%

Error		Description
average error	68	Measure bias; the forecast under-estimates demand
MAD	208/6 = 35	Measure accuracy; the difference between forecast and demand is 35 units
MSE	14494/6 = 2416	Squared error is difficult to explain. This term is used to determine root mean squared error in the next row.
RMSE	$\sqrt{2416} = 49$	Measure accuracy; the difference between forecast and demand is 49 units.
MPE	7.6%/6 = 1.3%	Measure bias; the forecast under-estimates demand by 1.3%.
MAPE	31.4%/6 =5.2%	Measure accuracy; the forecast error is 5.2%.

5.4.2.2 Tracking signal

Tracking signals is the ratio of the sum of forecast errors (the difference between forecasted demand and actual demand) and the mean absolute deviation (MAD). Tracking signal is used to signal the forecaster when the forecasting model needs to be modified.

$$\text{Tracking Signal (TS): } TS = \frac{\sum_{t=1}^{n}(D_t - F_t)}{MAD} \qquad (5.11)$$

A tracking signal can be used to monitor the quality of the forecast. In general, when the value of tracking signal is between ± 4 to ± 8, the forecast method is considered acceptable for most exponential smoothing forecasting. Several procedures are used for tracking signal. The one presented in this section (formula 5.11) is a simple method. The following is an example of tracking signal.

Example Problem 5.7: Tracking Signal

Given the following historical data, use the tracking signal critical value of 4. Determine in which period the forecast should be reviewed. Apply formula 5.11 to determine tracking signal.

Solution for example Problem 5.7

The tracking signals for the four periods are all met the critical value of 4 (see the table below). No review should be made now. The tracking signal is recalculated each period when MAD is calculated and compared with tracking signal critical value, which is 4 in this problem.

Period	Sales	Forecast	Error	Cumulative Error	Absolute Error	MAD	Tracking signal
1	89	88	1	1	1	1	1
2	102	121	-19	-18	19	10	-1.8
3	108	112	-4	-22	4	8	-2.75
4	99	108	-9	-31	9	8.25	-3.76

Bias exits when cumulative actual demand varies from forecast. The problem is in guessing whether the variance is due to random variation or bias, which is identifiable. If the error is due to random variation, the error will correct itself. If the error is due to bias, then the forecast should be corrected.

In this example, if the Tracking Signal at any period is outside the range $\pm$ 4, it is a signal that the forecast is biased and is either under or overestimating the demand. If the forecast method under-estimate the demand that means there may be a trend component that has not been included. If this is the case, a trend forecast method should be considered.

5.4.3 Reduce demand variability and increase production flexibility

Demand variability is a common phenomenon. Therefore, there is no way to eliminate it. If demand is higher than the average demand, stock out is a problem. Whereas, if demand is lower than the average demand, there will have too much inventory. Excessive inventory is also a problem. Managers spend considerable amount of time and resource dealing with variability from the demand. Three things a manager can do.

  (i) Increase safety stock to hedge demand uncertainty in quantity and timing. For example, retailers do not know precisely when customers will buy Quaker oatmeal and how much they will buy, so they increase safety stock to prevent shortage; and

  (ii) Increase the flexibility of the production system for assembling the final product as it is needed. For example, Dell Inc. runs a flexible manufacturing system to meet customer demand.

Either case will require investment. The third way (iii) is to proactively manage demand that reduces demand variability

In general, it is easy to plan average demand. However, the problem is the deviation from the average demand. Managers should first try to reduce and eliminate identifiable variability, then try to reduce unavoidable variability through increasing supply chain flexibility. Reduce variability and increase accuracy of forecast will give a supply chain competitive edge in the market place.

5.5 Demand Management: Forecasting in e-Biz Environment

5.5.1 Enhance value through synchronize demand forecast

In an e-Biz environment, collaborative planning, forecasting and replenishment is applied to synchronize demand forecast. For a CPFR system to be successful, it is crucial that all trading partners monitor the accuracy of the collaborative forecasts. In other words, determine if the customer routinely buys a quantity close to what the system has forecast. The following suggests a few methods that can enhance to synchronize demand forecast in supply chain.

(1) Developing an order-fill forecast based on the length of supply chain cycle time. First, estimate an initial production quantity. When the demand stabilizes, a more reasonable forecast can be projected based on the sales order data. For example, Sport Obermeyer focuses on keeping raw material and factory production capacity undifferentiated as long as possible. Sport Obermeyer keeps raw materials in stock and books factory capacity for the peak production periods well in advance but does not specify the exact styles to be manufactured until a later date. Sport Obermeyer assumes the risk of supplying the correct raw materials to the factory and the factory agrees to hold production capacity for Sport Obermeyer to be used later[4]. In this way, Sport Obermeyer can reduce the variability of demand for the final product, which is more costly than stocking raw material. The manufacturer provides production flexibility.

(2) Supporting manufacturing strategy with appropriate forecasting method. A company's choice of delivering products to market affects its demand management. The choices can be make-to-stock, make-to-order, assembly-to-order, or engineer-to-order. This decision influences the choice of forecast methods. If it is a make-to-stock supply chain, forecast units will be the final products. Whereas, if it is a make-to-order supply chain, forecast will focus on production capacity cushion and the speed at which the product can be supplied to customer.

(3) Fostering supply chain communication. In a CPFR situation, data and forecast may be communicated with customers, suppliers. However, a firm needs to determine what data and forecast will be shared with other supply chain members. For instance, SKU-level forecast is jointly

developed by retailers and next-tier suppliers. Even when electronic collaborative forecasting system has not been implemented, trading partners may simply ask other members of the supply chain about their future projects and needs on a regular basis.

(4) Aligning supply chain strategy with uncertainty from both the customer and the supply. From the supplier, uncertainty may come from lead-time, quantity, and quality. From the customer, the uncertainty may come from timing and quantity. Uncertainty increases variability. Supply chain managers should work to reduce uncertainty or develop mechanisms to control uncertainty. Understand data and information needed to generate forecast, utilize data warehouse, and data mining, to improve the accuracy of forecast.

5.5.2 Delayed differentiation and postponement

Delayed differentiation and postponement is a relative new initiative to manage demand uncertainty. Recently, many manufacturers and retailers apply postponement or a delayed differentiation strategy to reduce forecast variability and to strike the right inventory level. By holding inventory at the parts and components stage, companies are able to offer customized products. However, postponement calls for a high degree of collaboration among supply chain trading partners[5].

Designing standard and configurable products provides a basis for the postponement of producing end items because products can be differentiated quickly and inexpensively once actually demand is known. The Oracle/Cap Gemini Ernest & Young survey found that by implementing successful postponement strategy the industry leaders have reduced inventory costs by as much as 40 percent[5]. This model allows companies to move from the push oriented supply chain to pull oriented supply chain, and to a demand driven supply chain.

---

[5] Matthews, P. and Syed, N. (2004). "The power of postponement." *Supply Chain Management Review*, 8(3), 28-34.

5.6 Demand Management Performance Metrics

The performance of the forecast process should be measured. The forecast performance metrics is used to improve forecast accuracy, reduce inventory investment, and improve customer service level. The following is a set of measures that can be applied to evaluate forecast performance. Important issues for demand management:

- Error management - wrong product or specification, wrong amount, wrong shipping date
- Number of backorders and units
- Customer service policy issues
- Order responsiveness
- Order lead-time management
- Order scheduling
- Customer priority rules
- Resource allocations
- Product substitution or upgrade
- On-time performance
- Lead-time management
- Safety stock investment
- Production safety capacity

5.7 Summary

Demand management and customer order forecast are important components of supply chain management. This chapter examines how companies manage the linkage of their production with their customers' needs using demand management measures and forecasting procedures. We have discussed collaborative forecasting, various forecast process, forecast models, variability reduction, and performance evaluation. Collaborative forecast should be considered in conjunction with collaborative planning and replenishment, which will be discussed in Chapters 6 and 7 respectively.

Questions for Pondering

1. Why and to what extent is the supply chain manager interested in demand management? How do you suppose the interest might be different if the supply chain manager were associated with
   a. A food manufacturer?
   b. An aircraft producer?
   c. A large retail chain?
   d. A hospital?
2. Give illustrations of
   a. Spatial versus temporal demand
   b. Lumpy versus regular demand
   c. Derived versus independent demand
3. Why should a manager be suspicious if forecaster claims to forecast historical demand without any forecast error?
4. What is the problem if a manager uses the previous year's sale's data instead of the previous year's demand to forecast demand for the coming year?
5. Some people have argued that it is more important to have low bias (mean deviation) than to have low mean absolute deviation (MAD). Do you agree? Give an example to support your argument.

Problems

1. If the forecast for January is 150 units and actual demand 85 units, what is the exponential smoothing forecast for February, assuming Alpha is 0.3.

2. Estimate the forecasts for August, September, October, November, December, and January nest year using exponential smoothing method. The smoothing factor, alpha is 0.3, and the forecast for July is 250.

Month	Actual Demand	Forecast
July	245	
August	260	
September	250	
October	235	
November	255	
December	260	

3. Demand information for the past 6 months is given in the following table.

Month	Actual Demand	Forecast
June	78	
July	46	
August	53	
September	80	
October	68	
November	70	
December		

   a. Graph the demand pattern.

   b. What is forecast for October, November, and December using three-month moving average.

   c. Calculate the forecasts using exponential smoothing method, alpha = 0.3. The forecast for June is 69.

   d. Using error measure methods to compare the results of two different forecast methods. Which forecast approach will you recommend to the manager? Why?

4. Using the following information to estimate the forecast for each period using the double exponential smoothing method for trended data. Alpha = 0.3, beta = 0.3, $Level_1$ = 100, $Trend_1$ = 50.

Period	Demand	Level	Trend	Forecast	Error
1	350	100	50		
2	450				
3	468				
4	520				

5. Calculate the seasonal indices for each period based on the following demand information.

Period	Demand	Seasonal Index	Period	Demand	Seasonal Index
1	112		7	30	
2	127		8	50	
3	247		9	85	
4	90		10	257	
5	60		11	137	
6	25		12	115	

    a. Calculate the seasonal indices for each period based on the demand information in the table.
    b. Suppose the forecasted annual demand for next year is 1750 units, what will be the expected demand for each period? Using seasonal indices in part a.

6. A company uses a tracking signal trigger of +/- 6 to decide whether a forecast should be reviewed. MAD is 20. Is there any indication that the forecast should be revised given the following information?

Month	Demand	Forecast	Error	Cumulative Deviation	Tracking Signal
August	110	105			
Sept.	115	120			
Oct.	120	115			
Nov.	125	135			
Dec.	140	125			

Supplement 5.1

Synchronizing Production and Inventory Management in Supply Chain: Introduction to Beer Game

1. Introduction

The goal of supply chain is to fulfill customer demands and requests through the process of transforming raw materials to the finished goods. Consequently, the transformation process is associated with material flow, information flow and fund flow as we discussed in Chapter 1. The transformation process may include multiple companies and can be modeled in a simple supply chain that contains a retailer, a wholesaler, a distributor, and a manufacturer. Beer Game is a simulation game for users to imitate the dynamics of production capacity and inventory management in a supply chain.

In the 1960s, Beer Game was first introduced by the faculty at the Massachusetts Institute of Technology's Sloan School of Management to illustrate the bullwhip effect. This simulation game shows what happens in a hypothetical supply chain and how to coordinate the actions of different companies in a supply chain.

In his book *The Fifth Discipline*, Peter M. Senge uses a hypothetical scenario to show how the bullwhip effect gathers momentum and what can be done to avoid it[6]. The beer game starts with retailers experiencing a sudden but small increase in customer demand for a certain brand of beer called Lover's Beer. Orders are batched up by retailers and passed on to the distributors who deliver the beer. Initially, these orders exceed the distributor's on-hand inventory so they ration out their supplies of Lover's Beer to the retailers and place even larger orders for the beer with the brewery who makes Lover's Beer. The brewery cannot instantly increase production of the beer so it rations out the beer it can produce to the distributors and begins building additional production capacity.

The scarcity of the beer prompts panic buying. After a couple of weeks, the demand on the manufacturer can be hundreds of cases a day

---

[6] Senge, Peter M. (1990) *The Fifth Discipline* (*The Fifth Discipline: The Art and Practice of the Learning Organization*, New York: Doubleday/Currency.

while was only four cases up to a total of eight cases at the retailer. Then as the brewery increases its production outputs and ships the product in large quantities, the orders that had been steadily increasing due to panic buying suddenly decline. The opposite effect occurs. The retailer has too much inventory than is needed and decided to order zero quantity for several days. This eventually transmitted back upstream of the supply chain and the manufacturer has to stop production. The shortage then flows downstream back to the retailer. The whole mess starts all over again. The bullwhip occurs. The real change in order from consumer is only four cases a day.

In this case, all the members in the supply chain bear the costs of the bullwhip effect. The brewery increases production capacity to satisfy an order stream that is much higher than actual demand. The distributor stocks extra inventory to handle the volatility in order levels. Retailers experience problems with product availability and extended replenishment lead times. During periods of high demand, there are times when the available capacity and inventory in the supply chain cannot cover the orders being placed. This results in product rationing, longer order replenishment cycles, and lost sales due to lack of inventory.

The scenario occurs in the real world every day. The actual fluctuation in monthly demand in automotive industry is less than 10%, but the second and third tier suppliers often adjust their capacity by as much as 50%. In the apparel industry, the seasonal fluctuation compounds the demand variation along the supply chain. The high and low waves of demand continue to occur in the supply chain despite the demand of the end user being relatively flat.

2. Play the Beer Game

The Beer Game is a simulation game that models a supply chain of beer production and distribution. This game can be played with a group of four people. There are four players in the game, the retailer, wholesaler, distributor, and manufacturer. Order starts from the retailer and goes back to the wholesaler, the distributor, and finally to the manufacturer as illustrated in Figure 5.4. The sequence of delivering beer is from factory to the distributor, then to the wholesaler, and finally to the retailer. The main task of the retailer, wholesaler, and distributor is managing inventory, while the main task of the manufacturer is managing production capacity.

Order sequence

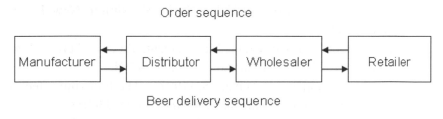

Beer delivery sequence

Figure 5.4. Beer game

The average daily demand for beer is four kegs. The demand can be as low as 2 units and as high as 6 units. The maximum change in order from consumer is four kegs a day.

There is a two-week transportation delay between each pair of the trading partners. For example, beer shipped from factory in week one will be received by the distributor in week three.

Only two relevant costs are considered in the game: inventory holding cost that is $0.50 a week for each keg of beer, and backorder cost that is $1.00 a week for each keg of beer. The total cost is computed weekly.

The group can play 30 weeks. After that a summary of 30 weeks' performance on holding cost, backorder cost, and total cost are analyzed, as well as Bullwhip effects.

References

APICS (1998). *Dictionary*, 9th edition. Falls Church, VA
Arnold, J.R.T. (1998). *Introduction to Materials Management*, 3rd edition. Prentice Hall: New Jersey.

Ballou, R.H. (1992). *Business Logistics Management*. Prentice Hall: Englewood Cliffs, New Hersey

Fredendall, L.D. and Hill, E. (2001). *Basics of Supply Chain Management*. The St. Lucie Press: New York.

Krajewski, L.J., Ritzman, L.P., and Malhotr, M. (2007). *Operations Management: Process and Value Chain*, 8th edition. New Jersey: Prentice Hall.

Lambert, D. (2006). Supply Chain Management: Process, Partnerships, Performance, 2nd edition. Sarasota, Florida: SCMI.

Lee, H.L., Padmanabhan, V., Whang S. (1997). The bullwhip effect in supply chains. *Sloan Management Review*, 38(3), 93-103.

Schreibfeder, Jon (2005). *Achieving Effective Inventory Management*, 3rd edition. Coppell, TX: Effective Inventory Management, Inc.

Chapter 6

Transforming Demand in Supply Chain: Production Planning and Scheduling

6.1 Transforming Demand through Production Planning

A company has to manage its production in order to transform customer orders to products and to add value to the product. The question is how to smoothly transform customer orders to the end-user products in the supply chain. The answer lies in the effective manufacturing planning and control system.

A company usually belongs to one supply chain. However, many companies belong to more than one supply chain. Production planning is a mechanism to coordinate not only the activities within operations, but also other functions in the firm such as marketing, sales, human resources, engineering, accounting, and the entire supply chain.

The goal of the production planning is to ensure that planned production matches customer demand. Nevertheless, demand uncertainty and variation are inevitable. There are two approaches to manage demand fluctuation: one is to increase production capacity flexibility so that production can be scheduled when demand is there. The other is to raise or lower inventory to meet demand. Both solutions require resources. Consequently, production planning is to balance the resources such as workforce, inventory, and overtime that are required to manufacture products to meet customer demand. The customer demand, which is an output of demand management activity discussed in the previous chapter (Chapter 5), is a crucial input to production planning.

Figure 6.1 illustrates a hierarchical production planning process. The production planning is based on product family. This plan provides an overall balance of what the customer needs and what the manufacturer can produce. Master production schedule (MPS) is planned on stock-keeping-unit (SKU) items, which are the items that are shipped out of the factory (Figure 6.1). For example, at the production planning stage, garden sprayers are stated in the units of product family, which does not specify the demand for various colors or sizes. The MPS, on the other hand, derives from the number of garden sprayers stated in the production plan and disaggregate to SKU items. Production quantity and time for each SKU item is specified in the master production plan. Rough-cut capacity planning is conducted at the master production schedule level to ensure the company has adequate capacity.

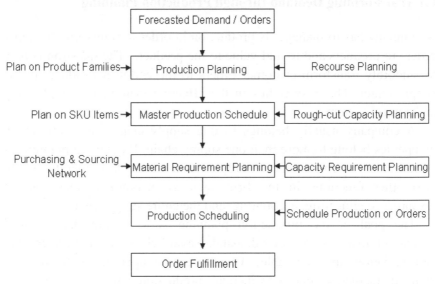

Figure 6.1. An overview of production planning and scheduling

Material requirement planning (MRP) translates the master product schedule into requirements needed for producing the product such as raw material, parts and components. MRP is a software that assists managers in ordering materials and scheduling inventory replenishment. At the MRP stage, capacity requirement planning is performed to ensure capacity of key workstations.

Scheduling is the last manufacturing stage to transform demand. At this stage, capacity and materials are ready for customer orders to be launched to the shop floor for production. After this stage, orders are ready to be shipped out of the factory.

In moving from traditional materials management to supply chain management, demand transformation is more visible in terms of planning, forecasting and replenishment. The transformation process allocates available capacity and inventory to satisfy customer orders. When a product or component is not available at a certain place, a system-wide check can identify alternative locations and/or locate a substitutable item. Manufacturing planning and control is crucial to the transformation of customer orders to products and to making a firm successful in the market place.

6.1.1 Aggregate planning

Production planning is also called aggregate planning because the plan aggregates demand on product family. Production planning is a statement of time-phased production rates, work-force levels, and inventory holdings based on customer requirements and capacity limitations. It serves as a link between strategic goals of a company and plans for individual items and components. Based on forecasted demand, production plan is typically prepared for the next 12 months. Companies usually update their production plan to recognize the changes in demand. They may do this by reviewing the plan monthly and updating it quarterly. Given the objectives set by a company's business plan, production planning will determine the following:

- The quantity of each product family to be produced in each period
- The desired inventory level for each period
- The allowed backorder level for each period
- The allowed stockout level for each period
- The resources (labor, material, and other resources) required to support the production for each period.

The objective of production planning is to minimize the costs of change in production level, cost of holding inventory, cost of stockout and subcontracting. The information needed to make a production plan includes:

- Forecasted demand for the planning horizon
- Beginning inventory and desired ending inventory
- Back orders
- Subcontract
- Resources needed for production

There are three basic strategies commonly used in production planning. They are level strategy, chase strategy, and mixed strategy. More discussion is provided in Section 6.1.4.

6.1.2 Dimensions of production planning

Production planning has three dimensions: products (or services), labor, and time. The plan aggregates all three.
  (i) Product families
- Groups similar markets and manufacturing processes
- Relevant units of measurement include: units, barrels, tons, dollars, standard hours, etc.
  (ii) Labor
- Plans on the level of work-force needed, it doesn't specify the type of skills needed
  (iii) Time
- Updates monthly or quarterly
- Planning periods are in terms of month or quarter, not week or day.

6.1.3 Planning alternatives

Production planning uses various alternatives to manage demand uncertainty and capacity constraints. Typically, two approaches are used: reactive approach and proactive approach.

Reactive approach includes work-force adjustment through hiring and firing, using overtime and under-time, adjusting vacation schedules, building up anticipation inventory, using subcontractors, and allowing backlogs, backorders, and stockouts.

Proactive alternative intends to adjust demand pattern. Commonly used methods include producing complementary products to manage the seasonal nature of the demand, and using creative pricing and promotion methods to level demands in high season and slow season.

6.1.4 Planning Strategies

Usually, companies use three planning strategies for production plan: level strategy, chase strategy, and mixed strategy.

Level strategy. Level strategy maintains a constant output rate or work force level over the planning horizon by cumulating anticipation inventory and/or using under-time. Level strategy keeps a stable workforce level or output rate to match the demand for the planning horizon. Anticipation inventory, backorders, stockout, and under-time are used.

Chase strategy. Chase strategy adjusts output rates or work-force levels to match the demand over the planning horizon without using anticipation inventory or under-time. Chase strategy is accomplished through hires and layoffs, overtime, extra shifts or subcontracting.

Mixed strategy. Mixed strategy covers a range of strategies, such as level strategy and chase strategy. The best strategy may be a mix of some anticipation inventory, some work-force level changes, and some overtime.

6.2 Master Production Schedule

6.2.1 The basics of master production schedule

Master Production Schedule (MPS) is disaggregated from production plan. MPS is not a sales forecast. Rather, it is the detailed production plan for the end item to be produced by the plant. It is constrained by the production plan. For example, if the production plan calls for 400 window blinds to be produced in June. This may mean 100 window blinds in ivory color in week one, 100 in white color in week two, 100 in gray color in week three, and 100 in light blue in week four. This process of identifying each end item is called disaggregation. The demand for each Stock Keeping Unit (SKU) end item may be determined at the retail stores when the item is scanned at the checkout. MPS takes into account the forecast, the aggregate plan, available capacity, and available material. MPS must be feasible because the following planning steps in material and capacity assume that the MPS is reliable.

At the master production planning stage, rough cut capacity planning is used to check the feasibility of MPS (Figure 6.1). Rough cut capacity planning is medium-term capacity planning. The length of time ranges from one week to three months and depends on the company and the industry. If there is not enough capacity, then some demand has to be pushed ahead or postponed. Alternatively, some capacity is added.

Master production schedule is changed and updated more frequently than the production plan. It is a detailed plan and does not extend as far into the future as the production plan. Therefore, it can be viewed as a contract among different functional areas within a company.

In the time horizon in which the MPS is frozen, production will produce everything that is stated on the schedule and the rest of the firm will sell what is produced. The company will decide when the MPS should be updated. In Figure 6.2, the MPS is broken into three time periods and divided by a curve line. The points below the curve line are orders received from customers. Points above the curve line indicate available production capacity and available to promise inventory.

The first time period is the one most close to the present and MPS is frozen. The frozen section indicates that production has started or the firm is committed to the materials that it purchased from its vendors. No changes are allowed in this time period. The second period is from week 2 to 8. A certain level of commitment has been made. For example, a request for parts and components has been sent to the upstream suppliers. At this stage, changes will result in costs, but can be negotiated. In the third time period changes can be made without penalty. The agreement of time fence is to achieve coordination both within and outside the firm. It provides insight to a firm's ability to respond to changes.

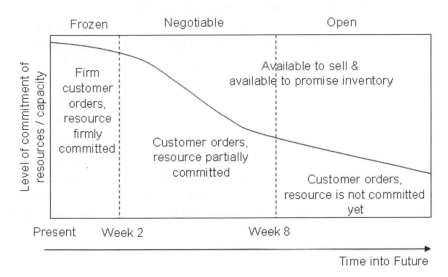

Figure 6.2. Time fence in master production schedule

Determining the length of frozen periods, negotiable periods, and open periods is a strategic issue, since it will influence the relationship of the firm to the other members of the supply chain. Where to place the time fence determines the overall flexibility of the firm and the supply chain to respond to changes in customer demand. For example, if the company supplies window blinds, fabric has a four-week time fence. It is difficult for the retailer to make changes if the end user wants to change the fabric color three weeks before delivery. However, if the fabric producer has a three-week time fence, then changes can be made close to the delivery time.

If one partner in the supply chain cannot produce an accurate MPS, then the entire supply chain will be affected. A large amount of variance in MPS will lead to a longer lead-time and large inventories in the supply chain. Therefore, a firm should try its best to plan and schedule production accurately.

Once a firm has a feasible MPS, material requirement planning is conducted. To produce the MPS end items a firm needs to procure or produce intermediate materials. For example, window blinds are assembled from rods, fabric, and string. The material needed is calculated at the material requirement planning stage.

The material requirement plan becomes inputs to the shop-floor scheduling system. The detailed requirements are sent to the suppliers to make sure that required parts, components or raw material will be delivered on time and in the right quantity.

The sales person needs to know what is available to fulfill the customer orders. Available to promise (APT) in the master production plan provides such information. In a make-to-stock production environment, orders are fulfilled from inventory; while in a make-to-order or assemble-to-order production environment, orders are fulfilled from production capacity. The portion of inventory or planned production capacity that is not consumed by actual customer orders is available to promise to customers.

The following is an example of master production schedule.

Example Problem 6.1: Master Production Schedule

Window blinds are made in lot size of 90 units. The beginning inventory is 75 units. Forecasted demand is 80 units for weeks 1 to 4, 95 units for weeks 5 and 6, and 90 units for weeks 7 and 8. Customer orders received are as follows:

Week 1 – 85   Week 4 – 22
Week 2 – 50   Week 5 – 8
Week 3 – 30   Week 6 – 2

Compute projected on hand inventory, MPS and ATP.

Solution to example Problem 6.1

The complete solution to example problem 6.1 is shown in the table below. First, enter forecast quantity and customer orders to the customer orders row.

(1) Projected on-hand inventory at the end of week 1, January:

On-hand = On-hand inventory at the end of last period + MPS quantity

$$- \max (\text{forecast, customer order}) \qquad (6.1)$$

Week 1, January: since on-hand inventory at the beginning of week 1 is not enough to cover the order of 85 units, a MPS of 90 units should be scheduled. On-hand inventory by the end of week 1 is computed as:
On-hand$_1$ = 75 + 90 − 85 = 80

	January				February			
Week	1	2	3	4	5	6	7	8
Forecast	80	80	80	80	95	95	90	90
Customer orders (committed)	85	50	30	22	8	2		
Projected on-hand inventory (75)	80	0	10	20	15	10	10	10
MPS	90		90	90	90	90	90	90
Available to promises	30		60	68	82	88	90	90

Week 2: since 80 units of on-hand inventory is available at the beginning of week 2 that is enough to cover the forecasted demand of 80 units; no new MPS should be scheduled. On-hand inventory for week 2 is computed as:
On-hand$_2$ = 80 + 0 − 80 = 0

Repeat the same step until all the on-hand inventories are computed.

(2) Available to promise for the 1st period of the planning horizon:
    ATP = On-hand inventory at the end of last period + MPS quantity − customer orders due before next MPS   (6.2)
    ATP$_1$ = 75 + 90 − (85 + 50) = 30

(3) Available to promise for periods after the 1st period:
    ATP = MPS quantity − customer orders due before next MPS   (6.3)
    ATP$_3$ = 90 − 30 = 60
    ATP$_4$ = 90 − 22 = 68

(4) Repeat the same step until all ATPs are computed.

6.2.2 Available to promise

In the example problem 6.1, the available-to-promise for the first week is 30 units. This information indicates to the sales department that it can promise as many as 30 units until next MPS quantity is delivered at the beginning of week 3. In week 3, there will be 60 units uncommitted and are available to promise to new orders.

If actual customer order quantity exceeds the ATP quantity, the MPS should be adjusted before more orders can be taken. Alternatively, the customer can be given a later delivery date, which can be the date of the next MPS arriving date.

6.2.3 Available to sell

Available to sell is to project the full visibility of uncommitted supply potential across the entire MPS planning horizon, for example 8 weeks in example problem 6.1. The idea is to go beyond on-hand uncommitted inventory, which is available to promise. Available to sell includes uncommitted inventory, as well as uncommitted capacity that can sell. For example, HP launched an initiative to create an available to sell capability[1]. A SKU-level available-to-sell report indicates upstream uncommitted capacity. This provides sales teams the information they need to steer demand and promotions into SKUs level, so as to avoid busy season when SKU is in tight supply.

6.2.4 E-Business solution – Global available to promise

To win and maintain the confidence of customers over time, industries strive to provide realistic product delivery dates based on actual and planned material availability, current production capacity and vendor lead times. In recent years, software companies such as MySAP, QAD, and Made-2-Manage have promoted an e-Business solution, global

---

[1] Scott Culbertson, Ike Harris, & Steve Radosevich (2005). Synchronization – HP style. *Supply Chain Management Review*, Mar 2005, 9(2), 24-31.

available-to-promise (ATP) that automates the search for available production capacity, as well as inventory in multiple warehouses, distribution centers, and manufacturing facilities to maximize customer service level.

Global ATP helps the supply chain keep its promises and improves customer satisfaction. The e-Business solution enables supply chain to view the existing inventory, check over production in progress, and identify substitutable products that can be used to fill orders. Additionally, the software allows the supply chain to reallocate its inventory system-wide, based on changing customer needs and market dynamics. By doing this, the supply chain is able to set delivery dates based on available capacity and material constraints to avoid over promising and under promising on customer orders.

The Global Available-to-Promise uses a rule-based strategy, which allows manufacturers to move from a "what if" scenario to "what's the best" decision. Consequently, asset utilization is improved through inventory and capacity checks along the supply chain in real time to ensure that supply matches demand.

6.3 Collaborative Planning

6.3.1 Overview of collaborative planning

In an openly communicative supply chain, firms may share their production plans with each other to encourage coordinated planning into the future. In this type of environment it is much more likely that all sources of demand are accounted for and there will be fewer surprises that disturb the production plan. Consequently, the production plan is based more on actual demand than forecasted demand.

A challenging issue facing production planning is demand variation. Retailers, wholesalers, and distributors place orders in batches periodically to minimize their order cost, transportation cost, and administrative effort. However, when orders are grouped to batches, the orders vary from the size of actual demand from customers. As the orders move up the supply chain, the size of the order gets larger and larger and the demand variance gets bigger and bigger. This is the bullwhip phenomenon as discussed in Chapter One, which disrupts production planning.

As supply chain evolves, collaborative planning, forecasting, and replenishment (CPFR) emerges as new supply chain strategy and technology. To react to the variation in demand and supply, companies start to link their demand and supply functions using CPFR. For example, in recent years, retailers have established collaborative agreements with their supply chain partners and have an on going planning, forecasting, and replenishment process in place with their suppliers. To facilitate the coordination that is needed in supply chains, the Voluntary Interindustry Commerce Standards (VICS) has set up a committee to establish certain procedures for CPFR issues. This committee documents best practices for CPFR and creates guidelines for implementing CPFR.

Innovative consumer goods manufacturers and retailers are forging partnership to advance the implementation of CPFR. Compaq is working with 850 of its trading partners to conduct purchasing planning over the Internet. Thomson Electronics is doing CPFR with 50 of its retailers. More trading partners have launched pilots. Canadian Tire is treading new ground with seven of its suppliers, and New Balance and Timberland are setting the pace in the shoe industry with selected retailers. Lane and Broyhill work with a Midwest furniture company, Wickes. Schering Plough and Johnson & Johnson are taking the lead with Eckerd Drug. Mitsubishi Motors is collaborating with its dealers to reduce customer lead time to two weeks[2]. Each player in the supply chain needs to perform its portion of the collaborative forecasting and planning as accurately as possible. The result is a smoother flow of small orders that distributors and manufacturers are able to handle more efficiently.

Collaboration in planning production, forecasting demand, and replenishing inventory brings a number of benefits. It helps smooth production flow, balance capacity, reduce inventory, reduce safety stock,

---

[2] Dion, Calvin, (2000). The growing pace of CPFR, Jan/Feb 2000. www.consumergoods.com.

and reduce stock outs. Furthermore, CPFR reduces the bullwhip effect because all the companies in the supply chain have access to sales data and share sales forecasts. This allows every player in the same supply chain to develop a better production plan, keep ideal inventory levels, and make realistic delivery schedules. Companies that are able to put CPFR into action have already gained significant competitive edges over their competitors. Wal-Mart, Dell Inc., and Proctor & Gamble, to name a few, share point of sales and inventory data with all the other companies in their respective supply chains and have yielded better efficiencies and profits for themselves and the supply chain as a whole.

Nevertheless, collaboration is not easy to implement and it will take time to become more common in business. Integrating disconnected forecasting and planning in the entire supply chain is challenging. A key issue in improving collaborative efforts is to have supply chain partners get their organization in order and have accurate data.

6.3.2 Pull and push boundary in production planning

Where to draw a line to determine a supply chain's push-pull boundary depends on the manufacturing production environment. The customer order decoupling point may move from finished goods inventory back to the raw material suppliers. Those who serve their customers from finished goods inventory have a make-to-stock production environment. Those who assemble products from available product choices have an assembly-to-order manufacturing environment. Those who produce tailored goods such as machine tools employ build-to-order or engineer-to-order production systems. Production details vary significantly among make-to-stock, assemble-to-stock, and build-to-order production environments. Table 6.1 illustrates some of the features that relate to pull-push boundary in production planning as well as the level of flexibility that the supply chain intends to achieve.

Table 6.1 indicates that make-to-stock production environment focuses on the maintenance of finished goods inventories. The push-pull boundary is located at the finished goods inventory. For the make-to-stock production environment, there are very few customer orders since demand is forecasted and a push system is applied. Flexibility is low.

Table 6.1. Push-pull boundary and manufacturing environment

	Engineer-to-order	Make-to-order	Assembly-to-order	Make-to-stock
Volume	One-of-kind	Small	Medium	Large
Push/Pull boundary	Design & raw materials	Raw material & common components	Components & subassembly units	Finished products
Production planning	Engineering capacity	Determine capacity flexibility & cushion	Determine production & delivery cycle time and dates	Forecast finished goods inventory level
Master Production Schedule	Final production	Final production	Mix forecasts & actual demands	Forecasted demands
Capacity flexibility	High	High	Moderate	Low
Key performance metrics	Delivery due date & capacity flexibility level	Delivery due date & capacity flexibility level	Delivery due date	Customer service level

The assembly-to-order manufacturing environment handles numerous end-item configurations and is an option for mass-customization. A combination of push-pull system is implemented. The push-pull boundary locates at the beginning of assembly. The demand management is to define the customer orders in terms of alternatives and options. In the assembly-to-order production environment, customer orders have booked for several periods into the future. Capacity flexibility is reserved to accommodate the promises of the delivery date. Master Production Schedule is typically set up in the form of Final Assembly Schedule (FAS).

Make-to-order, on the other hand, produces customized products in low volume after the manufacturer receives the orders. In a make-to-order production environment, the challenge is to manage a large backlog of customer orders. A large capacity cushion is needed to satisfy customer needs since what the customer will order is uncertain. The push-pull boundary locates at components and subassembly units. In the make-to-order production environment, the production plan is based on orders received. Instead of fulfilling the orders from inventory, companies with a make-to-order strategy use backlogs to fulfill customer orders. Backlog is the customer orders received but not yet shipped.

Engineer-to-order produces products with unique parts and drawings required by customers. Engineering resource is important in this production environment. Communication between the manufacturing firm and the customer is crucial to make sure customers' special needs are satisfied and delivery due dates are met. The push-pull boundary locates at the design stage of the product.

6.3.3 Manufacturing flexibility

Supply chain flexibility means to have a system that adapts to environment changes quickly, modifies the process and product configuration with a little cost and time. Flexibility can be expressed in five areas[3]:

- Volume flexibility. Volume flexibility is the ability to operate economically at different production volume.
- Mix flexibility. Mix flexibility is the ability to change the variety of products being made in a period.

---

[3] Giovani J.C. da Silveria (2005). "Effects of simplicity and discipline on operational flexibility: An empirical reexamination of rigid flexibility model." *Journal of Operations Management.*

- Product flexibility. Product flexibility is the ability to design new products or modify existing ones.
- Process flexibility. Process flexibility is the ability to produce a certain product using alternative routes.
- Delivery flexibility. Delivery flexibility is to deliver orders at the time customer wants and to the place customer wants.

Flexibility is needed to respond to market and customer requirements with less time and cost, especially when the manufacturing system needs to respond to a wide range of product variability. The challenge is to plan for the right degree of manufacturing flexibility because increased manufacturing flexibility means increased cost and investment in excess production capacity. Lot size and cycle time, which vary by products, markets, or product life cycle phase, should be well analyzed to determine the flexibility level. A trade-off between stocking inventory and keeping capacity cushion is a strategic issue that reflects a supply chain's overall objective. Since flexibility requires investment, it should match the design nature of both the product and manufacturing system.

Two manufacturing initiatives that are popularized in recent years are lean manufacturing and agile manufacturing. Both approaches aim at satisfying customer needs at a competitive cost structure and increased system flexibility.

The lean system that initiated in a Toyota production system had as its goal to eliminate waste from the production system through cycle time reduction and pull system implementation. When cycle time is reduced the system is more flexible to respond to customer needs. Lean manufacturing system is most suitable for a line processing production environment and efficient supply chain, where components are fairly standardized and the product variety is low.

The agile manufacturing system is created in response to mass customization. One of the best examples is Dell Computer's assembly system, which can quickly respond to varied demand in product complexity, volume, variety, and delivery schedule. An agile approach is preferred when there is a large amount of product variety, demand is highly unpredictable, new products introduction is fast, and product life cycle is short. The agile method suits a responsive supply chain.

In order to make the system more flexible in the process of demand transformation, supply chain collaboration in capacity planning is desirable. For example, Sport Obmeyer continuously refines its forecast procedure to better predict customer needs. In addition to forecasting finished goods demand, it forecasts the need for production capacity, so that it can reserve its supplier's capacity for making products in a later date. Reserving capacity cushion gives Sport Obmeyer flexibility to meet customer needs in terms of size, color, and style, and avoid mismatches in supply and demand.

6.3.4 Synchronization – HP example

When it is implemented right, CPFR is an effective tool that can generate significant value. When Hewlett-Packard's Imaging and Printing business division realized that it regularly produced too many wrong products and not enough of the right ones, it decided to synchronize its supply chain through working back from customers.

In 1999, HP Imaging and Printing business division employed a top-down forecast method for long-range production planning, and a bottom-up CPFR process for detailed information about a retailer's sales plan, promotion, and operational policies needed for production[4]. After receiving a 12-week order forecast every week from account teams, HP Imaging and Printing business division sets up a spreadsheet database to keep track of changes in orders. Then changes in demand are aggregated and analyzed. Short-term forecast rolls up weekly based on the account level demand information. The primary output of the collaborative demand analyst is a short-term SKU-level order, which is an important input for master production schedule.

The next step is to match supply with demand through integrating the results from the previous week. With weekly updated demand forecast, all previous weeks requests will be satisfied first before the new demand will be allocated. Retailers will be informed what they are going to

---

[4] Scott Culbertson, Ike Harris, and Steve Radosevich (2005). Synchronization – HP style. *Supply Chain Management Review*, 9(2), 24-31.

receive in the next 12 weeks in response to their weekly forecast. Three fundamental changes have been made through CPFR.

(1) The factory moved to weekly production measures and weekly execution of the delivery plan instead of monthly. With a weekly plan, the channel members have more up-to-date information about the synchronized demand plan and CPFR process.

(2) HP factory has trimmed the number of weeks frozen in the master production plan from five to two weeks, in order to make the system more flexible. At the same time, a biweekly cycle for deciding product mix and volumes within specified guideline is implemented.

(3) The upstream supplier's responsiveness has increased. Their Asian suppliers have reserved more capacity cushion for the HP factory. This leads to less inventory in HP's factory as compared to the inventory level they had before synchronization was implemented.

At the same time, the HP Imaging and Printing business division launched a team to create an available-to-sell capability. The idea is to go beyond on-hand uncommitted inventory. This gives account teams the information they need to steer demand and promotions into the SKU level, so as to avoid busy season when SKU is in tight supply.

With solid production plans, the synchronization initiative has achieved a number of encouraging results as listed below:

- As compared to the baseline year 1999, inventory investment across the supply chain is reduced by 20 percent.
- At the outset, the division could only meet 70% of a four-week forecast, but the number has climbed to 97% and stayed there.
- SKU level forecast and data quality have improved as well.

6.4 Demand Transformation

6.4.1 Enhancing value through demand transformation in supply chain

A supply chain is a sequence of activities that add value at each stage of production. For example, a supply chain of bread starts with forecasting customer demand, wheat production, flour production, scheduling production, inventory management, transportation, distribution, and extends all the way to the final customers. In this process, production adds a considerable amount of value as the product moves through the supply chain.

Value-add in demand transformation is enhanced by the appropriate choice of manufacturing system. The right manufacturing system increases flexibility and agility, reduces bullwhip effects, and bottlenecks, and improves the order fulfillment rate. Manufacturing systems, such as make-to-order and make-to-stock, have their own capability constraints, which are critical in achieving the order fulfill objective. Capacity constraints expressed in bottleneck may happen in equipment or labor. Therefore, constraints need to be identified and communicated well in advance with supply chain partners to ensure a smooth demand transformation process.

Well connected value-add points in the supply chain are important to smooth production flow and order. That is to say, there are many value-add points in a supply chain. Given each company as a member of the chain contributes its own value add point, a seamlessly connected chain is desirable for optimum demand transformation flow. This can be done through identifying push-pull boundary that a company desires to set. Where should a company start the value-add point? Should the value-add point be at the parts production stage, or the sub-assembly stage, or the final assembly stage? This question can be answered according to the role the company plays in the supply chain, the nature of the product, and the manufacturing system. When the pull-push decoupling points of various partners of a supply chain are determined, production flows better in the supply chain and customers orders are transformed properly.

6.4.2 Demand transformation performance metrics

Traditionally, the metrics for production management focuses on efficiency and cost reduction. This performance criterion leads to large volume production of standardized products.

In recent years, mass customization has become a common practice. Demand transformation process focuses on better manufacturing flow management, consistent availability of products that meet customer needs, and a higher sales and profit margin. The following is a set of measures that can be applied to evaluate demand transformation performance:

- Reduction of production cost. Production cost can be reduced as a result of reduced labor and material costs, better capacity management through better forecasting customer needs and scheduling customer orders.
- Reduction of non-manufacturing expense. Non-manufacturing expense can be reduced through appropriate manufacturing system choice and the number of expedited shipments and rush orders.
- Reduction of inventory investment. Better flow management reduces inventory investment, improves inventory turns, accommodates demand with the right product, and reduces inventory obsolescence. As a result, asset utilization improves.
- Improved customer service level. Good customer service level can be achieved through better order fill rate, on-time shipments, and shortened cycle time.

6.5 Summary

Demand transform is to realize what customers need through converting raw materials to finished goods. The process of demand transformation is a value-add process and is a critical component of supply chain management. This chapter examines how companies select a manufacturing system that best fits the product nature and the demand pattern. In this chapter, we have discussed aggregate planning, master production scheduling, push-pull boundary determination, and application of flexible and agile manufacturing. Pertinent performance metrics are suggested as well. Collaborative planning and forecasting should be considered in conjunction with collaborative replenishment of inventory in supply chain, which will be discussed in chapter 7.

Questions for Pondering

1. In recent years, some leading companies, such as HP, focus more on master production schedule than on aggregate planning. What makes available-to-promise, available-to-sell, and capability-to-promise gain more attention than aggregate planning in supply chain management?

2. The linear decision model for aggregate production planning developed by Holt, Modigliani, Muth, and Simon in the 1950s has been considered a classical piece of aggregate planning. Later many modified versions of aggregate planning have been developed to guide production planning. Is aggregate planning no longer useful in supply chain management? Support your argument with reasons and examples.

3. How to apply various aggregate planning strategies to various manufacturing environment with different level of demand uncertainty?

Problems

1. (MPS) The Best Pump, Inc. forecasted requirements for a medium size pump for the next six weeks: 25, 55, 20, 30, 60, and 45. The marketing department has received four orders for week1, 2, 3 and 4 in the quantity of 30, 40, 20, and 35. Currently there are 35 units in inventory. MPS quantity is 55 units and lead time is 1 week.
   a. Develop the MPS record for the pump.
   b. A utility company placed an order of 26 units. What is the appropriate shipping date for the order?

2. The following table gives the information of desk clock for the MPS.
   a. Complete the MPS for desk clock.
   b. Five new customer orders arrive in sequence. Assume the sequence of order cannot be changed and orders have to be delivered on the required date. Which orders can be fulfilled?

Item: desk clock			MPS quantity: 50				
Beginning inventory on hand: 35			Lead time: 1 weeks				
	Week						
	1	2	3	4	5	6	7	8
Forecast	57	28	38	47	32	33	22	28
Customer orders booked	32	33	25	27	18	10	8	8
Projected on-hand inventory								
MPS quantity	50							
MPS start								
Available to promise								

New Orders	Quantity	Desired Delivery Date
1	48	4
2	43	5
3	30	1
4	20	7
5	20	6

References

APICS dictionary 9th edition (1998). *APICS – The Education Society for Resource Management*. Fall Church, VA.

Arnold, J.R.T. (1998). *Introduction to Materials Management*, 3rd edition. New Jersey: Prentice Hall.

Dion, Calvin (2000). The Growing Pace of CPFR, Jan/Feb 2000. www.consumergoods.com.

Hugos, Mecheal (2003). *Essentials of Supply Chain Management*. New York: John Wiley & Son, Inc.

Ritzman, L.P. and Krajewski, L.J. (2003). *Foundations of Operations Management*. New Jersey: Prentice Hall.

Vollmann, T.E., Bill Berry, D. Clay Whybark, and F. Robert Jacobs (2005). *Manufacturing Planning and Control for Supply Chain Management*, 5th edition. New York: McGraw-Hill.

Chapter 7

Managing Inventories in Supply Chain

7.1 Brief History of Inventory Management

To a country, inventory is the artery and represents the material wealth of a nation. To a company and its supply chain, inventory is assets. As such, inventory management is crucially important. For example, when Hurricane Katrina hit New Orleans in the summer of 2005, The Food Bank supplied 2.4 million pounds of food from its inventory to people who lived in emergency shelters and helped disaster communities survive the difficult time[1].

Inventory is everywhere. When we buy a gallon of milk for a week's supply, we create inventory at home. Our intuition tells us inventory makes our life convenient. Inventory is more important to a manufacturing company that produces commodities. For example, a bakery will stock flour and sugar for further production.

Since the industrial revolution, manufacturers have favored large-scale production, which creates quantities greater than consumption and generates inventory. As such, many inventory management models have been developed. Table 1 provides a brief summary of the few seminal models that influence both inventory theories and practices.

Written records of inventory management can be traced back to the creation of Economic Order Quantity model (EOQ), a formula that primarily controls an independent demand inventory system. The origin of the EOQ model was recorded in a 1913 article by Ford Whitman

---

[1] David B. Caruso, "Some food banks say Katrina Drained aid." Associated Press, November 23, 2005.

Harris in *Factory: the Magazine of Management* and in a *Harvard Business Review* article by R.H. Wilson in 1934[2].

The EOQ model illustrates the concept of total cost of holding inventory. The decision rules of EOQ model dictates the best order quantity that minimizes the total cost associated with the quantity. Balancing the annual order costs against the annual carrying costs is the basis for arriving at the economic order quantity.

Table 7.1. History of materials management

Topic	Contributor	Date
EOQ	Ford Whitman Harris	1913
	R.H. Wilson	1934
MRP	IBM developed BOM software	Late 1960s
	George Plossl & John Orlicky	
JIT	Toyota production system	Early 1970s
MRPII	Evolved from MRP	1980s
CPFR	The Voluntary Interindustry Commerce Standards	1990s

Nevertheless the EOQ model does not provide lead-time visibility, a critical factor, to dependent demand inventory management. When a product has many layers, the lead-time associated with each level should be integrated into the model. IBM was the first to introduce Bill of Material (BOM) software that tackled dependent demand inventory management issues in the 1960s. In the late 1960s, Material Requirement Planning (MRP) was introduced by George Plossl and John Orlicky. The significance of MRP is to identify what product the customer requires. It compares the required quantity to the on-hand inventory level and determines the quantity and timing of the required items that need to be produced. Later, MRP evolved to Manufacturing Resource Planning (MRPII) to include financial and other resources needed for production.

---

[2] Bill Roach, (2005). "Origin of the economic order quantity formula; transcription or transformation?" *Management Decision*, 43 (9), 1262-1268.

Meanwhile, the Just-In-Time (JIT) production method was popularized in 1970s, which has an emphasis on lean production and supplier relationships. The philosophy of JIT is to eliminate waste by cutting excess inventory and to remove non-value added activities. JIT was first adopted by Toyota manufacturing plants under the direction of Taiichi Ohno. The main concern at that time was to meet consumer demands. After the successful introduction of JIT system by Toyota, many companies followed up and around the mid 1970s' and early 80s, it was used broadly by companies worldwide.

The idea of collaborative planning, forecasting, and replenishment (CPFR) advances the concept of inventory control in supply chain management. The enabler of CPFR is information technology. For example, Wal-Mart has engaged in CPFR with about 600 trading partners[3]. Its collaboration is evident in so many parts of the business, such as vendor-managed inventory, sharing information with vendors without charge, and the cross-docking inventory distribution method. Wal-Mart's inventory management is revolutionary and is a model of best practices. Consequently, inventory is of strategic importance to supply chain management.

7.2 Inventory Concepts

7.2.1 Definition of inventory

Inventory is the stock of any item or resource used in an organization. *An inventory system* is a set of policies and procedures that determines what inventory levels should be maintained, when stock should be replenished and how large orders should be.

Manufacturing inventory types include:
- Raw Materials
- Work-in-Process inventory (include component parts)
- Finished products inventory

---

[3] Dave Cutler, "CPFR: Time for the breakthrough." *Supply Chain Management Review*, May/June 2003, 54-60.

Inventory holds at distribution centers and retailer's warehouses is usually finished goods inventory.

7.2.2 Purpose of holding inventory

Inventory is created when supply exceeds the demand. The purpose of holding inventory is to achieve economies of scale, protect suppliers from stockout due to uneven and uncertain demand, and shelter demand variation during lead-time. The following discusses cycle inventory, safety stock, seasonal inventory, and in-transit inventory.

Cycle Inventory. Cycle Inventory is the inventory that accrues in the supply chain as the result of purchasing or producing larger lots than currently demanded by customers. Cycle inventory exists because each stage of the supply chain attempts to exploit economies of scale and thus reduce total costs.

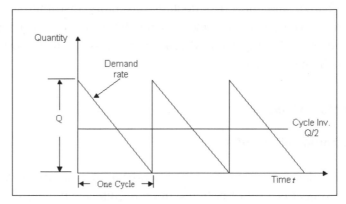

Figure 7.1. Cycle inventory

Figure 7.1 illustrates the cycle inventory level. This is a two-dimensional inventory problem. The horizontal direction shows time. From the beginning of a cycle to the end of the cycle indicates time between orders. The vertical direction shows quantity of inventory on hand. We assume that there is no safety stock. When inventory reaches zero, an order is placed and received simultaneously. Two questions regarding the two dimensional problem are: "When to place order?" and

"How much to order?" Two costs associated with the two questions are ordering cost and inventory holding cost. The total cost is the sum of ordering cost and inventory holding cost.

Safety Inventory. Safety inventory is created to protect against fluctuations and uncertainty in demand, supply, and lead-time. There are two major sources of uncertainty: quantity and timing.

The quantity of demand from the customer side fluctuates from period to period. Sometime, demand exceeds the forecasted sales, other times demand is lower than the expected sales. Thus, safety stock is required.

From the supplier side, replenishments from suppliers may have quality problems that result in fewer usable units than originally ordered. Additionally, suppliers may not be able to deliver orders on time. Safety stock is used to hedge quality and late delivery problems.

Seasonal Inventory. When demand is seasonal, seasonal inventory is created to absorb uneven rates of demand.

In-transit Inventory. In-transit inventory is a function of demand during lead-time. In-transit inventory provides a safeguard during supply delivery time.

7.2.3 Inventory for independent and dependent demand

Independent demand comes from many sources external to the firm and is not a part of other products. In other words, it is unrelated to demand for other products.

Dependent demand, on the other hand, is derived demand based on production levels; the need for one item is directly related to the need for some other item. For example, a furniture producer forecasts demand for dining tables, which is an independent demand. However, the number of table legs the manufacturer needs to produce is derived from the number of tables it is going to produce. Therefore, table legs are dependent demand.

7.2.4 Inventory costs

Inventory is used to improve customer service level. However, money invested in inventory is an opportunity cost to the company and its supply chain. Therefore, the supply chain manager needs to balance the advantage and disadvantage of both low and high inventory. There are two major costs associated with inventory. One is holding cost and the other is ordering or set-up costs.

The primary reason for keeping inventory low is due to the cost of holding inventory. Money invested in inventory cannot be used for other investment. Inventory holding cost includes storage, facilities, handling, insurance, pilferage, breakage, obsolescence, depreciation, taxes, and the opportunity cost of capital.

The primary reason for keeping inventory high is due to the cost of replenishing inventory. Ordering cost or set-up cost are the two major costs. Ordering cost includes managerial and clerical costs associated with preparing the purchase. Setup cost consists of equipment setups, filling out required papers, and material handling activities.

To calculate the annual inventory cost, three pieces of data are required.

(i) Inventory holding cost, which is the percent of item cost. The annual cost of carrying inventory is a percentage of inventory value, including financing, devaluation, storage, theft, and scrap.

(ii) Ordering cost, which may include purchasing, administrative handling and transportation costs.

(iii) Customer service level is expressed in the amount of safety stock held. For example, the numbers of locations that are required to meet the most stringent customer service requirements. This data is available from marketing and sales department.

7.2.5 The cost of inaccurate inventory

Many companies try to manage their inventory more effectively because inventory is treated as an asset. It is not unusual to learn that a member of the customer service department is constantly going to the warehouse to check warehouse inventory against inventory listed by the computer system. Warehouse clerks spend hours searching for items that have been misplaced, damaged, and stolen. Purchasers constantly fill back orders for items that have been received but cannot be located. Inaccurate inventory can cost a company or a supply chain thousands or millions of dollars affecting profit margins, inventory turns, order fill rate, and customer service levels. Additionally, inaccurate inventory disrupts purchasing and warehouse operations.

Let's consider a hypothetical situation. Assume your company earns a 5% net profit before taxes. You lost $150 every month due to inaccurate inventory. How much will this cost the company annually? How much in new sales revenue should your company generate to make up for the loss of $150 a month?

New sales in dollars * % of net profit before taxes = loss   (1)
New sales in dollars * 5% = $150
$3000 * 5% = $150

If we divided $150 by 5% we get $3,000. That means your company has to generate $3,000 new sales per month to make up for the loss of $150 due to inaccurate inventory. Now pick a number in column one of Table 7.2 and see how much it costs your company if your inventory is not accurate.

Table 7.2. Effect of inaccurate inventory

Value of loss due to inaccurate inventory per month	Net Profit Before Tax			
	1%	2%	5%	10%
	New sales needed to makeup the loss per month			
$10	$1,000	$500	$200	$100
$100	$10,000	$5,000	$2,000	$1,000
$1,000	$100,000	$50,000	$20,000	$10,000
$10,000	$1,000,000	$500,000	$200,000	$100,000

7.2.6 Inventory measures

Inventory measures evaluate how effective a supply chain uses its resource to satisfy customer demand. Inventory measures starts with physical counting of units, weight, or volume. Three measures of inventory are commonly used, the average aggregate inventory value, inventory turnovers, and weeks of supply.

Average aggregate inventory. Average aggregate inventory includes raw materials, work-in-process inventory, and finished goods inventory a company holds for the year. It is usually expressed in dollar value.

Inventory turnover. Inventory turnover measures the speed inventory can be sold in a year. A higher turnover rate usually generates high profits and is more desirable. The formula used to compute inventory turnover (IT) is as follows:

IT = annual cost of sales / average aggregate inventory value   (2)

Weeks of Supply. Weeks of Supply means the number of weeks' supply a company holds as on-hand inventory that can be used to fulfill orders. From the inventory cost perspective, the fewer the weeks of supply, the less the inventory cost. Weeks of inventory supply (WS) is determined as follows.

WS = average aggregate inventory value / weekly sales at cost   (3)

Example Problem 7.1: Inventory Measures

A recent accounting statement of EXUL, Inc. showed average aggregate inventory value that includes raw material, work-in-process inventory and finished goods to be $10,000,000. This year's cost of goods sold is $20 million. The company operates 50 weeks a year. How many weeks of supply are being held? What is the number of inventory turnovers?

Solution to example Problem 7.1

Weeks of supply (WS) is computed as follows:
WS = average aggregate inventory value / weekly sales at cost
    = $10,000,000 / ($20,000,000 / 50) = 25 weeks

Inventory turns (IT) = annual cost of sales/average aggregate inv. value
= \$20,000,000 / \$10,000,000 = 2 turns

7.3 Managing Inventory Cost – EOQ-Based Inventory Models

7.3.1 Economic order quantity

Economic Order Quantity (EOQ) is to minimize total annual ordering cost and inventory holding cost through ordering an optimal lot size and achieve economies of scale. A few assumptions needed to implement EOQ model are:
1. Demand is fixed, known, and constant
2. Holding and ordering costs are the only relevant inventory costs
3. Holding and ordering costs are fixed, known, and constant
4. Inventory lots are received all at once
5. There are no price discounts and joint order of multiple items

As stated above, the only costs relevant to this model are holding and ordering costs. Based on this information, a total cost equation for a given order quantity is given as follows.

$$\text{Total Cost} = \left(\frac{D}{Q}\right)S + \left(\frac{Q}{2}\right)H \tag{4}$$

Where:
Q = Order Quantity
h = holding cost percentage
C = cost per unit purchased
H = hC, annual holding cost per unit
S = Cost to place an order or set up cost in manufacturing / per order
D = Annual demand

Ordering costs or set up costs are fixed costs that are incurred each time an order is placed. These costs do not vary with order quantity. Ordering costs include the managerial and clerical costs associated with ordering, as well as shipping and receiving costs. Total annual ordering costs decrease with increased order quantity.

Generally speaking, inventory holding costs are a function of capital cost, insurance, taxes, damage, and obsolescence, etc. Total holding cost increases as lot size and average cycle inventory increases.

The EOQ is found by determining the minimum cost point. The minimum cost point can be found by taking the first derivative of the total cost curve with respect to quantity. Alternatively, making holding cost equals ordering cost will help to solve for the optimal quantity.

$$\frac{Q}{2}H = \frac{D}{Q}S$$

Economic order quantity (EOQ) = $\sqrt{\dfrac{2\,DS}{H}}$ \hfill (5)

Using the above equation, it is important to make sure that the time units for demand and holding cost are the same. For example, if demand is expressed as annual demand, then holding cost per unit will be annual cost. The EOQ model indicates that the manager must make a fundamental trade-off between holding costs and ordering costs when selecting an order quantity. For example, when Toyota implemented the JIT system, it significantly reduced setup time leading to a reduction in setup cost. Small setup cost makes JIT small lot size possible. Small lot sizes reduce inventory-holding costs.

The Optimal Time between Orders. The optimal time between orders (TBO) or optimal order frequency is given in year according to the following equation.

Time Between Orders (TBO) $= \dfrac{EOQ}{D}$ \hfill (6)

TBO can be expressed in weeks or months, as you prefer. For example, if you want TBO in weeks, multiply TBO by the number of working weeks in a year. Example problem 7.2 gives detailed instruction.

Example Problem 7.2: EOQ and TBO

Quik Motors uses 50,000 gear assemblies each year and purchases them at $2.40 per unit. It costs $50 to process and receive each order and it costs $.90 to hold one unit in inventory for a whole year. What is the

Economic Order Quantity? How frequently will orders be placed if the EOQ is used?

Solution to example Problem 7.2

$$EOQ = Q^* = \sqrt{\frac{2(50,000)(50)}{.90}} = 2,357$$

When EOQ is used, time between orders can be expressed in various time frames as shown below.

$$TBO_{eoq} = \frac{EOQ}{D} * (1 \text{ year}) = \frac{2,357}{50,000} \ (1) = 0.047 \text{ year}$$

$$TBO_{eoq} = \frac{EOQ}{D} * (12 \text{ month a year}) = \frac{2,357}{50,000} \ (12) = 0.57 \text{ month}$$

$$TBO_{eoq} = \frac{EOQ}{D} * (52 \text{ weeks a year}) = \frac{2,357}{50,000} \ (52) = 2.45 \text{ weeks}$$

7.3.2 Inventory replenishment – Reorder point system

Reorder point system, which is also known as Continuous Review System, is an inventory policy that tracks inventory position. Whenever inventory level reaches the reorder point, an order is placed to replenish inventory. The reorder point has two components: (i) average demand during lead-time and (ii) safety stock. Reorder point is calculated as follows.

$$R = d'L + z\sigma\sqrt{L} \tag{7}$$

Where:

R = reorder point   d' = average demand
L = replenish lead time   z = z-score
σ = standard deviation of demand per period

Example Problem 7.3: Reorder Point System

The distributor of the TV sets is trying to set inventory policies at the warehouse for one of the TV models. Suppose lead-time is 2 weeks. The distributor would like to ensure that the service level is 97%. The average weekly demand is 200 units and standard deviation of weekly demand is 50 units. It costs $60 to process and receive each order and it costs $1.20 to hold one unit in inventory for a whole year.

    a. What is the safety stock?

    b. What is the reorder point?

    c. What is the order quantity?

    d. How many weeks of demand (average weekly demand) can on-hand inventory at the reorder point supply?

Solution to example Problem 7.3

    a. For a service level of 97%, the Z score is 1.88 from the Normal Table (Table A).

$$\text{Safety stock} = z\sigma \sqrt{L} = 1.88 * 50 * \sqrt{2} = 133 \text{ units}$$

    b. Reorder point $= d' L + z\sigma \sqrt{L} = 200(2) + 1.88\,(50)\,\sqrt{2} = 533$ units

    c. Order quantity: $EOQ = \sqrt{\dfrac{2(50{,}000)(60)}{1.20}} = 1019.8 = 1020$ units

    d. Weeks of demand can be supplied at the reorder point:

    533 / 200 = 2.67 weeks

Note:

- A stockout can only occur during lead-time. A stockout occurs when demand during lead-time exceeds the Reorder Point, which is the quantity available from stock during lead-time.
- During a stock shortage, demand is either backordered or lost.

7.3.3 Inventory replenishment – Periodic review system

Periodic review system is to review inventory position in a fixed time interval. This inventory system simplifies delivery schedule because it follows a routine replenishing cycle. A periodic review system also has two components: (i) average demand during lead time plus fixed time interval and (ii) safety stock. The formula is as follows.

Target Order Level (TOL) =

average demand during LT and order interval + safety stock

$$TOL = d' (L + OI) + z\sigma \sqrt{L + OI} \qquad (8)$$

Where:

d' = average demand

L = lead time

OI = order interval or time between orders

σ = standard deviation of demand per period

z = z score

Example Problem 7.4: Periodic Review Policy

Weekly demand for GameKid at a Game-Rus store is normally distributed with an average weekly demand of 1500 units and a weekly standard deviation of 200. The replenishment lead-time is two weeks. The store manager wants to have 95% cycle service level and has decided to review inventory every four weeks.

a. Using periodic review policy to evaluate safety inventory and target order-level.

b. Currently there are 1275 units on hand. How much should the store manager order now?

Solution to example Problem 7.4

a. Find the z score for the probability of 95% from the Normal Table (Table A). 95% cycle service level has a z score of 1.645.

Safety inventory: $z\sigma \sqrt{L + OI}$ = 1.645 (200) $\sqrt{2 + 4}$ = 806

TOL = d' (L + OI) + $z\sigma \sqrt{L+OI}$ = 1500 (2+4) + 806 = 9,806

b. Number of units should be ordered: 9,806 - 1,275 = 8,531

7.4 Improving Customer Service Level – Managing Safety Stock

7.4.1 Safety stock

In general, there are two reasons to keep safety stock. The first reason for keeping safety stock is to protect against demand variation. The second reason for keeping safety stock is to protect against time and quantity variation from the supply side. Suppliers may deliver the orders later than the promised due date or there are defects in the delivered items. In these cases, the usable quantity is reduced and safety stock can be used to protect shortage. The amount of safety stock is the difference between the average demand during lead-time and inventory on-hand.

Safety stock is related to forecasting error in demand. In Chapter 5, we discussed deviations between forecasted demand and actual demand. This kind of deviation is inevitable and can be offset by safety stock.

7.4.2 Cycle service level

Cycle service level, a term that is widely used in supply chain management, is the probability that all demand will be satisfied from available stock during any given replenishment cycle. Stock out is a situation that exists when demand exceeds the quantity on hand during lead-time. Cycle service level can be ensured using safety stock. Cycle service level and safety stock are expressed as follows.

$$\text{Cycle Service Level (CSL)} = 1.0 - p \text{ (stock out)} \tag{9}$$

$$\text{Safety stock} = z * s * \sqrt{\frac{L}{FP}} \tag{10}$$

Where:
    z: z-score   s: standard deviation of demand
    L: lead time   FP: forecast periods

Example Problem 7.7: Safety Stock

How much safety stock is needed if desired cycle service level is 98%, lead time is 3 weeks, the time period used for forecast is in week, and standard deviation of weekly demand is 35 units?

Solution to example Problem 7.7

Using the Normal Table (Table A), we find out that cycle service level of 98% has a z score of 2.05. Forecast period is in week.

$$\text{Safety stock} = z * s * \sqrt{\frac{L}{FP}} = 2.05 * 35 * \sqrt{3/1} = 124.3 \text{ units}$$

7.4.3 Fill rate

Fill rate is the probability that any given random selected demand will be instantaneously satisfied from available inventory. Fill rate is computed using the following formula.

$$\text{Fill Rate (FR)} = 1.0 - \frac{E(US)}{Q} \qquad (11)$$

Where:

  Q = order quantity or lot size

  $E\,(US)$ = expected units short per replenishment cycle

When demand is normally distributed, we can use the "The Table of Unit Normal Loss Integrals (Table B)." This table converts z score into standard deviation's worth of expected units short. The fill rate achieved by a given amount of safety stock can be found as:

$$FR = 1.0 - \frac{N[z]s}{Q} \qquad (12)$$

where

  $E\,(US) = N\,[z]\,s$

  $N\,[z]$ is z score conversed

  S = standard deviation of demand.

The value of $N\,[z]$ can be found in The Unusual Normal Table (Table B). The safety stock needed to achieve a given fill rate can be found by calculating the necessary $N\,[z]$ value:

$$N[z] = \frac{(1.0 - FR)Q}{s} \qquad (13)$$

In this case, the z factor is needed to achieve the desired fill rate.

188   *Supply Chain Management: Concepts, Techniques, and Practices*

Table A. Normal distribution table

z	0.00	0.01	0.02	0.03	0.04	0.05	0.06	0.07	0.08	0.09
0.0	0.5000	0.5040	0.5080	0.5120	0.5160	0.5199	0.5239	0.5279	0.5319	0.5359
0.1	0.5398	0.5438	0.5478	0.5517	0.5557	0.5596	0.5636	0.5675	0.5714	0.5753
0.2	0.5793	0.5832	0.5871	0.5910	0.5948	0.5987	0.6026	0.6064	0.6103	0.6141
0.3	0.6179	0.6217	0.6255	0.6293	0.6331	0.6368	0.6406	0.6443	0.6480	0.6517
0.4	0.6554	0.6591	0.6628	0.6664	0.6700	0.6736	0.6772	0.6808	0.6844	0.6879
0.5	0.6915	0.6950	0.6985	0.7019	0.7054	0.7088	0.7123	0.7157	0.7190	0.7224
0.6	0.7257	0.7291	0.7324	0.7357	0.7389	0.7422	0.7454	0.7486	0.7517	0.7549
0.7	0.7580	0.7611	0.7642	0.7673	0.7704	0.7734	0.7764	0.7794	0.7823	0.7852
0.8	0.7881	0.7910	0.7939	0.7967	0.7995	0.8023	0.8051	0.8078	0.8106	0.8133
0.9	0.8159	0.8186	0.8212	0.8238	0.8264	0.8289	0.8315	0.8340	0.8365	0.8389
1.0	0.8413	0.8438	0.8461	0.8485	0.8508	0.8531	0.8554	0.8577	0.8599	0.8621
1.1	0.8643	0.8665	0.8686	0.8708	0.8729	0.8749	0.8770	0.8790	0.8810	0.8830
1.2	0.8849	0.8869	0.8888	0.8907	0.8925	0.8944	0.8962	0.8980	0.8997	0.9015
1.3	0.9032	0.9049	0.9066	0.9082	0.9099	0.9115	0.9131	0.9147	0.9162	0.9177
1.4	0.9192	0.9207	0.9222	0.9236	0.9251	0.9265	0.9279	0.9292	0.9306	0.9319
1.5	0.9332	0.9345	0.9357	0.9370	0.9382	0.9394	0.9406	0.9418	0.9429	0.9441
1.6	0.9452	0.9463	0.9474	0.9484	0.9495	0.9505	0.9515	0.9525	0.9535	0.9545
1.7	0.9554	0.9564	0.9573	0.9582	0.9591	0.9599	0.9608	0.9616	0.9625	0.9633
1.8	0.9641	0.9649	0.9656	0.9664	0.9671	0.9678	0.9686	0.9693	0.9699	0.9706
1.9	0.9713	0.9719	0.9726	0.9732	0.9738	0.9744	0.9750	0.9756	0.9761	0.9767
2.0	0.9772	0.9778	0.9783	0.9788	0.9793	0.9798	0.9803	0.9808	0.9812	0.9817
2.1	0.9821	0.9826	0.9830	0.9834	0.9838	0.9842	0.9846	0.9850	0.9854	0.9857
2.2	0.9861	0.9864	0.9868	0.9871	0.9875	0.9878	0.9881	0.9884	0.9887	0.9890
2.3	0.9893	0.9896	0.9898	0.9901	0.9904	0.9906	0.9909	0.9911	0.9913	0.9916
2.4	0.9918	0.9920	0.9922	0.9925	0.9927	0.9929	0.9931	0.9932	0.9934	0.9936
2.5	0.9938	0.9940	0.9941	0.9943	0.9945	0.9946	0.9948	0.9949	0.9951	0.9952
2.6	0.9953	0.9955	0.9956	0.9957	0.9959	0.9960	0.9961	0.9962	0.9963	0.9964
2.7	0.9965	0.9966	0.9967	0.9968	0.9969	0.9970	0.9971	0.9972	0.9973	0.9974
2.8	0.9974	0.9975	0.9976	0.9977	0.9977	0.9978	0.9979	0.9979	0.9980	0.9981
2.9	0.9981	0.9982	0.9982	0.9983	0.9984	0.9984	0.9985	0.9985	0.9986	0.9986
3.0	0.9987	0.9987	0.9987	0.9988	0.9988	0.9989	0.9989	0.9989	0.9990	0.9990
3.1	0.9990	0.9991	0.9991	0.9991	0.9992	0.9992	0.9992	0.9992	0.9993	0.9993
3.2	0.9993	0.9993	0.9994	0.9994	0.9994	0.9994	0.9994	0.9995	0.9995	0.9995
3.3	0.9995	0.9995	0.9995	0.9996	0.9996	0.9996	0.9996	0.9996	0.9996	0.9997

Table B. An unusual normal distribution table

{z Factor / N[z] Conversion}

z	.00	.01	.02	.03	.04	.05	.06	.07	.08	.09
0.0	.3989	.3940	.3890	.3841	.3793	.3744	.3697	.3649	.3602	.3556
0.1	.3509	.3464	.3418	.3373	.3328	.3284	.3240	.3197	.3154	.3111
0.2	.3069	.3027	.2986	.2944	.2904	.2863	.2824	.2784	.2745	.2706
0.3	.2668	.2630	.2592	.2555	.2518	.2481	.2445	.2409	.2374	.2339
0.4	.2304	.2270	.2236	.2203	.2169	.2137	.2104	.2072	.2040	.2009
0.5	.1978	.1947	.1917	.1887	.1857	.1828	.1799	.1771	.1742	.1714
0.6	.1687	.1659	.1633	.1606	.1580	.1554	.1528	.1503	.1478	.1453
0.7	.1429	.1405	.1381	.1358	.1334	.1312	.1289	.1267	.1245	.1223
0.8	.1202	.1181	.1160	.1140	.1120	.1100	.1080	.1061	.1042	.1023
0.9	.1004	.09860	.09680	.09503	.09328	.09156	.08986	.08819	.08654	.08491
1.0	.08332	.08174	.08019	.07866	.07716	.07568	.07422	.07279	.07138	.06999
1.1	.06862	.06727	.06595	.06465	.06336	.06210	.06086	.05964	.05844	.05726
1.2	.05610	.05496	.05384	.05274	.05165	.05059	.04954	.04851	.04750	.04650
1.3	.04553	.04457	.04363	.04270	.04179	.04090	.04002	.03916	.03831	.03748
1.4	.03667	.03587	.03508	.03431	.03356	.03281	.03208	.03208	.03137	.02998
1.5	.02931	.02865	.02800	.02736	.02674	.02612	.02552	.02494	.02436	.02380
1.6	.02324	.02270	.02217	.02165	.02114	.02064	.02015	.01967	.01920	.01874
1.7	.01829	.01785	.01742	.01699	.01658	.01617	.01578	.01539	.01501	.01464
1.8	.01428	.01392	.01357	.01323	.01290	.01257	.01226	.01195	.01164	.01134
1.9	.01105	.01077	.01049	.01022	.009957	.009698	.009445	.009198	.008957	.008721
2.0	.008491	.008266	.008046	.007832	.007623	.007418	.007219	.007024	.006835	.006649
2.1	.006468	.006292	.006120	.005952	.005788	.005628	.005472	.005320	.005172	.005028
2.2	.004887	.004750	.004616	.004486	.004358	.004235	.004114	.003996	.003882	.003770
2.3	.003662	.003556	.003453	.003352	.003255	.003159	.003067	.002977	.002889	.002804
2.4	.002720	.002640	.002561	.000248	.002410	.002337	.002267	.002199	.002132	.002067
2.5	.002005	.001943	.001883	.001826	.001769	.001715	.001662	.001610	.001560	.001511
3.0	.000382	.000369	.000356	.000344	.000332	.0003199	.000309	.000298	.000287	.000277

Example Problem 7.8: Compare Cycle Service Level and Fill Rate

GameKid Co. uses the order quantity of 1,000 units. Standard deviation of weekly demand is 100 units. Replenish lead time is 1 week. Compare fill rate and cycle service level.

Solution to example Problem 7.8

We use Table A, the Normal Table, to determine the cycle service level and use Table B, An Unusual Normal Distribution Table, to determine the fill rate. For the same z factor, fill rate is much higher than the cycle service level. Let us look at Table 7.3. For example, when z score = 1, cycle service level is 84% and fill rate is about 99%; the actual expected units short is about 8.

Talking about 69% service level may make supply chain managers anxious because they envision 30% stock-out rates. Actually, 69% cycle service levels typically lead to a 98% fill rate. In general, an increase in safety stock will improve both the fill rate and the cycle service level.

Table 7.3.

	Cycle Service Level			Fill Rate	
z	Cycle Service Level	Probability of Stockout	N [z]	Expected Units Short; N [z]*std	Fill Rate
0.50	0.6915	0.3085	0.1978	19.78	0.98022
1.00	0.841	0.159	0.083320	8.33200	0.99167
1.50	0.933	0.067	0.029310	2.93100	0.99707
1.65	0.951	0.050	0.020640	2.06400	0.99794
1.96	0.975	0.025	0.009445	0.94450	0.99906
2.00	0.977	0.023	0.008491	0.84910	0.99915
2.33	0.990	0.010	0.003352	0.33520	0.99966
3.00	0.999	0.001	0.000382	0.03822	0.99996

7.5 New Initiatives of Inventory Management in e-Business Environment

Inventory is a core component of e-Business and has direct impact on business performance. Today, supply chain management is transforming inventory management both in theory and practice. Vendor managed inventory (VIM), Everyday Low Price (EDLP), pull system, to name a few are impacting the way inventory is managed.

7.5.1 Bullwhip effects and information sharing

The bullwhip effect is an ineffective situation that happens due to lack of information sharing and communication in the supply chain. The bullwhip effect uses excessive safety stock and triggers exponential movements down the supply chain. Suppliers hold extra inventory for the safety stock wholesalers hold. Wholesalers need extra inventory for the safety stock retailers hold. Incongruent information across the supply chain leads to overreact to backlog and building of excessive inventory in order to prevent stock-outs.

As we discussed in Chapter One, the bullwhip effect is essentially the artificial distortion of consumer demand figures as they are transmitted back to the suppliers from the retailer. Many leading companies have developed countermeasures to address the bullwhip effects. The following are a few countermeasures that can be considered to reduce the bullwhip effects:

- Countermeasure 1 – reduce demand uncertainty. Provide centralized demand information on actual customer demand and focus on SKU demand information.
- Countermeasure 2 – reduce demand variability. Possible approaches on managing customer demand variability include Everyday Low Price (EDLP), which can lead to a stable demand pattern. On the supplier side, vendor managed inventory (VIM) can reduce order variability to the upstream of the supply chain.
- Countermeasure 3 – shorten lead time. Shortening lead-time through communicating and sharing information with trading partners to reduced supply lead-time.

- Countermeasure 4 – improve information accuracy. Forge strategic partnership within the supply chain to share demand, inventory, and production information to reduce inventory. Provide trading partners with point-of-sale data. CPFR can be used as a vehicle to do so.
- Countermeasure 5 – reduce order size. Reduce order cost by implementing Electronic Data Interchange (EDI) and inventory control information system. Use 3rd party logistic service to counter full-truck load economies. Order small lot sizes frequently to reduce inventory.

A successfully integrated supply chain is important to decrease a company's overall inventory supply costs. Information is important in achieving equilibrium between responsiveness and efficiency in a supply chain. Bullwhip effects can be reduced if information is accurate, relevant and timely.

7.5.2 Push-pull strategy in inventory management

In the e-Business environment, production and inventory are driven by either a push or a pull system. To push inventory down the supply chain without knowing customer needs often creates a phenomena of sending the wrong products to a wrong location. Meanwhile, the market is starving of the right merchandise and the retailers lose money. If a product takes three weeks to replenish, the demand variability is much larger than the same product that takes three days to replenish. In other words, the retailer could carry much less inventory if lead time is three days instead of three weeks. As such, the pull inventory approach becomes very attractive to supply chain managers.

For a long time, John Deere used a "basic rule of thumb" to maintain 30 percent of annual sales in inventory for each dealer. But this rule of thumb didn't take into account seasonal variability and the specific requirements of individual dealers. To overcome this deficiency, the commercial and consumer equipment division of John Deere decided to move from push inventory management approach to a pull inventory management system. Since the project began in 2002, John Deere invested in $3-million supply-chain optimization software called

SmartOps. It moved from traditional push inventory management approach to a pull inventory management model. The return on investment has been dramatic. John Deere reduced the inventory-to-sales ratio by half and the value of inventory by $1 billion[4].

SmartOps loaded the data from three John Deere plants and 25 dealers into its Multistage Inventory Planning and Optimization (MIPO) module. Products include everything from ride-on lawn mowers to golf course maintenance equipment, aerators, and utility tractors. By designing a model that forecasts what products should be at which locations each week, the MIPO system makes the pull inventory system possible at Deere. Customer service levels have been improved while safety stock investment is reduced.

The key purpose of converting a push system to a pull system is to better manage the amount of inventory a supply chain carries to cover the variability in both supply and demand.

7.5.3 Vendor managed inventory

Vendor Managed Inventory (VMI) is a coordinated approach to manage inventory in supply chain. The manufacturer is responsible for the inventory level of the wholesaler or retailer. The manufacturer receives electronic data using EDI or via the Internet that tells him the distributor's sales and stock levels. At the same time, the manufacturer has access to the wholesaler's or retailer's inventory data, and can view every item that the distributor has in inventory. Under VMI, the manufacturer is responsible for creating and maintaining the inventory plan, not the distributor or retailer. The purpose of VMI is to optimize inventory management in supply chain.

Both manufacturing and service firms have applied VMI. Baxter, a hospital supply company, developed a new type of partnership with its hospital customers. A set of clear, predetermined criteria is used to

---

[4] Ephraim Schwartz, "John Deere's Supply-Chain Victory." *InfoWorld* 05/13/05, http://www.crmbuyer.com/story/43103.html.

select target accounts[5]. Large buyers are willing to enter into volume contracts, geographically clustered for economical service provision, and management stability to an information system known as ValueLink. The hospital specifies its stock requirements for each ward. An on-site Baxter employee counts the stock in each ward each day or every few days. The vendor's employee enters this information into a hand-held device and transmits it to Baxter's warehouse, where a replenishment order is derived at the warehouse. The order is picked into ward specific containers and is delivered the following day, or in a few days directly to the ward. Finally, Baxter sends the invoice to the hospital.

The vendor managed inventory system creates a powerful new channel that has changed the ground rules for all other hospital supply companies. The stockless system was very attractive to big accounts because hospitals literally outsource a non-core function. Nevertheless, the stockless system required significant delegation of account control to operations managers and multidisciplinary account teams.

7.5.4 Inventory reduction: Lean inventory system

Generally speaking, a lean inventory system has been applied in many different industries, such as automotive, computer, and distribution. For example, Dell Inc. has discovered the profitability of lean inventory systems by implementing a direct selling model with no pre-assembled finished goods inventory.

Before the introduction of the lean system, there were a lot of manufacturing defects at Toyota, such as large lot production, long setup time, excessive inventory, and late deliveries. Consequently, lean manufacturing management was developed as a mechanism to control these problems. Instead of producing large lots of one type of products, Toyota conducted research on setup time reduction and produced more diversified goods to gain efficiencies from frequent deliveries of small quantities to meet immediate demands. As a result of implementing the

---

[5] William C. Copacino and Jonathan L. S. Byrnes (2002). "How to become a supply chain master." *Supply Chain Yearbook*, 37-42.

lean system, cycle inventory has been reduced, so has inventory at all levels of the organization.

Electronic Data Interchange (EDI) is a useful tool for implementing lean operations within a company and across a supply chain. Through EDI, customers can pull off inventory by a remote center control point. It is the integration of computer systems and information sharing that makes the demand and inventory data flow within the supply network. Additionally, when implementing a lean inventory system, trading partners of a supply chain have to develop trust and good relationships with each other because lean practice requires a stable, fast and flexible supply of materials.

Differentiating various stock-keeping units (SKU) by demand pattern is one of lean inventory management strategies to control costs and inventory. Traditionally, supply chain treats every SKU the same way. Retailers place large orders of all SKUs and manufacturers produce large quantities of SKUs. Today, manufacturers produce more styles and sizes than ever before. Some are slow-selling items and some are fast movers. The risk faced by the supply chain is that it has to absorb a huge financial loss if slow selling items are out of favor. Recently, large retail chains such as Wal-Mart and Home Depot have initiated lean retailing strategy by requesting manufacturers to deliver small lots to retailing stores on an on-going basis[6]. Various SKU items should be treated with different sourcing methods. Large usage volume, low variance, and fast moving SKUs can be replenished on an on-going base and use offshore vendors to reduce costs. Long-term contracts can be negotiated with cost, delivery and service terms. On the other hand, small usage items with large variance, or slow moving SKUs should be taken care of by local vendors to reduce sourcing lead time. By fine-tuning inventory according to SKU-levels, supply chains can increase profits and reduce inventory risks.

---

[6] Frederick H. Abernathy, John T. Dunlop, Janice H. Hammond, and David Well (2000). "Control your inventory in a world of lean retailing." *Harvard Business Review*, 169-176.

7.5.5 Issues related to information technology

Most computer systems provide a lot of information. Management and employees depend on the analysis and reports generated by computer software to make critical business decisions without knowing what factors were used for calculation and how these numbers were generated.

Let us consider an example. A soft drink distributor noticed a drop in sales of a particular soft drink called Sweeter than Sugar, but the inventory software produced reports that suggest more inventory for the product. The usage history is illustrated in Table 7.4.

From Table 7.4 we can tell that the usage for the soft drink decreased since January 2006. Yet the inventory system generated a demand for September 2006 of 138 cases. Inventory analyst described that demand forecast was based on an average of what was sold in the past. As such the average demand of the product was calculated over the entire time it had been in inventory. The item had been stocked for 18 months at the distribution center. During that time the company had sold 2,215 cases of the product, or about 138 cases per month. Consequently, the predicted usage for September 2006 is 138 cases. The inventory manager explained that the inventory information system analyzed the need according to the way it was programmed.

Table 7.4.

Year 2005	Usage	Year 2006	Usage
May	214	January	98
June	256	February	88
July	276	March	76
August	252	April	82
September	178	May	78
October	162	June	80
November	118	July	75
December	106	August	76

Let us consider another example. A distributor experienced a decrease in demand for an item. However, the inventory information system was projecting a 7% increase in demand for the item. The increase trend was calculated by comparing the sales recorded during the past three months this year to the sales recorded in the same months last year. Recent sales data indicated that the product had a 5% decrease in the number of units sold in the past 5 months. Further investigation showed that the inventory information system was designed to calculate trend factors based on the cost of goods sold, not the number of units sold. This year there had been a 12% increase in cost of goods sold over the previous year. Therefore, the computer system automatically projected an increase in demand. As a result, the distribution center had faced an overstock of wrong product.

Supply chain professionals have to realize that information systems are only as good as they are designed and programmed. Human intelligence is critical to managing demand and inventory.

7.6 Enhancing Value through Inventory Management in Supply Chain

Peter Drucker describes the myth of inventory management by saying that we know little more about distribution today than Napoleon's contemporaries knew about the interior of Africa. This is why economic downturns affect inventory so much. During the contraction period of 1981-1982, GNP in the US fell by $105 billion while inventory investment was reduced by $95 billion[7] that means that the reduction in inventory accounts for almost 90 percent of the reduction in GNP. This phenomenon indicates the importance of inventory management to a nation's wealth.

The single most important control point of a supply chain is the markets or customers served. A supply chain can be synchronized by focusing on this control point and arranging all other resources around this point. Synchronizing the links of a supply chain through CPFR is a solution to treat the supply chain as one entity driven by the actual

---

[7] Heng, M.S.H., Wang Y.C.W. and He, X. (2005). Supply chain management and business cycles. *Supply Chain Management: An International Journal*, 10(3), 157-161.

market demand.   Orders are consolidated from all retailers and production is planned accordingly.   Safety stock is determined by the size of variation from customer demand, and production capacity; flexibility is reserved to protect large demand surges.

A supply chain's success is not only dependent on sales, it also depends on its ability to ensure the right item in stock at the right place and at the time a customer needs it.   Better inventory control puts the supply chain in a unique advantageous position in the marketplace as evidenced by the best practices of Wal-Mart.   After playing the Beer Game, we realize that the key to keeping costs down and improving customer service level is to have a joint business plan of the entire supply chain, develop a feasible sales forecast for all the participating firms, and develop an efficient production and delivery schedule.

7.7 Inventory Management Performance Metrics

Regarding inventory management performance metrics, most logistics managers rate accounts receivables, return-on-assets, and cash-to-cash cycle times as the most important inventory metrics[8].   This is a good summary of how industry evaluates inventory performance.   More detailed metrics can be as follows:
- Reduce inventory handling cost
- Implement new order fulfillment models
- Provide reliable delivery dates
- Eliminate unnecessary shipping and handling costs
- Improve order fill rate
- Improve customer service level
- Reduction in transit time
- Reduction in manufacture cost
- Increasing in management efficiency and effectiveness

The goal is to maintain good customer service level at a reasonable cost.

---

[8] Rene Jones, "Inventory control is perhaps the most powerful tool you have for containing your warehousing costs." November 26, 2005, www.trginternational.com.

7.8 Summary

In this chapter, we have discussed history of material management, managing cycle inventory, safety stock, and customer service. The EOQ model described in this chapter can be extended to analyze various inventory management issues. Reorder point system and periodic review system are based on EOQ model.

Many new initiatives emerge in recent years that reflect new inventory management initiatives. Vendor managed inventory, pull-push strategy, lean inventory system and the countermeasures to bullwhip effects all significantly contribute to a supply chain's overall business strategy. Inventory is the physical item that flows in the supply chain.

Questions for Pondering

1. CPFR has only seen modest growth to date despite being embraced by retail giants such as Wal-Mart and Target. Why do industries hesitant to embrace such a promising practice?
2. Under what conditions should a supplier offer quantity discounts? What are the appropriate pricing schedules that a supplier should offer?
3. Does inventory reduction really reduce inventory in the entire supply chain? Or do some giant trading partners push inventory back to their suppliers?

Problems

1. The annual demand for the screwdrivers at Tool Mart is 2250 units. Tool Mart incurs a fixed order placement, transportation, and receiving cost of $40 each time an order is placed. Each screwdriver costs Tool Mart $10, and the retailer has a holding cost of 20 percent of the cost of screwdriver.

    a. Evaluate the number of screwdrivers that the store manager should order in each replenishment lot.

    b. If the store manager would like to reduce the optimal lot size to 200, how much the order cost per lot should be reduced?

2. Best Pharmacy Store uses the reorder point system to replenish inventory. It operates 52 weeks a year. One of the drugs it sells has the following characteristics:

Annual demand: 260 cases	Lead-time: 3 weeks
Ordering cost: $35 / per order	Cycle service level: 95%
Unit cost: $100 per case	On-hand inventory: 5 cases
Holding cost: 20 % of the unit cost	
Standard deviation of wkly demand: 3 cases	

    a. Calculate EOQ for this drug.

    b. Calculate the safety stock.

    c. What is the reorder point?

    d. A withdrawal of 2 cases just occurred. Is it time to reorder? If so, how much should be ordered?

    e. What is the cost implication if the store replaces the current inventory policy (EOQ = 50 and reorder point = 28) with the reorder point policy you have just developed in part c?

3. A grocery store sells a special brand cheese that has the following characteristics.

    Annual demand = 3640 units
    Unit purchasing cost = 25.65
    Inventory holding cost = 25% of unit cost
    Standard deviation of weekly demand 30 units
    The operates 52 weeks a year

    a. What reorder point will yield a service level of 85%, 90%, 95%, and 99%? What will the fill rate be?

    b. What will be a fill rate if the store wants to have high customer satisfaction level? Consider the trade-off between inventory costs and customer satisfaction?

4. A recent accounting statement of Quik Machine Company showed raw material, work-in-process inventory and finished goods inventory to be $1,020,000 (as shown in the table below). This year's sales revenue is $3 million. The company operates 52 weeks per year. The inventory turns of the machine industry is 4 times a year.

Item	# of Units	Unit Value	Total Value
Raw material AA	1000	50	50,000
Raw material BB	2000	40	80,000
Work-in-progress MM	500	80	40,000
Work-in-progress NN	1500	100	150,000
Finished product XX	1000	300	300,000
Finished product YY	2000	200	400,000
Total			1,020,000

a. How many weeks of supply are being held?
b. What is the inventory turns?
c. Comment on Quik Machine's inventory management performance.

Supplement 7.1

Quantity Discount

One of the assumptions of EOQ model is that materials costs remain constant regardless of the quantity purchased. Now we want to explore the impact of quantity discount by relaxing the no-quantity-discount assumption of the EOQ model.

Two commonly used lot size-based discount schemes are:
(1) All units quantity discount
(2) Marginal unit quantity discount

(1) All-unit quantity discounts

Quantity discount is a common practice in supply chain. For example, a manufacturer may offer $10 per unit for an order between 1 - 49 units, $9.80 per unit for an order between 50 - 99 units, and $9.60 per unit for an order of 100 units or more.

EOQ model is applied to determine the order quantity with respect to each price break quantity. The EOQ at a particular price break level may be feasible, but it may not have the lowest total cost as compared to the total cost at other price levels. In this case, the lowest total cost option is chosen. The solution procedure is as follows:

Step 1: Computer the EOQ for each price break, starting with the lowest price, until a feasible EOQ is found. The feasible EOQ is the one that is within the price break quantity.

Step 2: If the first feasible EOQ is for the lowest price break, the lot size is the optimal lot size. Otherwise, compute the total cost for the first feasible lot size and the total cost of each lot size with lower price break. Then settle on the lot size that minimizes the overall cost.

The total costs are a function of material acquisition costs, holding costs, and ordering cost. Each of these costs varies with lot size Q.

$$Total \ \ Annual \ \ Cost = \left(\frac{Q}{2}\right)H + \left(\frac{D}{Q}\right)S + PD \tag{14}$$

Example problem: All-unit quantity discount

Toy Mall is an on-line retailer of toys. GameKid represents a significant percentage of its sales. Demand for GameKid is 2,000 per month. Toy Mall incurs a fixed order placement, transportation, and receiving cost of $300 each time an order for GameKid is placed with the manufacturer. Toy Mall incurs a holding cost of 20 percent of the purchasing price. The price charged by the manufacturer varies according to the following all-unit discount-pricing schedule. Evaluate the number of GameKid that the Toy Mall manager should order in each lot.

Order Quantity	Unit Price
0 up to 1,000	$ 30.00
1,000 up to 2,000	$ 29.00
2,000 or more	$ 28.00

The solution to this problem is presented in Excel spreadsheet format on the next two pages.   The company should take $28 unit price approach because this option generates lowest total cost.

Solution to example problem: All-unit quantity discount in Excel format

	A	B	C	D
1	**All Units Quantity Discount**			
2				
3	Demand = 2,000/month		2,000	
4	Operating 12 mon / year		12	
5	Annual demand (D)		24000	
6	Ordering cost (S)		$300	
7	Holding cost (h)		0.2	
8				
9	Order Quantity	Unit Price (C_i)		
10	0	$30		
11	1,000	$29		
12	2,000	$28		
13				
14	Index	$i=2$	$i=1$	$i=0$
15	C_i	$28	$29	$30
16	Price Break Q	2,000	1,000	0
17	EOQ[C_i]	1,604	1,576	1,549
18	Q_{ci}	2,000	1,576	1,549
19	DC_i	672,000	696,000	720,000
20	$S*(D/Q_{ci})$	3,600	4,569	4,648
21	$hC_i(Q_{ci}/2)$	5,600	4,569	4,648
22	TC[Q_{ci}]	681,200	705,139	729,295

Excel Codes for All Units Quantity Discount

	A	B	C	D
1	All Units Quantity Discount			
2				
3	Demand = 2,000/month		2000	
4	Operating 12 mon / year		12	
5	Annual demand (D)		=C3*C4	
6	Ordering cost (S)		300	
7	Holding cost (h)		0.2	
8				
9	Order Quantity	Unit Price (C_i)		
10	0	30		
11	1000	29		
12	2000	28		
13				
14	Index	i=2	i=1	i=0
15	C_i	28	29	30
16	Price Break Q	=A12	=A11	=A10
17	EOQ[C_i]	=SQRT((2*$C$5*$C$6)/($C$7*B12))	=SQRT((2*$C$5*$C$6)/($C$7*B11))	=SQRT((2*$C$5*$C$6)/($C$7*B10))
18	Q_{ai}	=MAX(B16:B17)	=MAX(C16:C17)	=MAX(D16:D17)
19	DC_i	=C$5*B15	=C$5*C15	=C$5*D15
20	S*(D/Q_{ai})	=$C$6*($C$5/B18)	=$C$6*($C$5/C18)	=$C$6*($C$5/D18)
21	$hC_i(Q_{ai}/2)$	=($C$7*B15)*(B18/2)	=($C$7*C15)*(C18/2)	=($C$7*D15)*(D18/2)
22	TC[Q_{ai}]	=SUM(B19:B21)	=SUM(C19:C21)	=SUM(D19:D21)

(2) Marginal unit quantity discount

Marginal unit quantity discount is another price discount method in supply chain. For example, a manufacturer may offer $10 per unit for an order between 1 - 49 units, starting from unit 50, the price is $9.80 per unit for the range of 50 - 99 units, and starting from unit 100 and more, the price is $9.60 per unit.

The objective is to maximize profit, which, in this case, is equivalent to minimizing cost. The solution procedure evaluates the optimal lot size for each marginal price and then settles on the lot size that minimizes the overall cost.

The solution procedure is as follows:

Step 1: Compute the marginal cost at each price break.

Step 2: Computer the EOQ for each price break, including marginal cost computed in Step 1 as part of the ordering cost. Start with the lowest price, until a feasible EOQ is found. The feasible EOQ is the one that is within the price break quantity.

Step 3: Compute average unit price using EOQ for each feasible price break, including marginal cost.

$$\text{Average unit price} = \frac{C_i(EOQ_{ci}) + MC_i}{EOQ_{ci}} \tag{15}$$

Where

C_i = price break cost

MC_i = marginal cost associates with price break

Step 4: Computer the total cost for the feasible lot size within the price break using formula (8) then settle on the lot size that minimizes the overall cost.

Example problem: Marginal unit discount

Toy Mall is an on-line retailer of toys. GameKid represents a significant percentage of its sales. Demand for GameKid is 3,000 per month. Toy Mall incurs a fixed order placement, transportation, and receiving cost of $350 each time an order for GameKid is placed with the manufacture. Toy Mall incurs a holding cost of 20 percent. The price charged by the manufacturer varies according to the following marginal unit's discount-pricing schedule.

Evaluate the number of GameKid that the Toy Mall manager should order in each lot.

Order Quantity	Marginal Unit Price
0 up to 1,000	$ 65.00
1,000 up to 2,000	$ 60.00
2,000 and more	$ 55.00

The solution to this problem is presented in Excel spreadsheet format on the next two pages. The company should take $55 unit price approach because this option generates lowest total cost.

Solution to marginal unit discount in Excel format

	A	B	C	D
1	**Marginal Unit Discount Algorithem**			
2				
3	Demand = 3,000/mon		3000	
4	Operating 12 mon / year		12	
5	Annual demand (D)		36000	
6	Ordering cost, S		350	
7	Holding cost, h		0.2	
8				
9	Order Quantity	Unit Price		
10	0	$65		
11	1,000	$60		
12	2,000	$55		
13				
14	Index	i=2	i=1	i=0
15	Purchase cost (C_i)	$55	$60	$65
16	Price break quantity (Q_i)	2,000	1,000	0
17	Fixed cost penalty (F_i)	$15,000	$5,000	$0
18	EOQ[C_i]	10,024	5,666	1,392
19	Order quantity (Q_{ci})	10,024	0	0
20	Average unit cost (Mci)	56.50		
21	Annual purchase cost (MCi * D)	2,033,873		
22	Annual order cost [$S*(D/Q_{ci})$]	1,257		
23	Annual holding cost [$(hMC_i)* (Q_{ci}/2)$]	56,630		
24	Total cost [Q_{ci}]	2,091,760		

Notes:

Row 17: The fixed cost penalty due to the incremental nature of the discount. $F_0 = 0$.

Row 18: The EOQ computed at C_i with Fi included as an ordering cost.

Row 19: If row 18 is within the interval of the discount, Row 19 = Row 18. Otherwise, Row 19 = 0, and stop.

Row 20: The average unit cost given the order size is
$MC_i = [(C_i * Q_i) + F_i] / Q_i$.

Solution to marginal unit discount in Excel codes

	A	B	C	D
1	Marginal Unit Discount Algorithm			
2				
3	Demand = 3,000/mon	3000		
4	Operating 12 mon / year	12		
5	Annual demand (D)	=C3*C4		
6	Ordering cost, S	350		
7	Holding cost, h	0.2		
8				
9	Order Quantity	Unit Price (C)		
10	0	65		
11	1000	60		
12	2000	55		
13				
14	Index	i=2	i=1	i=0
15	Purchase cost (C$_i$)	=B12	=B11	=B10
16	Price break quantity (Q$_i$)	=A12	=A11	=A10
17	Fixed cost penalty (F$_i$)	=C17+(C13-B13)*B16	=D16+(D15-C15)*C16	0
18	EOQ[C$_i$]	=SQRT((2*C5*($C36+B17))/($C$7*B13))	=SQRT((2*C5*($C36+C17))/($C$7*B11))	=SQRT((2*C5*($C36+D17))/($C$7*B10))
19	Order quantity (Q$_{ci}$)	=IF(B18=B16,B18)	=IF(C16<C18<B16,C18,0)	=IF(D16<C18<C16,D18,0)
20	Average unit cost (Mc$_i$)	=B12*B19+B17)/B19		
21	Annual purchase cost (MC$_i$ * D)	=B20*C5		
22	Annual order cost (S*(D/Q$_{ci}$))	=C6*(C5/B19)		
23	Annual holding cost (h*MC$_i$) * (Q$_{ci}$/2))	=($C$7*B20)*(B19/2)		
24	Total cost (Q$_{ci}$)	=SUM(B21:B23)		

Supplement 7.2

Risk Pooling

Risk pooling describes the relationship between the number of warehouses, inventory, and customer service level. The square-root rule for risk pooling and the number of warehouses is as follows.

$$I_2 = \sqrt{\frac{N_2}{N_1}} \ (I_1)$$
(16)

Where:

I_1 = Total system inventory for the N_1 warehouses

I_2 = Total system inventory for the N_2 warehouses

N_1 = Number of warehouses in the existing system

N_2 = Number of warehouses in the proposed system

Example problem: Risk pooling & warehouse location

Hot-topic Book Company currently operates a warehouse system of five warehouses with 3000 units of inventory at each warehouse. Determine and compare the average inventory levels if the number of warehouses is reduced to three; then reduce to one.

Solution to example problem risk pooling & warehouse location

Three warehouses: $I_2 = \sqrt{\frac{3}{6}} * 3{,}000 = 2121$ units

One warehouse: $I_2 = \sqrt{\frac{1}{6}} * 3{,}000 = 1225$ units

The five-warehouse system will have 3000 books; three-warehouse system will have 2121 books, and one-warehouse will have 1225 books. The lowest level is associated with one warehouse system.

References

Amaral, J. (2005). "How 'rough-cut' analysis smoothes HP's supply chain." *Supply Chain Management Review*, 9(6), 38-45.

Chopra, S. and Meindle, P. (2001). *Supply Chain Management*. Prentice Hall: New Jersey.

Fredendall, Lawrence D. and Hill, E. (2001). *Basics of Supply Chain Management*. The St. Lucie Press: New York.

Krajewski, L. J. and Ritzman, L. P. (2002). Operations Management, 6th edition. Prentice Hall: New Jersey.

Master, J. (1994). Logistic Management, Course Packet, Ohio State University, Columbus, Ohio.

Schreibfeder, Jon (2006). "Do You Know Where Your Information Comes From?" Effective Inventory Management, Inc., retrieved from http://www.effectiveinventory.com.

Simchi-Levi, D., P. Kaminsky, et al. (2003). *Designing and Managing the Supply Chain*, 2nd edition. New York, McGraw-Hill.

Zipkin, P. (2000). Foundation of Inventory Management. McGraw-Hill: Boston. http://www.vendormanagedinventory.com.

PART FOUR

Transportation and Logistics

Chapter 8
Logistic Network and Distribution

Chapter 9
Transportation Systems and e-Distribution

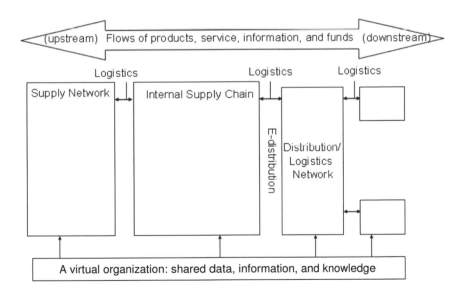

Chapter 8

Logistics Network and Distribution

8.1 Logistics in Supply Chain Management

The logistic network consists of the suppliers, the manufacturer, the distributor, the retailer, and the users as depicted in Figure 8.1. The purpose of an integrated logistic network in a supply chain is to fulfill customer orders through providing place utility to deliver products and services to the end users. Logistics is now being considered as more than simply an opportunity to minimize cost; it has developed into a core component of fulfilling customer orders in supply chain management.

The place utility is achieved by managing a number of key functions of a supply chain. The functions include the following:

- Demand management
- Inventory management
- Transportation
- Warehousing
- Order processing
- Information management

To configure a logistic network in a supply chain, we need data, analytical techniques, computer software, and information systems. The process that we apply to configure a logistic network determines the material and service flows.

Two important areas of logistic network design in an e-Business environment are global logistic network and the reversed logistic network for product recovery. The following two sections discuss these two issues.

8.1.1 Facility configuration of global supply chain

A supply chain is a network of plants, distribution centers and retail stores that transform raw materials, parts and components to finished

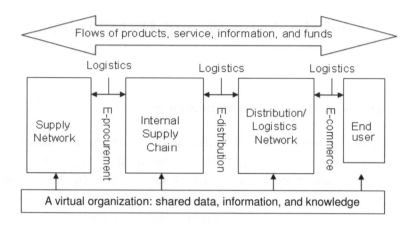

Figure 8.1. Logistics network

products, and then distribute these products to customers. As global competition gets more and more fierce, many companies are reengineering their supply chains by expanding their supply network worldwide to seek the most cost effective suppliers or to be closer to the markets that they serve. For example, McDonald's uses suppliers all over the world for their core product, hamburger. A Big Mac sold in Saudi Arabia uses lettuce from Holland, Cheese from New Zealand, beef from Spain, onion and pickles from the United States, sugar and oil from Brazil, buns from Saudi Arabia, and packaging from Germany[1]. Figure 8.2 presents an example of McDonald's global supply chain network, where raw material is procured from vendors worldwide, transported to distribution centers, and then assembled to the final product at McDonald's restaurants to be consumed by customers. Such a logistic network is complicated and sophisticated in terms of quality control, delivery timing, quantity scheduling, and costs analysis.

---

[1] "What is operations management," Operations Management Video Series, McGraw-Hill Company, Inc., 2005.

1. Saudi Arab	5. United States
2. Holland	6. Brazil
3. New Zealand	7. Germany
4. Spain	

Figure 8.2. McDonald's Saudi Arab supply network

Suppliers within the McDonald's system play a critical role to its success. McDonald's serves over 45 million customers every day of the year. As such, it is important for the company to locate reliable quality suppliers. In the US, McDonald's strategically locates its 40 distribution centers so that more than 12,000 restaurants in the country have convenient access to these distribution centers[2].

As the industries structure and restructure their product lines and market shares, they rebalance their logistic networks to reflect the changes in production and market needs. For example, the U.S. auto industry has reconfigured its facility network over the past 20 years. In 2006, both Ford and GM announced their plans to close down some of

---

[2] http://www.mcdonalds.com.

their production facilities in the US. Through 2008, Ford will idle the St. Louis assembly plant, the Atlanta assembly plant, the Wixom (Mich.) assembly plant, the Batavia (Ohio) Transmission, the Windsor Casting, and the Norfolk assembly plant. These restructuring plans will further shape the logistic network for the auto industry. Recently, American brand cars such as Ford Fusion are made in Mexico, while Japanese brand cars such as Toyota Camry and Honda Civic are made in the US. When Toyota established its product plant in Kentucky, it also established a network of supply facilities around its assembly factory.

In June 2005, Toyota announced that it would build a new plant in Woodstock, Ontario to produce RAV4 sport utility vehicle to serve the North America market. With the establishment of the new assembly factory, Toyota announced an expansion of Canadian Autoparts Toyota, Inc. in Delta, British Columbia[3]. In his discussion of the new investment via videotape broadcast, Katsuaki Watanabe, the president of Toyota Motor Corporation, noted that twenty years ago, Toyota management made two expansion decisions: (i) to make a sweeping commitment to manufacturing in North America and (ii) to make Canada a core part of that commitment. This expansion has strengthened Toyota's ties with its suppliers across North America and reconfigured its auto supply facilities and supply networks in North America.

8.1.2 Reversed logistic network

Recovery, remanufacturing and recycling of used products and materials have become issues of growing importance. Though reuse or remanufacturing is not a new phenomenon, developing a reverse logistic network is a challenging topic facing supply chain professionals. Some commonly accepted reasons for product recovery include legislative pressures on environment, commercial benefits, and economical viability.

---

[3] Toyota to expand in Canada; first new site for auto assembly plant in Canada in almost 20 years. Retrieved in June 2006 from http://origin.www.toyota.com/about/news/manufacturing/2006/02/10-1-tmmna.html.

Implementation of product recovery requires establishing a backward logistics network for the arising flows of used and recovered products. Physical locations, facilities, and transportation links need to be chosen to convey used products from their former users to a producer and to future markets again. For a reverse logistics context, however, a standard set of models has not yet been established. The question that arises here is whether traditional forward approaches can adequately be extended to a backward logistic network to recover products?

Fleischmann et al. briefly discussed a few case studies on recovery networks in different industries, including carpet recycling, electronics remanufacturing, reusable packages, sand recycling from demolition waste, and recycling of by-products from steel production[4]. For example, the design of a large-scale European recycling network for carpet waste is supported with a joint effort from both chemical companies and the European carpet industry. Through the network, used carpet is collected, sorted, and reprocessed for material recovery. In this case, large volume is identified as a critical factor for product recovery.

The electronics industry is one of the most prominent sectors in product recovery. Printer producers such as HP and Xerox created a backward logistics structure for reverse channel functions such as collection, inspection, and remanufacturing. For example, a few years ago, some unsold Uniden's cordless phones with a retail price of $34.98 each were sold to a salvage company for refurbishing. These phones were then sold for $48 in Mexico retail stores.

A sand recycling network is initiated by a consortium of construction waste processing companies in the Netherlands. Since sand is polluted from the demolition process, it needs to be cleaned before it can be reused for road construction. As such, the design of a logistics network is to include cleaning facilities and storage locations.

The recovery process is a closed loop structure. Figure 8.3 depicts an example of a printer recovery process. The supply network provides application-specific integrated circuits (ASIC), cartridges and PC boards.

---

[4] Fleischmann, Moritz, Beullens, Patrick, Bloemhof-Ruwaard, Jacqueline M, Van Wassenhove, Luk N, "The impact of product recovery on logistics network design," *Production and Operations Management*, Summer 2001.

The manufacturer assembles the printer. Distribution centers all over the world deliver the products to various customer zones. After the product is used or worn out, it is sent back through the reversed pipeline for remanufacturing. Typical phases included in the transition from the disposer to the reuse market include collection, sorting, inspection, reprocessing, redistribution, and back to the disposal phase. This role of recovery networks as an intermediate between the disposal and reuse markets and gives rise to the coordination between supply and demand. These unique characteristics ought to be taken into consideration when designing a product recovery logistic network.

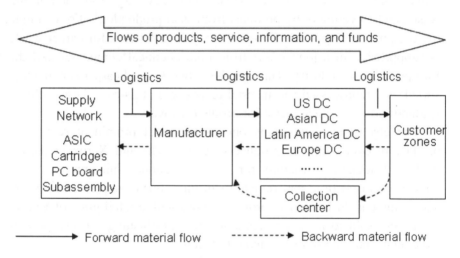

Figure 8.3. Product recover logistics network

8.2 Data for Logistic Network Planning

8.2.1 Data sources

Data internal and external to the firm can be used to plan a logistic network. Examples of major sources include business operating data files stored in an information system, accounts reports, logistic research, published information of the industry, previous experience, and predictions. Additionally, government also issues some statistics about logistics and transportation. For example, the US Department of Transportation publishes regulatory impact analysis, performance and accountability reports. More data and statistics about logistic issues are released by the Bureau of Transportation.

8.2.2 Data check list

Designing a logistic network requires a lot of business data. A list of data required is suggested below. Some data are organization or industry specific, other data can be generalized from published data sources.

- Customer demand: products, order time, order size, order frequency.
- Order processing: transit time, order transmittal times, and order fill rate.
- Customer service requirements: lead time, customer service level, and fill rate.
- Product: product families, product line, stock keeping unit (SKU), product weight, product size, product maintenance condition (such as temperature required).
- Locations: location of customers, retailers, service providers, suppliers, manufacturers, wholesalers, and distribution centers.
- Transportation: transportation rate or cost by mode, road condition, traffic hours, and one way street information.
- Facility costs: capital cost, facility rate or costs, utility, labor, insurance, operating cost, inventory holding cost.
- Material handling costs.

8.3 Techniques for Logistic Network Configuration

After gathering relevant data and information, the process for searching the best network design starts. This process is complicated and usually is assisted by mathematical modeling and computer simulation. The commonly applied techniques used in industry include:

- Optimization models
- Computer simulation

- Heuristics models
- Expert systems and decision support systems

8.3.1 Optimization model

Optimization models include linear programming, nonlinear programming, integer programming, dynamic programming models, calculus models, enumeration and sequencing models. These models provide the best solutions mathematically. The limitation of applying optimization models in network design is that they deal with static models such as annual demand or average demand and do not take into consideration changes over time.

8.3.2 Computer simulation

Simulation models take into account the dynamics of logistic network for a specific design and its performance. Simulating a logistic network involves replicating various constraints and cost structures, visualizing the proposed network system, simulating what-if questions regarding the logistic network, exploring operational issues, and integrating available resources. This replication is usually stochastic in nature and is done by the means of mathematical relationship. When the design of a logistic network requires substantial amount of details and optimization solutions are impossible, simulation is a reasonable option.

8.3.3 Heuristics model

Heuristic models integrate simulation approach and optimization method to find a feasible solution for a complex logistic network design problem. This approach is applied to solve some of the most difficult logistic network problems when too many factors need to be compromised to satisfy the requirements of optimization models. Heuristics does not guarantee an optimal solution but can generate feasible and very good network configuration solutions.

8.3.4 Expert systems and decision support systems

The designers of a logistic network may have accumulated a lot of working experience in how the problem should be solved. These experts can process incomplete data, fuzzy and partial information, as well as unstructured problems. Such experience and knowledge often transcends sophisticated mathematical models and can be used to generate solutions better than using simulation, optimization method, or heuristics models alone.

A decision support system integrates data, information, and techniques with the aid of computer programs to generate network configuration solutions. Managers use decision support information to make logistic network configuration decisions.

8.4 Facility Location and Configuration

We now move to the issue of a strategic plan for the logistic network configuration. Before doing this we need to make sure that relevant data are collected and a customer service level is determined.

Alfred Weber suggests that the weight of material can affect the logistic network design. For example, steel making is a weight loss process. Therefore, the facility that processes the raw material should be located close to the source of raw material so as to reduce transportation cost. Soft drink production, on the other hand, is a weight gaining process. Therefore, soft drink production should be placed close to the market so as to save transportation costs.

8.4.1 Single facility location

8.4.1.1 The center of gravity method

One of the most popular methods used to locate a single facility is the center of gravity method. This method only considers transportation cost in the design process. The transportation cost increases linearly as the quantity gets larger. The objective is to find a centroid location that will minimize the total transportation cost. The minimization formula is expressed as follows.

(1) Collect data on the coordinate points of supply and demand points, the quantity to be moved, and the linear transportation rate per weight unit per mile.

(2) Get an estimate of x', y', and d_i using the following formulas.

$$x' = \frac{\sum_{i=1}^{n} \frac{Q_i c_i x_i}{d_i}}{\sum_{i=1}^{n} \frac{Q_i c_i}{d_i}} \qquad (8.1)$$

$$y' = \frac{\sum_{i=1}^{n} \frac{Q_i c_i y_i}{d_i}}{\sum_{i=1}^{n} \frac{Q_i c_i}{d_i}} \qquad (8.2)$$

$$d_i = \sqrt{(x_i - x')^2 + (y_i - y')^2} \qquad (8.3)$$

Where:

x' and y' = estimated coordinates for the warehouse

x_i and y_i = coordinates of the plant and customer zones

d_i = distance from the facility to market i.

c_i = freight rate per unit / mile from the facility to market i.

Q_i = freight volume to be shipped from the facility to market i.

TC = total transportation cost from the distribution center to all the markets.

(3) Compute the total cost:

$$\text{Min TC} = \sum_{i=1}^{n} Q_i c_i d_i \qquad (8.4)$$

(4) Substitute the current estimates with the newly computed estimates, $x_i = x'$, $y_i = y'$,   TC = TC'. Repeat steps 2 and 4 until the newly

computed location (x', y') is almost the same as the current (x_i, y_i). Now stop.

Example Problem 8.1: The Center of Gravity Method

The window blinds produced by Zerk, Inc. serve three markets. Recently, the company wants to build a new warehouse in a location that minimizes the total transportation cost. Coordinate points, demand quantity, and transportation rates are given in Table 8.1.

Table 8.1.

Site	Coordinates		Freight volume	Freight rate cost
	x_i	y_i		
Factory	8	10	1000	0.25
Market A	12	9.5	250	0.5
Market B	11	7.5	350	0.5
Market C	6	5	400	0.5

Solution to example Problem 8.1: The Center of Gravity Method

Excel spreadsheet is employed to solve this problem. The detailed result is given in Table 8.2 and Excel spreadsheet codes are provided in Table 8.3.

Let's take row 2 (plant) of Table 8.2 as an example. We start with the estimation of x' = 0 and y' = 0. Column D shows the result of formula 8.3. Column G operationalizes the numerator of formula 8.1, Column H operationalizes the numerator of formula 8.2, and Column I denominator of formula 8.1 and 8.2:

(Column D, Row 2)

$$d_i = \sqrt{(x_i - x')^2 + (y_i - y')^2} = \sqrt{(8-0)^2 + (10-0)^2} = 12.81$$

(Column G, Row 2) $Q_i\, c_i\, x_i\, /\, d_i = 1000 * 0.25 * 8 / 12.81 = 156.13$

(Column H, Row 2) $Q_i\, c_i\, y_i\, /\, d_i = 1000 * 0.25 * 10 / 12.81 = 195.16$

(Column I, Row 2) $Q_i\, c_i\, /\, d_i\quad = 1000 * 0.25 / 12.81 = 19.52$

(Column G, Row 6)   Sum column G, rows 2 - 5

(Column H, Row 6)   Sum column H, rows 2 - 5

(Column I, Row 6)   Sum column I, rows 2 - 5
(Column C, Row 8)   Compute new x': 552.38 / 66.44 = 8.31
(Column E, Row 8)   Compute new y': 499.37 / 66.44 = 7.52

Please note that spreadsheet keeps many decimals. When compute by hand and keep a couple of decimals, the numbers may be a little different due to rounding.

Table 8.2. Iteration 0. Use (0, 0) coordinates as the initial warehouse location to start the problem.

	A	B	C	D	E	F	G	H	I
1	Site	x_i	y_i	d_i	Q_i	c_i	$Q_i c_i x_i /d_i$	$Q_i c_i y_i /d_i$	$Q_i c_i /d_i$
2	Plant	8	10	12.81	1000	0.25	156.13	195.16	19.52
3	Market A	12	9.5	15.31	250	0.5	97.98	77.56	8.16
4	Market B	11	7.5	13.31	350	0.5	144.63	98.61	13.15
5	Market C	6	5	7.81	400	0.5	153.65	128.04	25.61
6	Total				2000		552.38	499.37	66.44
7		x^0= 0.00		y^0= 0.00					
8		x'= 8.31		y'= 7.52					

We have repeated the computation nine times by substituting the current (x_i, y_i) with the most recently computed estimates (x_i = x', y_i = y') until the newly computed location (x', y') is almost the same as the current (x_i, y_i). Table 8.4 shows that iterations 8 and 9 obtain the same coordinates (9.01, 8.60) and the same total cost. We stop here.

This procedure can easily be done using an Excel spreadsheet. Excel codes are provided in Table 8.3. You can accomplish the task simply by applying the copy and paste features of Excel. Caution should be taken because the solution generated here may not be feasible for a real situation. For instance, the coordinates may be located in the middle of a lake. However, the result provides managers with the information of the lowest total transportation cost option. As such, a reasonable location that is close to the coordinates (9.01, 8.60) can be identified to locate the distribution center.

Table 8.3. Excel codes for the problem solved in Table 8.2

	A	B	C	D	E	F	G	H	I
1	Site	x_i	y_i	d_i	Q_i	c_i	$Q_i c_i x_i / d_i$	$Q_i c_i y_i / d_i$	$Q_i c_i / d_i$
2	Plant	8	10	=ROUND(SQRT((B2-$C$7)^2+(C2-$E$7)^2),2)	1000	0.25	=(E2*F2*B2)/D2	=(E2*F2*C2)/D2	=(E2*F2)/D2
3	Market A	12	9.5	=ROUND(SQRT((B3-$C$7)^2+(C3-$E$7)^2),2)	250	0.5	=(E3*F3*B3)/D3	=(E3*F3*C3)/D3	=(E3*F3)/D3
4	Market B	11	7.5	=ROUND(SQRT((B4-$C$7)^2+(C4-$E$7)^2),2)	350	0.5	=(E4*F4*B4)/D4	=(E4*F4*C4)/D4	=(E4*F4)/D4
5	Market C	6	5	=ROUND(SQRT((B5-$C$7)^2+(C5-$E$7)^2),2)	400	0.5	=(E5*F5*B5)/D5	=(E5*F5*C5)/D5	=(E5*F5)/D5
6	Total				=SUM(E2:E5)		=SUM(G2:G5)	=SUM(H2:H5)	=SUM(I2:I5)
7		$x^0 = 0$		$y^0 = 0$					
8		$x^1 =$ =G6/I6		$y^1 =$ =H6/I6					

Table 8.4. Summary of nine iterations

Iteration	x'	y'	Total Cost
0	8.31	7.52	
1	8.78	8.15	2195.50
2	9.05	8.49	2164.25
3	9.05	8.54	2159.25
4	9.04	8.56	2158.25
5	9.03	8.58	2160.00
6	9.02	8.59	2158.00
7	9.01	8.60	2158.50
8	9.01	8.60	2157.75
9	9.01	8.60	2157.75

8.4.1.2 The median method

The median method yields an optimal solution when the relevant metric is rectilinear distance. It uses median instead of mean for x_i and y_i. The procedure is as follows:

(1) Move across the grid horizontally from left to right, and accumulate the weight at each location reached until 50% or more of the total weight has been accumulated. This method is called median approach. The value of x that puts you at or over 50% is x_m.

(2) Move across the grid vertically from top to bottom, and accumulate the weight at each location reached until 50% or more of the total weight has been accumulated. The value of y that puts you at or over 50% is y_m.

Where:
  x_i and y_i = coordinates of customer zones
  x_m and y_m = identified median coordinates

Example Problem 8.2: Median Method

The x and y coordinates of five sites are given in Table 8.5, as is the demand quantity for each site. Determine a central warehouse location that minimizes the total transportation cost using the median method.

Table 8.5.

Customer zone	x_i	y_i	Demand (w_i)
A	2	3	35
B	4	9	65
C	5	7	65
D	6	5	80
E	9	8	55
Total			300

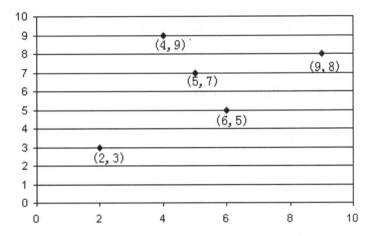

Solution to example Problem 8.2: Median Method

Applying steps (1) and (2), the total demand from customer zones A, B and C is over 50% of the total weight, we get $x_m = 5$, and $y_m = 7$. Then we compute the rectilinear distance and the total cost. The detailed computation is given in Table 8.6.

Table 8.6.

Customer zone	x_i	y_i	Demand (w_i)	$|x_i - x_m| + |y_i - y_m|$	d_i	$w_i * d_i$
A	2	3	35	$|2-5| + |3-7| = 7$	7	245
B	4	9	65	$|4-5| + |9-7| = 3$	3	195
C	5	7	65	$|5-5| + |7-7| = 0$	0	0
D	6	5	80	$|6-5| + |5-7| = 3$	3	240
E	9	8	55	$|9-5| + |8-7| = 5$	5	275
					Total Cost	955

In the median method, one of the customer zones is sometimes the optimal location. Sometimes the optimal location falls anywhere on a line segment or anywhere within a rectangle. When applying rectilinear distance, the orientation of the grid is an essential part of the input data. Therefore, changing the grid orientation changes the problem itself.

When choosing between a Euclidean model such as center of gravity and a rectilinear model such as median model, the decision should be consistent with the distance measurement that is under consideration. The rectilinear model will almost always produce a higher ton/mile total than a Euclidean model. This is because the straight line is shorter than the right angle distance.

8.4.2 Configure multiple facilities

Companies often need to configure two or more facilities in a network simultaneously. The possible configurations can be enormous, so this type of problem is more complicated. The goal is to determine the number of facilities needed, the size of each facility, and the location of each facility in a logistic network. A number of techniques have been developed to solve multi-location problem, including linear programming, mixed integer programming, dynamic programming, and simulation among others.

Major costs of designing a multiple facility supply chain network include:

- Fixed facility cost
- Inventory costs
- Transportation costs
- Production costs
- Other costs such as overhead, coordination costs

The Linear programming method can be used to allocate demand in a logistic network and the Mixed Integer Programming method can be employed when both fixed and variable costs are considered. The Linear programming and Mixed Integer programming methods are introduced below.

Example Problem 8.3: Allocating Markets to Existing Warehouses

GamesRus Inc. has three warehouses that serve four markets. Managers of the three warehouses need to decide how to allocate the demand to their facility. Fixed cost associated with each plant is not included in the total cost analysis. Only transportation cost is considered. As the cost and demand change, the managers will revise the facility configuration. Table 8.7 provides demand and capacity data. Transportation cost information is given in the middle of the table. For example, to transport a 1 ton product from Warehouse 1 to Virginia Beach costs 8 dollars.

Table 8.7.

	Virginia Beach	Norfolk	Chesapeake	Suffolk	Capacity
Warehouse 1	8	6	10	9	50
Warehouse 2	9	12	13	7	75
Warehouse 3	12	9	13	6.5	100
Demand (in ton)	45	25	28	30	

The manager wants to know which warehouse will serve which markets, and the total cost of the configuration.

The linear programming method is used for allocating demand to warehouses. All the demands are met. The available supply of the plants cannot be exceeded. Demand from one customer zone can be supplied from one or more warehouses.

Objective Function:

$$\text{Min } \sum_{i=1}^{n}\sum_{j=1}^{m} vc_{ij}x_{ij} \tag{8.5}$$

Subject to

$$\sum_{i=1}^{n} x_{ij} = D_j \tag{8.6}$$

$$\sum_{j=1}^{m} x_{ij} \leq Q_i \tag{8.7}$$

$$x_{ij} \geq 0 \tag{8.8}$$

Where:

Decision variable:
   x_{ij} = quantity shipped from warehouse i to customer zone j

Parameters:
   vc_{ij} = variable cost of one unit shipped from warehouse i to customer
      zone j per mile
   D_j = annual demand from customer zone j, j = 1 to n.
   Q_i = annual supply capacity of warehouse i, i = 1 to m.

   Equation 8.6 ensures that all demands are satisfied. Equation 8.7 is a capacity constraint that ensures that the total supply to customer zones will not exceed the warehouse capacity. *Excel Solve* is applied to solve the problem. Table 8.8 shows that the total cost is $1,039. Warehouse 1 will serve demand from Norfolk, Chesapeake, and Suffolk. Warehouse 2 will serve demand from Virginia Beach and Warehouse 3 will serve the Suffolk market. Solver codes are given in Table 8.9.

Example Problem 8.4: Developing a Logistic Network Considering Both Fix and Variable Costs

The CEO of GamesRus Inc. wants to know if they can save some fixed cost by closing one of the three warehouses they have now. In this case, one market may be served by more than one warehouse. The demand, capacity, transportation costs, and fixed costs are given in Table 8.10. Which warehouse to close and which to open? What is the total cost of the configuration?

Table 8.8. Solution to example Problem 8.3 using Excel Solver

	A	B	C	D	E	F
1	**Example 8.3 Allocating markets to existing warehouse**					
2						
3		Virginia	Norfolk	Chesapeake	Suffolk	Capacity
4	Warehouse 1	8	6	10	9	50
5	Warehouse 2	9	12	13	7	75
6	Warehouse 3	12	9	13	6.5	100
7	Demand	45	25	28	30	
8						
9						
10	*Decision Var*	irginia Beac	Norfolk	Chesapeake	Suffolk	
11	Warehouse 1	0	22	28	0	
12	Warehouse 2	45	0	0	0	
13	Warehouse 3	0	3	0	30	
14						
15	*Objective Fn*					
16	Cost =	1039				
17						
18						
19	*Constraints*	*Unused Capacity*	Virginia Beach	Norfolk	Chesapeake	Suffolk
20	Warehouse 1	0				
21	Warehouse 2	30				
22	Warehouse 3	67				
23	*Demand*		0	0	0	0

Table 8.9. Excel Solver codes for example Problem 8.3

	Formula	Cell	Excel Codes
Objective function	$\sum_{i=1}^{n}\sum_{j=1}^{m} vc_{ij}x_{ij}$	B16	= SUMPRODUCT(B4:E6,B11:E13)
Demand constraint	$\sum_{i=1}^{n} x_{ij} = D_j$	C23	=B7 – SUM(B11:B13)
		D23	=C7 – SUM(C11: C13)
		E23	=D7 – SUM(D11: D13)
		F23	=E7 – SUM(E11: E13)
Capacity constraint	$\sum_{j=1}^{m} x_{ij} \leq Q_i$	B20	=F4 - SUM(B11:E11)
		B21	= F5-SUM(B12:E12)
		B22	= F6-SUM(B13:E13)

Table 8.10. Example Problem 8.4 data

	Fixed cost	Virginia Beach	Norfolk	Chesapeake	Suffolk	Capacity
Warehouse 1	2250	8	6	10	9	50
Warehouse 2	3250	9	12	13	7	75
Warehouse 3	4200	12	9	13	6.5	100
Demand		45	25	28	30	

For the capacitated warehouse location model with multiple sourcing, when fixed cost is considered the problem is solved using Mixed Integer Programming. If the warehouse is open it is 1, otherwise it is 0.

Objective Function

$$\text{Min } \sum_{i=1}^{n}\sum_{j=1}^{m} vc_{ij}x_{ij} + \sum_{i=1}^{n} fc_i y_i \qquad (8.9)$$

Subject to

$$\sum_{i=1}^{n} x_{ij} = D_j \qquad (8.10)$$

$$\sum_{j=1}^{m} x_{ij} \leq Q_i y_i \qquad (8.11)$$

$$x_{ij} \geq 0 \qquad (8.12)$$

$$\sum_{i=1}^{n} y_i \leq N \; ; \; y_i \in \{0, 1\} \qquad (8.13)$$

Where
Decision variable:
   x_{ij} = quantity shipped from warehouse i to customer zone j
   y_i = 1 if the warehouse is open, 0 otherwise.

Parameters:
   vc_{ij} = variable cost of one unit shipped from warehouse i to customer zone j per mile
   fc_i = fixed cost of warehouse i
   D_j = annual demand from customer zone j.
   Q_i = annual capacity of warehouse i.
   N = the number of warehouse sites available.

Equation 8.10 ensures that all demands are satisfied. Equation 8.11 is a capacity constraint; it ensures that the total supply to customer zones will not exceed the warehouse capacity. Equation 8.12 is a non-negativity constraint. Equation 8.13 ensures that the total number of open warehouses will not exceed the current available number of warehouses.

Table 8.11 reports the results after the problem is solved using Excel Solver. Warehouses 1 and 3 will stay open and warehouse 2 will be closed. The total cost of this configuration is $7,579. The Virginia Beach market will be served by Warehouse 1. The Norfolk market will be supplied by warehouses 1 and 3. Both Chesapeake and Suffolk markets will be served by Warehouse 3. There will be 22 units still available for promising new orders after all the demands are satisfied. Solver codes are given in Table 8.12.

8.5 Warehouse

8.5.1 Nature and importance of warehouse

The warehouse is part of a supply chain's logistic network. It is used for the storage of inventory at all phases of a supply chain. Raw material, semi-finished components, and finished goods can all be stocked in warehouse.

Most companies use a warehouse as an intermediate point between the manufacturing plant and the customer. Some companies such as Sear's mail order catalog service use a warehouse as the point of origin or as sales headquarters.

Directly fulfilling orders from the warehouse becomes a new business model in the e-Business environment. e-Retailers such as Amazon.com take orders through their Web sites and fulfill orders directly from their warehouses. Amazon opened eight distribution centers in 2001 including five in 1999, so that it could handle shipping of its goods on its own. In general the functions of a warehouse include:

Table 8.11. Solution to example Problem 8.4 using Excel Solver

	A	B	C	D	E	F	G
1	**Example 8.4 Logistic network with both fix and variable costs**						
2							
3		Fixed	Virginia Beach	Norfolk	Chesapeake	Suffolk	Capacity
4	Warehouse 1	2250	8	6	10	9	50
5	Warehouse 2	3250	9	12	13	7	75
6	Warehouse 3	4200	12	9	13	6.5	100
7	Demand		45	25	28	30	
8							
9	*Decision Var*	Open/Close	Virginia Beach	Norfolk	Chesapeake	Suffolk	
10	Warehouse 1	1	45	5	0	0	
11	Warehouse 2	0	0	0	0	0	
12	Warehouse 3	1	0	20	28	30	
13							
14	*Objective Fn*						
15	Cost =	7,579					
16							
17	*Constraints*	*Unused Capacity*	Virginia Beach	Norfolk	Chesapeake	Suffolk	
18	Warehouse 1	0					
19	Warehouse 2	0					
20	Warehouse 3	22					
21	*Demand*		0.00	0.00	0.00	0.00	

Table 8.12. Example Problem 8.4 Excel Solver codes

	Formula	Cell	Excel Codes
Objective function	$\sum_{i=1}^{n}\sum_{j=1}^{m}vc_{ij}x_{ij} + \sum_{i=1}^{n}fc_i y_i$	B15	= SUMPRODUCT(C4:F6,C10:F12) + SUMPRODUCT(B4:B6, B10:B12)
Demand constraint	$\sum_{i=1}^{n}x_{ij} = D_j$	C21	=C7 – SUM(C10:C12)
		D21	=D7 – SUM(D10: D12)
		E21	=E7 – SUM(E10: E12)
		F21	=F7 – SUM(F10: F12)
Capacity constraint	$\sum_{j=1}^{m}x_{ij} \le Q_i y_i$	B18	=G4*B10 - SUM(C10:F10)
		B19	= G5*B11 - SUM(C11:F11)
		B20	= G6*B12 - SUM(C12:F12)

- Take advantage of production economies
- Take advantage of transportation economies
- Take advantage of purchasing discount
- Realize firms' customer service commitment
- Manage seasonal demand
- Provide place utility

As such, a warehouse is an integral component of a supply chain. However, warehousing is expensive and usually accounts for 2 to 5 percent of sales cost[5]. Therefore, trimming down warehousing cost has important implications for a supply chain's performance, specifically on the performance of return-on-assets. How to best balance warehousing cost containment and a high customer service level becomes the supply chain managers' charge.

8.5.2 Warehouse in supply chain

8.5.2.1 Public and private warehouses

There are a couple of warehouse options in a supply chain, mainly public warehouse and private warehouse. Usually, a rented facility is a public warehouse and an owned or leased facility is considered private warehouse. Companies may consider customer service and total cost to choose between public and private warehousing.

Some advantages of using a public warehouse include:

(1) Not needing the capital investment in building, land, material handling, etc.
(2) Being able to increase or decrease space for seasonal demand without a huge investment in facility;
(3) Having the flexibility to change warehouse location according to the changes in the market place or customer density;
(4) Having better estimates about the storage and handling cost, utility cost, and labor cost;

---

[5] Edward Frazelle (2002). *World-class Warehousing and Material Handling*. New York: McGraw Hill.

(5) Being able to take advantage of economies of scale when demand volume is low;

(6) Having a tax advantage when a firm does not own property in the state, and avoiding various state taxies; and

(7) Insulating labor disputes when the union is involved in a labor dispute with one of the customers. The US courts have ruled that a labor union does not have the right to strike against a public warehouse when the union is involved in a labor dispute with one of the customers of that public warehouse.

The disadvantages of using a public warehouse include:

(1) The lack of control of products stocked in the warehouse;

(2) Communication problem with the public warehouse;

(3) The lack of specialized services; and

(4) A public warehouse may not have extra space available when the company needs it.

A private warehouse also has some advantages and disadvantages. The advantages of using a private warehouse include:

(1) Having direct and a higher degree of control of the product;

(2) Having flexibility to design and operate the warehouse according to its own needs;

(3) Being less costly over the long term if the company is able to achieve sufficient utilization of the warehouse;

(4) The firm being able to utilize its present human resource; and

(5) Realizing tax benefits such as depreciation when a firm owns a warehouse.

The disadvantages of using a private warehouse include:

(1) The lack of flexibility due to its fixed space, utility cost, labor cost, and other overhead costs; and

(2) Requiring initial capital investment to build or buy a warehouse. Additional costs include purchasing material handling equipment, and recruiting and training employees.

8.5.2.2 Types of warehouses

Various products may require special warehousing arrangements. For example, Purdue Farm produces chicken products and requires refrigerated warehouses. In general, there are six types of warehouses:

- General merchandise warehouse for manufactured goods such as toys, bathroom tissues, etc.
- Refrigerated or cold storage warehouse for frozen foods.
- Bonded warehouse for storing goods authorized by customs officials until removal, without the payment of duties. Since this kind of warehouse holds bonded shipments, pending customs inspection, it must be secured. Dutiable goods need to be segregated from nondutiable goods.
- Household goods and furniture warehouse.
- Special commodity warehouse.
- Bulk storage warehouse such as Sam's Club and Costco.

8.5.3 Cross docking

The cross-docking approach is to accept the products at the receiving dock, where it is moved directly to the shipping dock. In this case, products are not put into the storage area so material handling and storage expenses can be saved. Outbound trailers serve as extensions of the distribution center. When cross-docking is chosen, more space will be allocated to the dock and less space will be allocated to the storage area.

Wal-Mart uses the concept of cross-docking to reduce its overall inventory costs. Products from different suppliers are exchanged at the depot between trucks so that each truck going to a retail store has products from different suppliers. Wal-Mart also allows its retail stores to exchange surplus and shortage items. Logistic network and transportation play an important role at Wal-Mart. This is to improve the matching of supply and demand so as to keep up the customer satisfaction goal while keeping costs low. However, when cross docking is applied, vehicle scheduling becomes important to reduce truck waiting time at the dock.

8.6 Enhancing Value through Logistics Management in Supply Chain

The logistic network is an integral part of a supply chain. It plays a vital role in providing a desired level of customer service at the lowest total cost possible. A well-designed, sophisticated logistic network makes a quick response supply chain possible. A quick response supply chain leads to reduced cycle time, better demand forecast due to short lead time, and increased supply chain profits.

As shown in Figure 8.1, logistics and distribution centers are the links among the suppliers, manufacturers, distributors, retailers and the customers. Traditional vertical integration of various production stages within a company is gradually losing its favor. For example, IBM was a fully integrated PC producer in the 1980s. It produced micro processors, wrote operating system codes, manufactured PCs, and even ran its own retail stores. Today, Dell computer purchases almost all the parts and components it needs for production, keeping the final assembly in house. This transition indicates that supply chain management is managing a logistic network, which integrates a set of tasks to produce the final products, and to provide place and product utilities to the customer. The reversed logistic network is adding value to the supply chain. For example, Sears shuttles customer-returned products from over 2,900 stores to three collection centers in the US. After remanufacturing or refurbishing, the company sells these recovered products for a profit. Over the past two decades, the logistic network has evolved from a relatively minor facet of a company to one of the most crucial functions in a supply chain.

8.7 Summary

In this chapter we have discussed the effects of global competition on logistic network configuration and reversed logistic network for recovery of products. An array of methods is introduced for designing a logistics network. Since the advancement of computer technology has made the computation much faster and easier, a real-world problem with a few hundred customer zones, more than a dozen warehouses, and several hundred product groups can be solved within a reasonable amount of time.

Questions for Pondering

1. In 2006 Ford motor announced its plan to close down 14 facilities in the US from now up until the year 2008. How does this decision affect Ford's logistic network configuration?
2. What benefits do cross-docking offer? If cross-docking is a solution to inventory reduction and fast inventory turn-over, why do we still need warehouses for stocking goods?
3. Amazon.com and Dell Inc. have changed the way a retailer conducts business. What role does a warehouse play in Amazon's e-Business model?
4. How would you determine performance metrics for a logistic network configuration? What key factors do you take into consideration when evaluating a logistic network?

Problems

1. Develop a list of factors that you think would be important in determining the location of
   - A fast food restaurant
   - A hospital
   - A shopping mall
   - A bottle water manufacturer
   - An auto component manufacturer

2. The following table gives the location of five demand points served by a central warehouse with coordinates of x=0 and y=0. The coordinates and annual freight volumes of the five markets are:

Market	x	y	weight
A	1	1	50
B	2	3	30
C	4	2	10
D	3	5	70
E	5	4	40

Determine the facility location that will provide minimum total ton-miles from the warehouse to the five customer locations. Compare the results from the center of gravity method to the median method.

3. Two warehouses are to serve three customer zones. Volume flowing either to or from each point and relevant transportation rates are given in the following table:

Site	X	Y	Freight volume	Freight rate
Warehouse 1	3.5	8	50	4
Warehouse 2	8	3	80	4
Customer A	6	4	35	9.5
Customer B	2	5	40	9.5
Customer C	8	8	55	9.8

a. Use the center of gravity method to find the optimal location for the warehouse.
b. Are there any factors that are not included in the model that you feel are important for a facility network problem? Explain how your manager can use the results from your analysis.

4. A company supplies goods to three customer zones through two warehouses. Demand from customer 1 is 40 units, from customer 2 is 50 units and from customer 3 is 35 units. Warehouse 1 has 80 units and warehouse 2 has 60 units available. The cost of shipping one unit of product to customer is given in the table below:

From	To		
	Customer 1	Customer 2	Customer 3
Warehouse 1	25	15	35
Warehouse 2	50	40	10

Please determine which customer is going to be served by which warehouse. Formulate the problem to minimize the total transportation cost and solve the problem using Excel Solver.

4. Regarding problem 3, the annual fixed cost for Warehouse 1 is $5,000, for Warehouse 2, the fixed cost is $9,000.
   a. What will be the logistic configuration if the company is going to redesign its logistic network?
   b. If demand from customer 1 is doubled and demand from customers 2 and 3 remain the same, what will the solutions be?

References

Ballou, R.H. (1992). *Business Logistics Management*, 3rd edition. Prentice Hall: New Jersey.

Chopra, S. and Meindl, P. (2002). *Supply Chain Management*. Prentice Hall: New Jersey.

Simchi-Levi, D., Kaminsky, P., and Simchi-Levi, E. (2003). *Designing and Managing the Supply Chain*, 2nd edition. McGraw-Hill Irwin: New York.

Prince, Theodore (2000). E-Commerce: Its Impact on Transportation, Logistics, and Supply Chain Management, 4/15/2000 *ASCET,* Volume 2.

Stock, J.R. and Lambert, D.M. (1987). *Strategic Logistic Management*, 2nd edition. Richard Irwin: Homewood, Illinois.

Chapter 9

Transportation Systems and e-Distribution

9.1 Transportation

Transportation moves products to geographically distanced markets to provide people allover the world with access to a wide variety of goods from various countries. For example, U.S. companies export agriculture products, lumber, medical equipment, chemicals, pharmaceuticals, manufactured goods, and many other products to overseas markets. Vice versa, American consumers enjoy beer from Holland, automobiles from Germany, leather shoes and bags from Italy, electronic appliances from Japan, garments from China, rugs and furniture from India, and coffee from Columbia. In this sense, transportation offers time and place utility to consumers.

According to the U.S. chamber of Commerce, U.S. international trade in goods and services has grown from 10.7% of GDP in 1970 to 26.9% in 2005. The trade flow benefits people throughout the U.S. and around the world. Meanwhile, transportation is inexpensive means that connects the world economy. According to the World Shipping Council, the annual cost of transporting America's liner imports is only slightly more than $130 per household, which is a small proportion of household expenses.

More recently, transportation and logistics companies have applied B2B practices and utilized e-commerce solutions to fulfill customer supply chain expectations. Therefore, the transportation function is an opportunity for supply chain managers to minimize cost and improve profitability.

9.1.1 Carriers

Carriers are those who provide transportation services to move goods from one point to another. For example, FedEx and UPS are carriers. A carrier such as airline, railroad, or trucking company needs to provide quality customer service at a competitive cost. When making investment decisions, a carrier needs to consider a range of costs, such as vehicle related cost, fixed operating cost, trip related cost, and overhead cost.

Vehicle related cost includes size and type of vehicles purchased or leased for moving goods around. Fixed costs include any cost associated with terminal fee, airport gate fee, and labor cost whether or not the vehicle is used. Trip related costs are the costs incurred when the vehicle is dispatched for service. These costs usually include fuel and labor expense, quantity related cost such as those associated with loading and unloading. Overhead costs include administrative expense, marketing expense, planning and scheduling transportation network, and investment in information technology.

9.1.2 Shippers

Shippers are those who require transportation services. For example, when Amazon requires FedEx and UPS to deliver books to its customers, Amazon is a shipper.

A shipper wants to provide responsive service while minimize the total cost of fulfilling a customer's order. When making transportation decisions, a shipper needs to consider transportation cost, inventory cost, order processing cost, as well as customer service level.

The transportation cost is the cost for purchasing transportation service from carrier. The cost of holding inventory incurred by the shipper's supply chain network can include interest, storage and handling, taxes, insurance, and shrinkage. Service level costs are the costs of not being able to meet the specified customer service objectives. These costs can be shortage cost, backorder cost, and compensation vouch.

9.2 Overview of Carrier Operations

A variety of transportation tools are available for people to move things around. Motor carrier, railroads, water, airlines, and pipeline are five major transportation modes. Additionally, several intermodal services such as rail-motor, water-rail, motor-water, and motor-air are available to offer a combination of more than one transportation tools. We give a brief discussion of each mode in this chapter. Interested readers may consult *Transportation* written by John Coyle, Edward Bardi, and Robert Novack for details.

9.2.1 Motor carrier

Motor carriage is the most popular transportation mode in the U.S. As the interstate system of highway developed from the 1950s, motor carriage gradually replaced rail carriage as the dominant form of freight transportation.

A motor carrier is classified either as a "for-hire-carrier" or a private carrier. For-hire-carriers provide service to the public and charge a fee for the service. Private carriers provide service to the organization without a charge. The organization usually owns or leases the vehicle.

A for-hire-motor carrier can be classified in a number of ways, including local vs. intercity, common vs. contract, and regulated vs. exempt. Additionally, it can be a truckload (TL) or a less- than-truckload (LTL) service provider. Figure 9.1 gives a classification of for-hire motor carriers.

A for-hire-carrier can either be a local or intercity service provider. If a carrier focuses on local service it will pick up and deliver the freight within the city; if it is an intercity carrier, it will operate between specified commercial zones or cities.

For-hire-exempt-carriers have the privilege of being exempt from economic regulation. The exempt status can be obtained by the type of commodity, such as agricultural items, it transports or the type of operation it uses to move goods, such as being a supplementary service to water transportation.

The common carrier, by law, provides services to the public for a fee. The US post office and UPS are examples of common carriers. The contract carriers, on the other hand, serve specific shippers with whom the carrier has a contract and does not provide service to the public. The contract carrier usually adapts its equipment or technology to meet the special requirements for the contracted shipper. For example, FWCC, Inc. is a contract carrier that provides transportation services to contracted customers. Its service includes long haul, truckload transportation of van and temperature controlled freight.

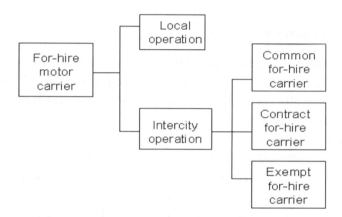

Figure 9.1. For-hire motor carrier classification

The truckload carriers provide service to shippers who meet the TL volume requirement and pay TL transportation rate. The TL carrier picks up the shipment at the origin and delivers the same truckload to the destination. The less-than-truck-load carrier provides services to shippers whose shipment volume is less than the truckload. The LTL carrier consolidates the small shipments for the intercity movement and then disaggregates the truckload at the destination city. The LTL rates are usually higher than TL rates. For example, Amazon.com hires UPS to deliver less-than truckload packages to its customers.

The cost structure of a motor carrier is determined by fixed and variable costs. The fixed cost is low because the highway cost is supported by the public, the size of the fleet is easy to adjust, and there are no requirements for terminals for TL operation. The variable costs include fuel, labor, and maintenance. In general, fixed cost counts for 10 to 30% and variable cost counts for 70 to 90 percent.

Major issues for TL include utilization, consistent service, and back hauls. Major issues for LTL include the location of consolidation facilities, vehicle routing and scheduling, customer service level, and vehicle utilization.

9.2.2 Railroads

Prior to WWII, the railroad industry was the dominant domestic transportation mode. Railroad main line mileage has been gradually shrinking from its maximum length of 390,000 miles in the 1930s to approximately 152,000 miles today in the US. However, railroad still plays an important role in today's economy. For example, rail revenue accounts for approximately one percent of GDP in 1997.

The ownership of the mileage is unequally divided among Class I and Class II railroads. Those with annual revenues of $87 million or more are classified Class I railroads and represent about 95 percent of the total railroad traffic in the US. A Class II classification is for short lines that connect shippers to the large railroads. By 2000, there were nine Class I railroads in the US. This oligopolistic market structure gives large firms the opportunity to control pricing. The railroad has the ownership of rights-of-way, which describes the equipment that the carrier uses to provide transportation service.

The railroad industry is facing competition from the trucking industry. To increase the level of railroad service, railroad management developed the piggyback service (also called intermodal) that combines trailer or container to railroad transportation. Intermodal includes trailer-on-flatcar (TOFC) and container-on-flatcar (COFC) services. To compete effectively with a motor carrier, the railroad invests in terminal facilities for loading and unloading, as well as changes in the railcars, trailers, and containers.

A railroad has high fixed cost and low variable costs. This situation exists because railroads, as well as pipelines, are the only transportation modes that own and maintain their own network and terminals. Initially, a large capital investment is required to invest in land, laying tracks, building bridges and terminals. Annual equipment maintenance costs and labor cost count for a large portion of variable cost. Fuel and power costs are the next largest groups of variable costs. Railroad is a good choice for large, heavy, high density and bulky commodity for a long haul at a low freight rate.

Major issues facing railroads include effective loading and freight scheduling to minimize both delays and early delivery because customers do not want to pay for extra storage.

The role of high technology will continue to expand and increase the ability of the railroads to provide better customer services. For example, Advanced Train Control Systems, a joint venture between the US and Canada, is developed to track the flow of the entire rail system. Additionally, new communication and signaling technology provides timely communication among dispatchers, yard workers, field workers, and the train crews.

9.2.3 Water carrier

Water carrier is the oldest economic mode of transportation and is still a viable part of the total transportation system. The water carrier system includes common, contract, exempt and private service providers. The majority of water carrier traffic is exempt from regulations.

Competition among water carriers is limited as long as there are sufficient commodities for water carriers to transport. The water carrier competes with railroads and pipelines for the movement of low value and bulky commodities. For example, railroads and water carriers compete for contract to move coals from West Virginia, Kentucky, and Pennsylvania to other parts of the US. Pipeline and water carriers compete to move petroleum and petroleum product.

The water carriers have high variable costs and low fixed costs. This is because water carriers pay for the use of right-of-way owned by the government. Additionally, the water carrier usually uses public-owned or shipper owned terminals. Labor cost is not high for water carrier service because water carriers hire people at the terminals for special types of loading and unloading operations. Water transportation is a very low-cost service, but the transit time of water service is long and subject to weather conditions.

9.2.4 Air carrier

In the early twentieth century, the airline industry began to grow. Both private and for-hire carriers operate as part of the airline transportation. The airline industry is dominated by the passenger services, but airfreight service is growing recently due to the increased volume of global sourcing. For example, Dell Inc. uses an airline carrier to ship chips from Taiwan to the US, and then uses motor carriers to ship computers to customers.

The deregulation of the airlines in 1977 allows all cargo carriers to set rates, serve routes, and use any size airplane. This new legislative decision gave an opportunity to cargo carriers such FedEx and Air Borne to penetrate the airline market.

Airlines use a hub-spoke network system to effectively manage their services. The hub-spoke model gets its name from the analogy of a bicycle wheel. The spokes spread out from the central hub. To consolidate traffic flows, commuter airplanes transport customers on low-density routes to a central hub, where customers assigned to larger planes fly the higher density routes. Sometimes, a customer may relay more than once, leading to a longer travel time.

Airlines have both a high variable cost and a low fixed cost structure. The relatively low fixed cost is due to the government investment and operations of airports and airways. Airlines usually pay for the use of publicly provided airways and terminals, which is a variable cost in nature. Fuel and labor costs are important expenses of airline service.

Major issues facing airlines include the number of hubs and their location, the location of fleet bases and crew bases, flight scheduling optimization, fleet assignment, and crew scheduling. Airline safety issues become especially important after 9.11. Recently, escalating fuel costs has caused airline revenue problems.

9.2.5 Pipeline

The pipeline transportation counts for a large portion of the transportation industry, but it is invisible to many people. Pipelines are a highly automated, efficient form of transportation and are very specialized in terms of the commodity that they can transport. Oil, natural gas, and chemical products move in large volume at a steady speed through pipelines. Pipeline service is slow and has limited accessibility. However, it is very reliable with little damage.

The development of pipelines began in the nineteenth century in Pennsylvania by the Pennsylvania Railroad. Oil companies gradually took the ownership of pipelines. Today, pipelines are owned by both oil and non-oil companies. Because of large capital investment, joint ownership of several companies becomes common.

Pipeline is a low-cost transportation mode. However, it has high level of fixed cost because of the heavy capital investment for the pipeline infrastructure. Labor cost is very low due to the highly automated operations.

9.2.6 Intermodal service

Intermodal transportation involves the joint efforts of two or more modes to complete the shipping movement. The most common forms of intermodal include piggyback (rail-truck), water-rail (container on flatcar), and truck-air. The container improves the freight interchange efficiency between the modes and enhances the value of intermodal service.

In June 2006, Dr. Patrick Sherry, co-director of the National Centre for Intermodal Transportation addressed the US House of Representatives' Committee on Transportation & Infrastructure on the issue of major challenges facing the nation's transportation system[1]. Dr. Sherry told the panel that congestion, competition, capacity, conservation and connectivity are the primary challenges facing the US logistics and transportation infrastructure today. Furthermore, he identified intermodal connectivity as the solution to the nation's transportation problems. A seamless intermodal transportation system can help maximize interconnectedness while improve the cost efficiencies of the various transportation modes.

---

[1] http://www.eyefortransport.com.

Meanwhile, the globalization trend gives rise to developing new transportation services to meeting the growing demand. In June 2006, Kansas City Southern (KCS) announced its strategic plan to provide a new daily service from Mexico to the southeastern US markets with its subsidiaries, Kansas City Southern de Mexico (KCSM) and The Kansas City Southern Railway Co (KCSR). This arrangement is to develop an International Intermodal Corridor, connecting Lazaro Cardenas to the southeast and central US with consistent and long haul rail moves.

In 2006, Norfolk Southern and Kansas City Southern announced their joint venture to expand capacity for intermodal traffic between the southeast and southwest parts of the US. Kansas City Southern contributes 320-mile line between Meridian, Miss. and Shreveport, Louisiana to the joint venture and Norfolk Southern will invest $300 million in cash for capital improvements to increase capacity and improve transit times over the line. This joint venture on transcontinental rail corridor and intermodal service supports the need for traffic growth efficiently and reliably.

9.2.7 Shipping containers

One of the most significant economic developments of international shipping in the second half of the 20th century is the introduction of shipping containers by Malcolm McLean. In the middle of 1950s, McLean came up with the idea of taking a fully loaded container from a tractor-trailer and placing it on a ship or a railroad car without breaking bulk. In this way, shipments are kept together and are protected from damage in handling. Labor costs went way down, cargo turnaround time in the port decreased significantly, and productive time for container ships increased.

Since the introduction of containerization operations, international trade has grown more than twice as fast as the global economy. It is estimated that 90 percent of the world's trade today moves in containers. Each year, about 100 million container cargos in over 5,000 container ships crisscross the oceans. The containerization allows dramatic improvement in port and ship productivity and helps to lower the cost of imported goods. For example, it took 50 days in 1970 for a standard shipment to travel from Hong Kong to New York, but it only takes 17 days today in containers.

An estimate is that the world trade will double by 2020 and container traffic will grow seven percent a year or more. The transportation infrastructure to support this level of growth in port and container operation is expected to face a shortage. Like the Port of Los Angeles, it will have two major infrastructure problems, one is limited available land left at a given site, and the other is the capacity investment rate. To further support ever-increasing world transit using containers, the major obstacles lie in infrastructure and the capital investment that transportation requires. This is not on a single country basis but on a global basis.

9.3 The Network of Shipper and Carrier in e-Distribution

The Internet has become part of our daily lives. Commercialization of the Internet spawned online shopping. Sell-side servers are electronic storefronts and catalogues that manage the purchase process from the selection of items through payment. Buy-side servers provide the capabilities for purchase orders entered and fulfilled. Usually there are well-established business rules that are incorporated into the e-commerce application. As customers want to know the exact location of their shipment, marketplace applications enable electronic communities, both buyers and sellers, to track and trace orders.

9.3.1 Carrier side e-Distribution

Today, transportation and logistics companies use the Internet to provide customer-side services. Transportation providers offer their customers the ability to log onto their Web sites to check their shipments. For example, US Postal Office and FedEx allow their customers to log onto web sites to track and trace their packages.

Many of these e-Business solutions were developed due to the market requirements. When a customer opts to visit a Web site instead of calling the service center, the company usually benefits, as the option requires no paid employee. This option not only eliminates the risk of any unfavorable exchange between the customer and the service representative, but also reduces costs. Internet service becomes even more desirable when the supply chain serves a global market, where customers can call 24 hours a day. The range of these solutions has varied. Some companies have tried to create a competitive advantage with their Web pages by developing signature options unique to their brands. Others provide a customized portal for each customer including offering languages other than English.

There are some obstacles in implementing carrier-side e-Commerce. For example, if a shipper wishes to track an individual shipment using intermodal service, he must go to a Web page of each logistics provider. Multiple shipments therefore require constant movements between Web pages. Additionally, carriers have to know their shipment ID, which they may not have handy, to locate their shipments online. When intermodal transportation movement is involved, truckers usually are the last link in the intermodal chain. They must know when equipment is ready for movement. However, very often they suffer from incomplete information.

Major port areas experience the same problem. Truckers have to log on to a number of Web sites for different steamship lines and marine terminals. Lacking timely information, the truckers are unable to maximize their transportation capacity. For example, they may leave a terminal with an empty truckload, not realizing that a return move is available.

9.3.2 Shipper side e-Distribution

Shipper-side e-Commerce determines the ultimate configuration of the market and the industry landscape. Although e-Commerce is still in its early stage, some companies have already generated significant savings by moving their transportation purchasing to the Internet. In many cases, multiple vendors offer sales to multiple shippers, which give the shipper the opportunity to select the most suitable carrier.

9.3.3 The network of shipper and carrier in e-Distribution

The transportation industry can be broken down to a couple of groups. At the basic level, a carrier provides services directly to a customer. Hence, a one-to-one relationship is formed. Shippers have numerous bilateral contracts with carriers, and carriers have many one-to-one contracts with shippers.

Beyond this basic arrangement, there are two other marketplace arrangements. One arrangement is to post announcements on bulletin boards at truck stops or rest places. Truckers post notes offering capacity and responding to requests for hauling capacity. This method is the simplest but requires an actual presence at the truck stop or rest place. The other arrangement is to let truck brokerages perform load matching task. Over time, truck brokerage has evolved into third party logistic providers (3PL).

The e-Commerce bulletin board grows out of the traditional method. Here, the provider gathers and posts information about available loads from carriers and desired loads by shippers. When shippers or carriers see an item, they can contact the other party. This eBusiness model is simple. The bulletin board provider charges a monthly subscription fee and offers levels of service.

Another type of marketplace e-Commerce is auction. Web sites serve as a freight rate auction marketplace. Shippers either place their desired bids on the site for carriers to view or offer bids or they may just request the carriers' best rates. Carriers also take advantage of e-Commerce. Some carriers advertise capacity and seek bids for it. This process usually is blind. At a predetermined date and time, the winning bid is announced.

Some carriers are afraid that e-Commerce penetration may drive freight rates down. People with this worry may consider the following three arguments.

First, e-Commerce penetration is determined by supply and demand in addition to market aggregation and intermediation. A market with a few major carriers such as the railroad industry and airlines will be harder to penetrate than one with numerous carriers such as interstate truckers.

Second, e-Commerce solutions can be introduced easier to markets that have well-established transportation intermediaries (the trucking industry) than to markets that do not traditionally rely on intermediaries.

Third, e-Commerce business models will not cause rates to fall further than they should, but may drive shipping rates to fall a little faster.

Concerns on the shipper's side lie on the decision of when to purchase transportation services. If shippers suspect that demand is close to, or exceeds supply, they will want contracts for their expected loads and transportation service. However, if they suspect that supply will exceed demand, they will tend to wait and purchase transportation service on the spot market.

Information is a critical component of the supply chain and will continue to drive change in the transportation and logistics markets. The number of transportation and logistics e-Commerce products proliferates daily. While many B2B sites claim to eliminate the need for intermediaries, many are becoming intermediaries in their own right.

9.4 The Rise of Intermediaries in Transportation

9.4.1 The rise of intermediaries

In recent years, an increased awareness of core competencies becomes part of competitive culture. As more sophisticated financial tools, such as activity-based costing and economic value-added activities entered the corporate mainstream, management began to consider outsourcing non-core functions and concentrate on their core competencies and customers. Outsourcing non-core function such as logistics and transportation allows a company to take advantage of greater operational flexibility. For example, Anheuser-Busch controls the majority of its supply chain functions including agricultural supply, brewing, and distribution, but it outsources logistics function such as warehousing to the third party providers.

Meanwhile, carriers may find pricing on the spot market unappealing. However, they lack accurate demand forecast, effective information systems, and personnel to handle such market dynamics. In order to avoid selling loading capacity at a steep discount, carriers seek contracts with 3PL providers for large cargo commitments. The rates for large volume may be lower than the smaller volume load, but this option requires fewer employees, less time, and less information technology.

As such, intermediaries provide functions such as shipment consolidation, marketing, information collection, and matching supply and demand from carriers and shippers. In general, intermediaries make purchased transportation decisions on two levels: buy and sell loading capacity and transportation services. Today, a transportation system is supported by a number of intermediary services, including shippers association, brokers, shipper's agents, owner-operators, and express companies. It has been estimated that more than 60% of Fortune 500 manufacturers used some form of third-party logistics services. The following two sections briefly discuss third party logistics and fourth party logistics since we have discussed both topics in Chapter 4, *Supply Relations and Strategic Sourcing*.

9.4.2 Third-party logistics in transportation services

Third-party logistics providers are firms that manage and execute certain value-add logistics and transportation functions on behalf of their customers, using their own assets and resources. Successful 3PLs provide service throughout the world using various modes such as surface, ocean, and air.

Third party transportation providers offer an array of logistics services, including carrier selection, route scheduling, shipment storage, partial assembly of parts, and transportation. Using 3PLs services, businesses are able to reduce operating costs and capital expenses. Some customers believe they can benefit from scope and scale economy that is unavailable from individual carriers. For example, Nortel Networks is a global leader in telecommunications equipment and supplies industry customers in 150 countries. Its customers require Nortel to deliver products just in time to their production sites. At the beginning of 2002, Nortel outsourced its entire $200 million in logistics operations to Kuehne & Nagel. Kuehne & Nagel created a separate company, KN Lead Logistics (KNLL), to handle Nortel's more than 80 primary and 200 secondary logistics service providers. After using 3PL service,

Nortel only needs to contact KNLL for a range of logistics and transportation operations such as warehouse storage, delivery, distribution network design, and global systems connectivity. Nortel is able to strengthen its core competencies that provide differentiated value to the customer. Both Nortel and KNLL are able to share the financial benefits of supply-chain performance improvement.

According to a recent survey of Fortune 500 companies on 3PLs conducted jointly by Northeastern University and Accenture, 83 percent of these companies use third-party logistics providers and nearly 60 percent use multiple 3PLs. According to a survey covering Global 1000 companies conducted by the Georgia Institute of Technology and Cap Gemini Ernst & Young, major U.S. companies spend 49 percent of their entire logistics budget on 3PLs. At the same time, large European companies spend 65 percent of their logistics budget to 3PLs[2].

9.4.3 Fourth-party logistics in transportation service

In general, people agree that fourth-party logistics providers emerged to cover informational technology needs in transportation. However, the true evolution of the 4PL is due to the growth of the global marketplace. Companies in the global marketplace become aware of the fact that logistics is not a commodity or a simple client - service relationship; it is a critical means to boosting their cost savings, enhancing their cash flow, and improving servicing levels for getting their products to market. In this sense, a 4PL provider is a supply chain integrator that synthesizes and manages the resources, capabilities, and technology of its own organization with those of complementary service providers to deliver an e-Commerce supply chain solution to its customers. A 4PL company provides strategy-consulting, reviews and redesigns its customer's business process, integrates various technologies, and leverages human resources. When a 4PL company provides 3PL services, it becomes known as an *infomediary*. A 4PL provider is a strategic partner instead of a tactical transportation service provider such as the 3PL.

---

[2] Thomas A. Foster, "The Trends Changing the Face of Logistics Outsourcing Worldwide." http://www.glscs.com, 2004.

9.5 Trade-Off of Transportation and Inventory Costs

When making transportation decisions, a number of factors need to be considered. These factors include inventory-holding cost, facility cost; order processing cost, transportations cost, and other relevant costs. Supply chain managers often consider the following trade-offs.

- Trade-off between inventory and transportation costs
- Trade-off between transportation mode and customer service target.

The following is an example problem regarding trade-offs between transportation choices and inventory costs.

Example Problem 9.1: Trade-Offs Between Transportation and Inventory Costs

Located near Norfolk, VA, Flow Pump Corporation offers a wide range of pump types, from pre-engineering process pumps to highly specialized purpose pumps and systems. It purchases all the motors for its pumps from Quik Motors, Inc. Flow Pump has an average demand of 30,000 motors annually. Each motor averages about 40 pounds in weight. Quik Motors charges $600 per motor. Usually, it takes one day for Quik Motors to process the orders from Flow Pump (i.e. if Quik Motors receives the order from Flow Pump on Monday, it will ship the order on Tuesday).

Flow Pump has an order processing cost of $50 per order. Inventory holding cost is 25% of the item-purchasing price. At its assembly plant, Flow Pump carries a safety inventory equals to 5 percent of the average demand during the carrier's delivery lead-time. Flow Pump operates 300 days a year.

The plant manager at Flow Pump wants to balance inventory costs and transportation costs before he selects a transportation option. Available transportation options are given below:

Carrier	Quantity shipped (pound)	Shipping cost($/lb)	Lead-time
Southern Railroad	20,000 & more	0.10	6 days
Southeast Trucking TL	10,000	0.15	3 days
Southeast Trucking LTL	no weight limit	0.20	4 days

The less-than-truck-load (LTL) option consolidates the small shipments for the intercity movement and then disaggregates the truckload at the destination. As such, the LTL option has a longer lead-time than Truckload (TL). The manager would like you to figure out the following issues.

a. What is the lot size for each option?
b. What is the number of orders for the year?
c. What is the cycle inventory?
d. What is the safety inventory?
e. What is the ordering cost?
f. What is the transportation cost?
g. What is the cycle inventory holding cost?
h. What is the safety stock holding cost?
i. What are the total costs that include cycle inventory cost, safety stock cost, order cost, and transportation cost for each option?
j. Which option would you recommend to the plant manager based on the cost analysis? What other relevant factors you would suggest to the manager?

Solution to example Problem 9.1

Below, we show detailed computational procedure for the choice of <u>Southern Railroad</u> service, answers to all three choices are presented in Table 9.1.

a. Lot size = $\dfrac{20,000 \text{ lb}}{40 \text{ lb}}$ = 500 units

b. Number of orders for a year = $\dfrac{30,000}{500}$ = 60 orders

c. Cycle inventory = $\dfrac{Q}{2} = \dfrac{500}{2}$ = 250 units

d. Safety inventory = $0.05 * 6 * \dfrac{30,000}{300}$ = 30 units

e. Ordering cost = $50 * 60 = \$3,000$

f. Transportation cost = $0.10 * (30,000*40) = \$120,000$

g. Cycle inventory cost = ($600 * 0.25) * 250 = $37,500

h. Safety inventory cost = ($600 * 0.25) * 30 = $4,500

i. Total cost = order cost + transportation cost + total inventory cost
   = $3,000 + $120,000 + ($37,500 + $4,500) = $165,000

j. Based on the cost analysis shown in Table 9.1, the plant manager decides to purchase transportation service from Truck-TL. The other factors can be considered include on time delivery, flexibility, customer service level, cash flow, etc.

9.6 Vehicle Routing and Scheduling

A good selection of transportation mode can provide a company with competitive cost advantage because transportation costs usually range from one-third to two-thirds of total logistics costs. An important decision problem in transportation is to find the best travel route that minimizes the distance or time that a vehicle can follow.

There are a number of factors need to be considered when develop a vehicle route and schedule. These factors include loading and unloading at each stop; multiple vehicles with similar or different capacities in volume and weight; maximum driving period limitation (e.g. an eight-hour shirt); time window for pick up and delivery to avoid traffic time or meet business office hour, such as deliver beer to a restaurant before dinner time.

One of the most important decisions in vehicle transportation management is select routes and schedule deliveries. Route is a sequence of pickup and / or delivery points which the vehicle must follow in order. Schedule is a set of arrival and departure times for the pickup and / or delivery points specified in the route.

When arrival times are specified at facilities on an existing road, we refer to the problem as a scheduling problem. When arrival times are unspecified, the problem is a straightforward routing problem. When time windows and precedence relationships exit, both routing and scheduling functions are performed.

Table 9.1. Summary of the cost structure of three options

	① lot size	② number of orders	③ cycle inventory	④ safety stock	⑤ order cost	⑥ transportation cost	⑦ inventory holding cost	⑧ safety stock cost	⑨ total cost
Railroad	500	60	250	30	3,000	120,000	37,500	4,500	165,000
Truck TL	250	120	125	15	6,000	180,000	18,750	2,250	207,000
Truck LTL	141	213	70.5	20	10,638.3	240,000	10,575	3,000	264,213.3

Note:
The lot size for truck (LTL) is computed as follows:

$$EOQ = \sqrt{\frac{2DS}{h*p}} = \sqrt{\frac{2(30000)50}{0.25(600)}} = 141 \text{ units}$$

9.6.1 Characteristics describing vehicle routing

The objective of motor services is to minimize routing costs incurred, minimize sum of fixed and variable costs, and provide the best service possible. There are a number of factors that a motor carrier needs to consider in offering motor services.

- Demand. The nature of demand can be stable or sporadic and delivery time can be specified in advance or unspecified.
- Facility and equipment. There are various kinds of facility and equipment. For example, there can be one terminal or several terminals. The type of vehicles can be one size or different sizes. Vehicle capacity constraints are imposed either consistently or at certain time windows. Routes are direct or indirect, or even mixed.
- Costs. There are a number of costs for providing service. For example, purchase a vehicle or lease a vehicle. Fixed operating costs such as terminals fee and airport gates ticket. Trip related cost such as labor cost and fuel expense. Quantity related cost such as loading and unloading cost, and overhead costs.
- Type of service. Type of service offered can be pick up only, drop off only such as UPS service. Alternatively, a mix of pick up and drop off service, such as post office mail carrier who picks up the out-going mail we leave in the mailbox and drops the in-coming mail in the mailbox.

There is a number of factors affect a shipper's decision. Various costs related to transportation are usually the important factors that affect shippers' decisions. These costs include mode related transportation cost, load-related inventory cost, facility cost, order-processing cost, and service level cost.

9.6.2 Solution procedure for vehicle routing and scheduling

The vehicle routing and scheduling problem is getting more complicated as more constraints are added to the problem. A number of solution procedures are developed over the years. Among them, the Saving Method suggested by Clarke and Wright is one that is able to handle a range of constraints. The following steps are taken to create routes and make travel schedules based on the model suggested by Clarke and Wright. The first three steps are used to assign customers to routes, and the fourth step creates schedule for each vehicle to minimize the distance traveled, to minimize the transportation cost.

1. Compute the distance matrix. The distance between the warehouse and the customer and a pair of customers is determined using the following formula.

Distance (between store and customer) =
$$\sqrt{(store_x - cust_{ix})^2 + (store_y - cust_{iy})^2} \qquad (9.1)$$
Where:

$Store_x$ = x coordinate of store

$Store_y$ = y coordinate of store

$Cust_{ix}$ = x coordinate of customer i

$Cust_{iy}$ = y coordinate of customer i

2. Compute the savings matrix. The savings in distance between tow customers i and j is determined by

Saving ($Cust_i$, $Cust_j$) = distance (store, $Cust_i$)

   + distance (store, $Cust_j$) – distance ($Cust_i$, $Cust_j$) $\qquad (9.2)$

3. Create routes. Assign customers to routes. Initially, we assume that there are as many routes as the number of customers. Search the Savings Matrix created in Step 2 for the intersection of customer$_i$ and customer$_j$ that has the largest savings. Consider combining route x with route y if add additional customer to the route will not exceed the vehicle capacity, and if neither route x nor route y has been combined to some other route. If a single customer's load exceeds the capacity of a truck, split the load to two vehicles.

4. Develop delivery schedule. First sequence customers within the route to make a schedule. The nearest insertion method is applied. Based on the distance matrix computed in Step 1, the customer closest to the current trip is inserted first.

The nearest insertion method. The procedure is called the nearest insertion method because it adds the customer that is closest to the route. The procedure is as follows.

- With a given route, determine the minimum increase in distance and insert the closest customer to the route.
- Continue this process until all customers assigned to the vehicle are inserted to the route.

Example Problem 9.2: Vehicle Routing and Scheduling

Farm Fresh, a grocery store, delivers customer orders that are placed on-line. One morning, the manager at Farm Fresh has orders from nine different customers that are to be delivered. Table 9.2 shows the locations of the store and the customers, and the customer order size. There are four minivans available, each capable of carrying up to 260 kilograms.

Table 9.2.

	X coordinate	Y coordinate	Order Size (kilogram)
Store	0	0	
Customer 1	5	13	38
Customer 2	2	9	91
Customer 3	8	16	57
Customer 4	9	11	47
Customer 5	13	2	30
Customer 6	18	1	56
Customer 7	15	-6	92
Customer 8	10	-9	43
Customer 9	4	-11	36

a. Using the Savings Method to determine the number of routes (minivans) needed to deliver orders that morning.
   - Create a distance matrix
   - Create a savings matrix
   - Assign customers to route (vehicle)

b. Make a schedule for each route (vehicle) using the Nearest Insertion Method.

Solution to Problem 9.2: Vehicle Routing and Scheduling

Step 1: Create distance matrix

Use equation 9.1 to compute distance matrix. The results of distances between the store and all the customers, and among the customers are reported in Table 9.3. For example, compute the distance from the store to customer 1:

$$\text{Distance (store, Cust 1)} = \sqrt{(0-5)^2 + (0-13)^2} = 13.93$$

Now let us compute the distance from customer 3 to customer 4:

$$\text{Distance (Cust 3, Cust 4)} = \sqrt{(8-9)^2 + (16-11)^2} = 5.10$$

Table 9.3. Distance matrix

	Store	Cust 1	Cust 2	Cust 3	Cust 4	Cust 5	Cust 6	Cust 7	Cust 8	Cust 9
Cust 1	13.93	0.00								
Cust 2	9.22	5.00	0.00							
Cust 3	17.89	4.24	9.22	0.00						
Cust 4	14.21	4.47	7.28	5.10	0.00					
Cust 5	13.15	13.60	13.04	14.87	9.85	0.00				
Cust 6	18.03	17.69	17.89	18.03	13.45	5.10	0.00			
Cust 7	16.16	21.47	19.85	23.09	18.03	8.25	7.62	0.00		
Cust 8	13.45	22.56	19.70	25.08	20.02	11.40	12.81	5.83	0.00	
Cust 9	11.70	24.02	20.10	27.29	22.56	15.81	18.44	12.08	6.32	0.00

Step 2: Create savings matrix

Use equation 9.2 to compute savings matrix. The results of savings between a pair of customers are reported in Table 9.4.

We assume that the minivan will travel to each customer from the store separately without saving. For example, the van travels from the store to customer 1, and then comes back from customer 1 to the store; travels from the store to customer 2, and then comes back from customer 2 to the store. The total distance is:

Distance (store ↔ customer 1, store ↔ customer 2)
= 13.93 + 13.93 + 9.22 + 9.22 = 46.30

If the van travels from the store to customer 1, then from customer 1 to customer 2, and travels back from customer 2 to the store. The total distance will be:

Distance (store → customer 1 → customer 2 → store)
= 13.93 + 5 + 9.22 = 28.15

Savings between customers 1 and 2 is:

Savings (Cust 1, Cust 2) = 46.30 − 28.15 = 18.15

Table 9.4. Savings matrix

	Cust 1	Cust 2	Cust 3	Cust 4	Cust 5	Cust 6	Cust 7	Cust 8	Cust 9
Cust 1	0.00								
Cust 2	18.15	0.00							
Cust 3	27.57	17.89	0.00						
Cust 4	23.67	16.15	27.00	0.00					
Cust 5	13.48	9.33	16.18	17.52	0.00				
Cust 6	14.26	9.36	17.89	18.79	26.08	0.00			
Cust 7	8.61	5.53	10.96	12.34	21.06	26.57	0.00		
Cust 8	4.82	2.98	6.26	7.64	15.20	18.68	23.78	0.00	
Cust 9	1.61	0.82	2.30	3.36	9.05	11.29	15.78	18.83	0.00

Step 3: Assign customers to routes

First, make each customer an independent route. There are nine routes to start with. Then, search for the largest savings between two customers from Table 9.4 the Savings Matrix. Saving between customers 1 and 3 is the largest, 27.57. Check order sizes and van capacity: 38 + 57 < 260. Customers 1 and 3 can be combined to form a new route. We call this route 1.

The next largest saving is 27, which is between customers 3 and 4. Check order sizes and van capacity: 38 + 57 + 47 < 260. Customer 4 can be combined to Route 1. Now Route 1 has three customers 1, 3, and 4.

The next largest saving is 26.57, which is between customers 6 and 7. Customers 6 and 7 do not intersect with the customers 1, 3, and 4 in Route 1. Besides, if both customer 6 and 7 are added to Route 1, the total order sizes of 5 customers will exceed the van capacity. Therefore, we create a new route for customers 6 and 7. This route is named Route 2.

Continue the search, Route 1 ends up with 4 customers (1, 3, 4, and 2) and a total load of 233 (38+57+47+91 = 233). The Route 2 has five customers (6, 7, 5, 8, and 9) and a total load of 257 (56 + 92 + 30 + 43 + 36 = 257).

Step 4: Sequence customers within the route to make a schedule

Next, we use the Distance Matrix in Table 3 to make travel schedules. Figure 9.2 shows the tow routes.

Route 1: The shortest distance from the store to customers 1, 2, 3, and 4 is between the store and customer 2. The route starts from the store to Customer 2. The next shortest distance between customer 2 and customers 1, 3, and 4 is between customer 2 and customer 1. The route is extended to store – Cust 2 – Cust 1. Continue this procedure, until the schedule is complete. Route 1 has the following schedule:

Store → Cust 2 → Cust 1 → Cust 3 → Cust 4 → store.
The total distance is: 9.22 + 5 + 4.24 + 5.10 + 14.21 = 37.77

Route 2 has the following schedule:
Store → Cust 9 → Cust 8 → Cust 7 → Cust 6 → Cust 5 → store.
The total distance is: 11.70+6.32+5.83+7.62+5.10+13.15 = 49.72

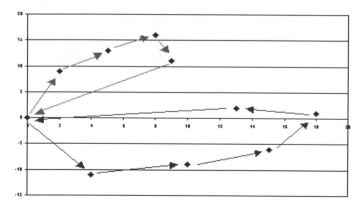

Figure 9.2. Routes

9.6.3 e-Business tools for creating routes

Some Internet search engines offer a convenient way to build delivery routes. For example, using google maps and Mapquest, readers can enter the addresses they want to visit and create a route. But these tools do not provide ways to handle delivery time window constraints and the weight capacity of vehicles. Consequently, human intelligence is needed to create delivery routes that take care of various constraints.

9.7 Railway Freight Car Scheduling

With the globalization of world economy and the birth of free-trade zones, railway freight services have played an important role in the development of modern transportation networks in Asia, Europe, the United States, and many other countries. The offshore sourcing of goods in the Pacific Rim countries leads to the increased use of water-rail-truck intermodal service. As such, railroad transportation has gained renewed attention for its capacity of transferring bulk commodities over long distances at a lower freight rate.

In practice, it is difficult to allocate the freight cars and to determine how to load varieties of goods into them in a large-scale railway network. Railway freight service requires sophisticated algorithms as well as flexibility. Both practitioners and researchers have indicated that a knowledge-based system can be useful for making decisions in railway freight services. Geng and Li have suggested a model for freight car loading and routing, and a knowledge-based system for railway freight service that is integrated into an existing railway information system[3]. The combination of loading rules, routing algorithms, logic programming and database technology provides railway managers with a practical way to manage railway freight service.

---

[3] Geng, G. and Li, L (2001) "Scheduling railway freight cars" *Knowledge-based Systems,* 14, 289-297.

9.7.1 Railway system

A railway system is a network of track sections connected to one another by stations and termini. The advantage of using railway service is that it delivers large volume, low value items over long distances at a low cost. With the advancement of supply chain management, the railroads have expanded their operations to intermodal services that lead to increased growth in loadings.

The carload is the basic unit of measurement of freight handled by the railroad. Therefore, loading and routing are two major operation issues to ensure reliable service for shippers. The overall objective is to maximize freight car utilization and minimize the distance traveled.

In railway service, there usually is a start station which dispatches a freight train; a stop station where the freight train complete the trip, and transfer stations that serves as a depot that covers a number of stations within a network of vertices. Commodities of smaller quantity from ordinary stations or other transfer stations are transported to the transfer station for consolidation, loading and unloading.

9.7.2 Characteristics describing railway freight scheduling

Freight car loading usually use some sort of priority rules. Loading priority is a function of commodity attribute, delivery due date, delivery time window, delivery date priority, core shipment status, and commodity weight.

Possible commodity attributes include fresh and live goods, coal, chemical and allied products, farm products, motor vehicles, equipment, military goods, food and kindred products, non-metallic minerals and other. A great number of chemicals and allied products are classified as hazardous.

Core shipment is a shipment of heavy weight. Railway authorities determine the weight; for example a shipment exceeds 5000 kilogram is a core shipment. The purpose of determining the core shipment is to realize 'more loading in a freight car with fewer stops'. A core shipment may include only one commodity. Several small shipments can be arranged to a core. Commodities of a core shipment are transported to the same stop station or transfer station. Using the core shipment priority method, the railway storage utilization will be improved, so will transportation efficiency.

In general, shipments with heavy weight but small-volume are not to be placed in the same freight car, nor are the goods with large-volume light weight to be placed in the same freight car. A mix of heavy weight, small-volume commodities and light weight, large-volume goods can better utilize freight car space.

When a train arrives at a transfer station, some goods are unloaded and additional goods are loaded onto the freight car. In this case, additional goods loaded to the rail car at the current stop should not disturb the unloading operation at the next station. This is to determine which item is to be loaded into the railcar first and which is to be loaded second. Transference range must be considered when loading additional goods.

Loading hazardous goods is a tough job. Any carelessness will result in an accident. Therefore, considerable attention is paid to loading hazardous goods.

The railway network is pre-existing. The length of legs between consecutive stations is fixed. The speed on the leg between any two stations is assumed constant. The selection of the best routes for each freight train determines the workloads and the general consolidation strategies for each station of the railway system.

The input information for arranging freight car loading and scheduling include commodity attribute, commodity weight, commodity volume, hazardous / perishable goods, number of days a commodity is in the rail yard, loading priority rating, neighbor distances, transfer range (the distance from a transfer station to every station within the transfer range) and transfer path (the shortest path between two transfer stations). The output of freight car scheduling include loading sequence of commodity by freight car, primary route, the 2nd and 3rd possible routes, freight car capacity utilization by each by freight car and by day of week.

9.8 Enhance Value through Transportation

The transportation industry is a vital, contributing group in world trade and economic growth. Over the past ten years, U.S. international trade in goods has doubled and this rate is not going to slow down in the next decade. The low transportation rates enhance the competitiveness of U.S. products in world markets and enable importers to bring a variety of industry and consumer goods to the US as well. For example, transportation adds a dollar to a VCR from Hong Kong to the US market; ocean shipping services from Asia added about 40 cents to the price of the sneakers[4]. As the supply chain is further extended, transportation service truly adds value to supply chain management.

Considering the biggest transportation and logistic issues facing the supply chain, a survey of managers from Fortune 500 companies conducted in 2005 indicated that tight carrier capacity, port congestion, and warehouse management were on the top of the list of the most pressing issues[5]. More investment is needed to support the expected doubling of freight volume by 2020. The US Federal Highway Administration anticipates the freight volume to grow by 70% by 2020. To support the U.S. trade flows and add value to the world economy, a seamless and efficient multi-modal transportation system is needed. The intermodal operation should be able to link large-size cargo vessels, complex cargo handling, effective storage operations, reliable rail service, and extensive trucking coverage.

Tight collaboration among supply chain companies will be more popular in the years to come. Mark Colombo, vice president for strategic marketing at FedEx, talked about a study of lean supply chain and manufacturing in the electronics industry[6]. In that survey, 87 percent of respondents said they expected their level of imports to increase beyond where it is now. These companies are already implementing global supply chains and may add another sub-production facility located in Asia or South America or even in Europe. In this case, they will

---

[4] The World Shipping Council.
[5] www.eyefortransport.com/supplychain.
[6] http://www.worldtrademag.com/CDA/Archives/.

transport their products from the production center to the customer-centered markets. The loads can start out as ground into air or ground into ocean. The issue is how integrated their logistic and transportation networks are going to support their supply chain needs. In the same survey, sixty-eight percent of the respondents said they expected collaboration and tight integration with their transportation providers, because their customers are expecting short lead times and high responsiveness.

9.9 Summary

In this chapter, we give an overview of various transportation modes and their role in supply chain management. The rise of intermediary, third party logistics and fourth party logistics have rapidly change the landscape of transportation industry in the US and world. E-Distribution becomes a new way of doing business in a global market. Transportation is no longer a minor function of a company. It has strategic importance to the success of a supply chain.

Questions for Pondering

1. Compare and contrast the cost structure, market structure, customer service policy, business infrastructure, and operations management of truckload and LTL segments of motor carrier industry in the US.
2. The railroad industry contributed significantly to the development and growth of cities and economic centers prior to WWII. The trucking industry contributed to the development and growth of cities and economic centers in the second half of the twentieth century. The airline industry has grown very fast after 1978 and is facing financial difficulties in recent years. Discuss the political, economic, social, technological and industry competitive factors that contribute to the growth and decline of various transportation modes. In your opinion, what will be the next dominant transportation mode? Why?

3. Discuss the advantage and disadvantages of the rise of intermediary, third and forth party logistics. Provide industry evidence with your discussions.

Problems

1. The Suzuki, Inc. supplies window fans to Best Appliances Distributor. Best Appliances Distributor is responsible for transportation arrangement and cost. Best Appliances Distributor purchases 100,000 units annually at an average of $10.00 per fan. Inventory cost is 25% of the unit purchasing cost. Order processing cost is $30 per order. Best Appliances operates 350 days a year.

The director of transportation at Best Appliances has collected the following information and hired you to complete the analysis. You need to present a solution that would minimize transportation and inventory costs. Consider the costs of cycle inventory and safety stocks, and transportation cost.

Transportation Mode	Transit Time	Rate Per Unit	Lot Size / Shipment Size
Railway	30 days	$1.00	1,000
Piggyback	12 days	$1.20	500
Truck	4 days	$1.30	200

2. A warehouse that distributes kitchen appliances is considering proposals from two trucking companies. Demand and inventory costs are given below.

Forecasted demand	5000 units /year
Order cost	$117 / order
Product price	$ 75 / unit
Inventory holding cost	25% of unit price

The warehouse operates 365 days a year and uses EOQ as its order quantity. The information about the two trucking companies is given below.

Trucking Company	Transit Time	Rate Per Unit	Variability in Delivery Time (std dev.)
Swift Trucking	3 days	$15	1day
OnTime Trucking	4 days	$13.5	2days

a. What is in-transit inventory without variability in delivery time?
b. What is in-transit inventory with variability in delivery time? Consider a one standard deviation case only.
c. What is the total cost?
d. Which trucking company should the warehouse select?
e. What other factors should be considered other than the cost?

3. FreshBread delivers customer orders daily to 10 grocery stores. One morning, the manager at FreshBread had the orders as shown in the following table. There are two vans available, each capable of carrying up to 500 loaves of bread.

	X coordinate	Y coordinate	Order Size
FreshBread warehouse	0	0	
Store 1	5	13	38
Store 2	2	9	91
Store 3	8	16	57
Store 4	9	11	47
Store 5	13	2	30
Store 6	18	1	56
Store 7	15	-6	92
Store 8	10	-9	43
Store 9	4	-11	36
Store 10	4	-11	36

a. Using the Savings Method to determine the number of routes (vans) needed to deliver orders that morning.
b. Make a schedule for each route (van) using the Nearest Insertion Method.

References

Ballou, R.H. (1992). *Business Logistics Management*, 3ʳᵈ edition. Prentice Hall: New Jersey.

Bodin, L. and Golden, B. (1981). Classification in Vehicle Routing and Scheduling, *Networks*, Vol. 11, 97-108.

Chopra, S. and Meindl, P. 2002. *Supply Chain Management*. Prentice Hall: New Jersey.

Clarke, G. and Wright, J.W. (1963). "Scheduling of vehicles form a central depot to a number of delivery points." *Operations Research*, Vol. 11, 568-581.

Coyle, John J., Bardi, Edward J., and Novack, Robert A. (1999). *Transportation*, 5ᵗʰ edition. South-western: Cincinnati, OH.

Prince, Theodore (2000). E-Commerce: It's Impact on Transportation, Logistics, and Supply Chain Management, 4/15/2000 *ASCET,* Volume 2.

Simchi-Levi, D., Kaminsky, P., and Simchi-Levi, E. (2003). *Designing and Managing the Supply Chain*, 2ⁿᵈ edition. McGraw-Hill Irwin: New York.

www.aar.org/AboutTheIndustry/AboutTheIndustry.asp.

Appendix 1

World Container Ports: Top 25 2001-2003							
Rank					2003	2002	2001
2003	2002	2001	Name of Port	Country	(millions TEUs)		
1	1	1	Hong Kong	China	20.499	19.14	17.83
2	2	2	Singapore	Singapore	18.411	16.94	15.57
3	4	5	Shanghai	China	11.28	8.61	6.34
4	6	8	Shenzhen	China	10.615	7.62	5.08
5	3	3	Pusan	South Korea	10.408	9.45	8.07
6	5	4	Kaohsiung	Taiwan	8.843	8.49	7.54
7	8	7	Los Angeles	USA	7.149	6.11	5.18
8	7	6	Rotterdam	Netherlands	7.107	6.52	6.1
9	9	9	Hamburg	Germany	6.138	5.37	4.69
10	10	11	Antwerp	Belgium	5.445	4.78	4.22
11	13	13	Dubai	United Arab Emirates	5.152	4.19	3.5
12	11	12	Port Kelang	Malaysia	4.84	4.53	3.76
13	12	10	Long Beach	USA	4.658	4.53	4.46
14	15	16	Qingdao	China	4.239	3.41	2.64
15	14	14	New York & New Jersey	USA	4.068	3.75	3.32
16	21	25	Tanjung Pelepas	Indonesea	3.487	2.66	2.05
17	19	17	Tokyo	Japan	3.314	2.78	2.61
18	16	15	Bremen/Bremerhaven	Germany	3.19	3.03	2.97
19	22	20	Laem Chabang	Thailand	3.181	2.6	2.37
20	17	18	Gioia Tauro	Italy	3.149	3.01	2.49
21	24	26	Tianjin	China	3.015	2.41	2.01
22	31	46	Ningbo	China	2.772	1.86	1.21
23	27	33	Guangzhou/Huangpu	China	2.762	2.17	1.74
24	20	19	Tanjung Priok (Jakarta)	Indonesea	2.758	2.7	2.5
25	23	21	Manila	Phillippines	2.552	2.46	2.3

source: www.oocl.com & www.infoplease.com

Appendix 2

Airport Cargo Loading & Unloading: Top 25 2001-2003						
Rank				2003	2002	2001
2003	2002	2001	Name of Airport	Tonnage		
1	1	1	MEMPHIS (MEM)	3,390,515	3,390,800	261,631
2	2	2	HONG KONG (HKG)	2,668,880	2,504,584	2,100,276
3	3	5	TOKYO (NRT)	2,154,691	2,001,822	1,680,937
4	5	3	ANCHORAGE (ANC)**	2,102,025	1,771,595	1,873,750
5	6	15	SEOUL (ICN)	1,843,055	1,705,880	1,196,843
6	4	4	LOS ANGELES (LAX)	1,833,300	1,779,855	1,774,402
7	9	8	PARIS (CDG)	1,723,700	1,626,400	1,591,310
8	8	7	FRANKFURT/MAIN (FRA)	1,650,476	1,631,322	1,613,179
9	10	6	MIAMI (MIA)	1,637,278	1,624,242	1,639,760
10	7	9	SINGAPORE (SIN)	1,632,409	1,660,404	1,529,930
11	11	11	NEW YORK (JFK)	1,626,722	1,589,648	1,430,727
12	12	10	LOUISVILLE (SDF)	1,618,336	1,524,181	1,468,837
13	13	12	CHICAGO (ORD)	1,510,746	1,473,980	1,299,628
14	14	16	TAIPEI (TPE)	1,500,071	1,380,748	1,189,874
15	16	14	AMSTERDAM (AMS)	1,353,760	1,288,626	1,234,161
16	15	13	LONDON (LHR)	1,300,420	1,310,615	1,263,572
17	26		SHANGHAI (PUG)*	1,189,303	634,966	
18	21	25	DUBAI (DXB)	956,795	784,997	632,224
19	17	19	BANGKOK (BKK)	950,136	956,790	841,150
20	18	17	INDIANAPOLIS (IND)	889,163	901,917	1,115,272
21	19	20	NEWARK (EWR)	874,641	850,050	795,584
22	22	22	ATLANTA (ATL)	798,501	734,083	739,927
23	20	18	OSAKA (KIX)	793,478	805,430	871,161
24	23	23	TOKYO (HND)	722,736	707,301	725,124
25	24	21	DALLAS/FT WORTH(DFW)	667,574	670,310	784,085

* new airport
** including transfer freight
source: Airport Council International

PART FIVE

E-Business Solutions

Chapter 10
E-Business Solutions: The Enabler of Global Supply Chain

Chapter 11
Business Intelligence in Supply Chain Management: Data, Information, and Knowledge

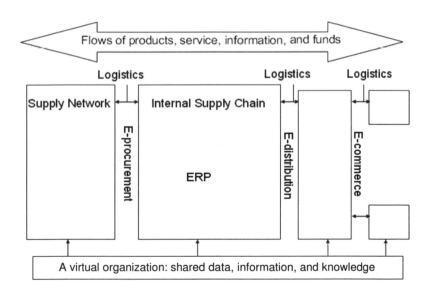

Chapter 10

e-Business Solutions: The Enabler of Global Supply Chain

10.1 e-Business Solutions: The Enabler of Global Supply Chain

10.1.1 Global supply chain

The growing interest in e-Business solutions is a result of global competition, the evolution of communication and Internet technology, and the convergence of local, regional and world markets. The term e-Business solutions started to appear in print in the mid 1990s when Internet technology began to penetrate the business world. As we enter the 21st century, globally expanding business models such as direct sell model, internet-based logistics model, and zero-inventory systems model are redefining supply chain operations.

However, an e-Business model is not just an e-Solution. Rather, it consists of a set of phases described below:

(1) A value proposition that reflects the competitive global market;
(2) A proactive business plan that determines products and markets;
(3) An innovative business model that relies on technical expertise to consolidate core competencies to carry out the business plan;
(4) A well-conceived supply chain network that smoothes information flows, material flows, service flows, and fund/cash flows;
(5) A cutting-edge information technology enabler that connects information flows; and
(6) An unprecedented level of performance creates value for the supply chain and its clients.

Let us consider Li & Fung, a premier textile trading company in Hong Kong, and observe how Li & Fung implements the above six steps. In the late 1970s, trading business was considered a sunset industry with very little hope to grow. Nevertheless, Li & Fung redirected its business to reflect the global competition. First, it creates a value proposition that focuses on providing one-stop shop from product design and development, raw material and factory sourcing, production planning and control, quality assurance and delivery documentation. This model is specifically valuable to those high-volume, time-sensitive apparel producers and retailers such as the Limited Brands. Then, a proactive business plan clearly determines its markets and business clients. Next, a business model called "Production Program" is initiated. Given a customer designer's sketch, Li & Fung searchs for the right material, and come up with a production program that specifies product mix and production schedules. They then follow up by ensuring quality inspection and on time delivery. A supply network that connects suppliers and producers of 41 countries that has been developed over the past 20 years ensures successful implementation of the new business model. When the sourcing concentration is on low cost, Asian suppliers usually have the priority to be selected; however, when quick response hits the top of the list, suppliers and producers in Eastern Europe, Mediterranean, and South America will be contracted to meet the delivery requirements in the same region. With such an expanded network, information technology becomes an inevitable enabler for Li & Fung to effectively communicate among 74 offices in 41 countries. e-Solutions such as email, fax, EDI, website, and e-Hub connect its worldwide supply network. By 2004, Li & Fung generated annual revenue of $7 billion and had 18,000 employees around world.

10.1.2 e-Solution outsourcing: A perceivable trend

As business spread out over the world, IT outsourcing becomes a golden opportunity for many corporations to generate high revenues. IT outsourcing model has been adopted by at least 40% of Fortune 500 companies. Corporations such as Microsoft, Lucent, Dell Inc., Wells

Fargo, and Motorola all have offshore divisions. Shortage of IT software development skills, reduction in direct and indirect costs, and decreases in delivery lead time brought major changes in IT sourcing arrangements. Additionally, offshore offices enable "follow-the-sun" office hours. When a US team finishes an eight-hour work day, the Indian office will pick up the duty.

Starting in 2001, Dell Inc. opened technical support centers for U.S. consumers and customers around the world. In 2006, Dell India was able to expand operations to include sales centers. Dell's two India service centers, Hyderabad and Bangalore, have over 6,000 staff members. Now Dell India not only focuses on customer service calls but also works on product development and testing.

However, there is a downside associated with offshore service centers. Some serious complaints about Dell's offshore call center has forced Dell to stop routing technical inquiries from some corporate customers to its overseas offices due to complaints about the poor quality of its offshore centers.

10.2 Enterprise Information Systems (EIS)

An Enterprise Information System (EIS) is an integrated information technology for streamlining business processes; it is able to facilitate the flow of data and information among all supply chain processes of a firm and among trading partners. Wikipedia Encyclopedia describes EIS as follows:

> Enterprise Information Systems provide a technology platform that enable organizations to integrate and coordinate their business processes. They provide a single system that is central to the organization and ensure that information can be shared across all functional levels and management hierarchies. Enterprise systems are invaluable in eliminating the problem of information fragmentation caused by multiple information systems in an organization, by creating a standard data structure[1].

---

[1] Wikipedia Encyclopedia, http://en.wikipedia.org.

An EIS formally called ERP (enterprise resource planning systems) is a system for a single enterprise or company, attempting to integrate most of the business activities within the company. One enterprise can be involved with one supply chain or with a number of supply chains for different product lines and markets. Many companies have begun to recognize EIS' potential to create a broader source of competitive advantage, and have capitalized on the increasingly cross-functional span of the technology.

EIS system expenditures were amongst the largest IT investments of the 1990s. EIS systems have been implemented in over 60% of multi-national firms. The license/maintenance revenue of the EIS market was $17.2 billion in 1998. Even major US software companies have adopted EIS products. For example, IBM and Microsoft now run most of their business on SAP R/3 ER software. The data released in the fourth quarter of 2000 indicates that the worldwide EIS market will grow at a rate of 24.9% and reach $73 billion in 2004. Recently, EIS is becoming popular in the small and medium enterprise market segment due to the sudden importance of Customer Relation Management (CRM), supply chain management, and business to customer (B2C) commerce in the business environment.

10.2.1 Business process reengineering – The foundation for implementing EIS

It is not the first time in the history that technology reshapes the existing business process. In the 1920s, Ford Motor production system utilized assembly line technology to speed up productivity and realized economy of scale. This technology altered the entire automobile production process. Today, computer and information technology have created a new way of doing business, which requires organizations to re-think and re-structure their business process. This initiative is called business process re-engineering.

Business process re-engineering is a method by which an organization examines and redesigns its business processes in accordance with its strategic objectives of implementing enterprise information systems.

EIS is a process oriented e-Business solution that keeps track of purchasing, business transactions, order fulfillment, and production planning and control activities. Consequently, one business process issue often has repercussions and effects for another process issue. Every company that has implemented an EIS system is faced with reengineering the company's existing way of doing business.

To successfully implement EIS systems, an organization needs to analyze its business process and produce a business blueprint. Process reengineering includes revising policies and procedures a business uses to run operations. Since the software does not allow people to do things in the old way, the reengineered process becomes the only way that people can work. Implementing EIS requires two key aspects of process reengineering. First, business processes should be placed in the center of organizational structure rather than being treated as individual functions; and second, business activities should not be divided according to the concept of specialization or the division of labor. Rather, the complete process should be systematically optimized in an enterprise-wide setting.

10.2.2 Legacy systems

Legacy system is a very broad label and applies to a wide variety of systems with applications that can range from order entry to manufacturing scheduling to order delivery. Before 1990s, legacy system was a popular technology solution to handle business transactions. During the 1990s, EIS systems became a replacement for legacy systems for many Fortune 500 companies. Two important characteristics of legacy systems are (i) narrow scope and visibility; and (ii) convenient at performing operational tasks.

The advantages of legacy systems include:
- Ability to accomplish operations without additional support such as process reengineering and user training expense; and
- Incremental features are less expensive to install compared to a client / server system.

The disadvantages of legacy systems include:
- Limited focus; only a small part of a firm or a supply chain's operations can be handled;

• Transactional capability only; and

• Less flexible to be modified due to mainframe technology.

Due to its narrow application scope, legacy system lost its favor when client / server technology was introduced to the market in the 1990s.

10.2.3 Client / server technology

The rapid pace of technology development in chips and microprocessors enables the full integration of business processes. In the 1990s, client / server technology became available and then was adopted by EIS systems. Client / server systems are more flexible than legacy systems. They are not a mainframe-oriented technology; instead, they can be linked via telephone lines or local area network.

The term, client / server, can be used for both hardware and software. The hardware based client / server system refers to the PC network operating systems such as Microsoft MS-Net, Novell NetWare, Microsoft LAN Manager, etc. In this case, the local network such as local area networks (LANs) is the server, and PCs and Desktops are clients.

The software based client / server system has a broader definition than the hardware-based client / server system. Software can be described as a client if it requests services or as a server if it provides services. Client / server systems can either be centralized on one computer or extended to many computers.

There are a variety of EIS systems based on client / server architectures, including centralized client/server, two-tier client / server, three-tier client / server, and others.

Centralized Client / Server has a central host computer. It performs all transactional and processing tasks involving presentations, applications, and a single database.

Two tier Client / Server uses PC or desktop systems to take care of both presentation and applications. The database system is separated from presentation and application.

Three tier Client / Server has separate systems for presentation, applications, and single database servers. Three tier Client / Server systems provide many benefits, including portability, investment protection, multilevel implementation, optimum load distribution and interoperability.

10.2.4 Major modules of EIS systems

EIS systems are a new form of business data system that focuses on systematic and integrated operations of various corporate activities. EIS systems not only integrate business functional areas such as marketing and sales, production planning, material management, and financial control of a company, but also link web sites and databases of all suppliers and customers of a supply chain. Under the integration concept, EIS systems connect standard business models, system functions, and data models that relate to all business activities. The major modules of EIS systems include marketing/sales, production, procurement, accounting, organization and human resource management, financial management, capital asset management, customer service, etc.

Current capabilities of EIS systems include:

- MRP / MRPII, which support engineering and manufacturing bills, engineering change control, product configuration capabilities, and online customized configuration.
- Purchasing, which supports contract purchases, blanket purchases, and Requests for Quotations (RFQ) capability; allows suppliers to update order status via the Internet or EDI; offers e-payment capabilities; and supports vendor release / control.
- Manufacturing Execution, providing support for advanced planning and scheduling, user-defined attributes, routings, and shop floor scheduling;
- Customer Relationship Management;
- Demand management and forecasting;
- Warehouse management and inventory control;
- Transportation and shipping;
- Financial management, including accounts payable and accounts receivable, order processing, general ledger, fixed asset accounting, and multinational monetary transaction function;

- Human resource management that include payroll, employee benefits, retirement accounts, training, etc; and
- Reporting that allows ad hoc reports. Operations results can be reported in financial terms and problematic situations will be labeled.

There are a number of emerging capabilities being tackled by EIS vendors:

- Enterprise application integration;
- Supply chain-wide visibility;
- Collaborative planning, forecasting and replenishment; and
- Web-enabled business applications.

10.2.5 Major EIS systems vendors

In the 1990s, the five largest EIS vendors were SAP, Oracle, PeopleSoft, J.D. Edwards, and Baan. These five vendors supplied the majority of EIS markets, also known as ERP markets. Among them, SAP is the leading EIS system producer. As we enter the 21st century, mergers and acquisitions are taking place to restructure the EIS market. PeopleSoft acquired J.D. Edward in 2003, and later Oracle and PeopleSoft merged in 2004. Nevertheless, there have been even more EIS vendors entering the EIS market in the past ten years. According to an EIS software directory compiled by capterra.com retrieved in June 2006, there are 122 EIS solutions, ranging from emphasizing consumer goods manufacturing to focusing on warehouse and inventory management, to emphasizing multi-sales channels.

SAP, the largest EIS vendor, stands for Systems, Applications and Products in Data Processing. SAP R/2 and R/3 are the trademarks in the United States. Established in 1972 in Germany, SAP has captured a significant share of worldwide client/server enterprise information systems software market. In the early 1980s, SAP developed R/2, a huge, mainframe legacy solution. In the late 1980s, SAP move to client / server technology and began developing R/3. In 1992, SAP introduced R/3 to the market, which is available in 14 languages. Today, SAP is a leading EIS client/server software company and has obtained a third of the world market share.

Oracle known for its database software has extended to EIS application section. Oracle Corporation was founded by Larry Ellison, along with Robert N. Miner and Edward A. Oates in 1977 in Redwood, California. They introduced the first Relational Database Management System based on the IBM System/R model and the first database management system utilizing IBM's Structured Query Language (SQL) technology.

Oracle's main competitors in application e-Business solutions like EIS were SAP, Peoplesoft, and BAAN. To strengthen its flagging applications division, Oracle, the No. 2 e-Business solution provider, acquired PeopleSoft, the third largest applications provider in early 2005. The adjustment and restructure after the merge is painstaking. It took a while before Oracle reported a 57 percent increase in its e-Business applications business in the 2nd quarter of 2005.

Founded by David Duffield and Ken Morris in 1987 at Pleasanton, California, PeopleSoft used to be the third largest EIS solution provider, focused on human resources applications. When PeopleSoft took over J.D. Edwards in 2003, it planned to rename PeopleSoft's EIS system as PeopleSoft Enterprise and J.D. Edwards' ERP product as PeopleSoft EnterpriseOne.

J.D. Edwards started out building cross-functional systems that were targeted toward midsize firms. Its EnterpriseOne EIS software is designed for the demand-driven environment, which optimizes effort within an organization and extends to supply chain management. PeopleSoft acquired J.D. Edwards in 2003.

Baan was a vendor of popular enterprise resource planning (ERP) software that is now owned by Infor Global Solutions. Baan used to focus on midsize companies and perform well in manufacturing environments. Jan Baan of Barneveld, Netherlands founded Baan in 1978 to provide financial and administrative consulting services. With the creation of his first application software, Jan Baan entered the ERP industry[2]. In June 2000, Baan was sold to Invensys, a UK automation

---

[2] http://en.wikipedia.org/wiki/Baan.

solutions group to create its new Software and Services Division. In June 2003, Invensys sold Baan to SSA Global Technologies for a cash consideration of 135 million US dollars. In May 2006, Infor Global Solutions of Atlanta acquired SSA.

10.2.6 Small and mid-size EIS market

It took a decade for the EIS vendors to realize the benefits they can take from the small and mid-size market. In 1990s, the small and medium business (SMB) markets were too small for the big five to compete. However, a recent estimation suggests that the value of demand from small and medium size companies is about $173 billion. This estimation opens the eyes of big EIS vendors such as SAP and IBM. By the end of 2001, IBM developed a business strategy to establish its position as a small and medium business market leader and secured a full contingent of products. It wants to tackle the small and medium business market with a combination of e-Business solutions and services that fit the needs of the small and mid-size market.

Microsoft catches up quickly and offers Dynamics NAV to the small and medium business market. Microsoft's Dynamics NAV integrates operations, distribution, e-commerce, financial, and customer data into a streamlined, comprehensive solution for mid-sized firms. This e-Solution is excellent for manufacturing environment and is easy to use.

Made2Manage positioned itself in the small and medium business market ever since it was founded in 1986 in Indianapolis, USA. From its early days, Made2Manage put all its effort to serve companies that have discrete manufacturing process and use MRP systems. Small manufacturing companies are also more comfortable dealing with a vendor of a size and corporate culture similar to theirs. During the last few years, Made2Manage has evolved to providing "one-stop-shop" enterprise business applications. It collaborates with vendors of customer relation management (CRM), business intelligence (BI), warehousing management systems (WMS), and advanced planning and scheduling components with its core ERP system.

10.3 Customer Relations Management

10.3.1 CRM's relation to supply chain management

Customer satisfaction is the key to success in a global supply chain environment. Therefore, many business organizations turn to a Customer Relationship Management (CRM) solution in seeking better customer relationship management tools. CRM can be independent software or a module of EIS systems, which is generally considered as the front office of an e-Solution. This is because CRM deals directly with customers, their needs and interests.

The purpose of CRM is to capture, consolidate, and analyze historical data from existing customers in order to retain current customers and attract potential customers. This process occurs throughout the entire process of marketing, sales, and order fulfillment, with the objective of better understanding customers and their interest in a company's products and / or services.

CRM systems and real time tracking information technology have captured tremendous amount of data on customer purchasing behavior and trend. After mining and analyzing historical data, patterns of what customers buy, when they buy, how they buy, and where they buy can reveal and potential customers can be identified.

Enabled with information technology, CRM offers a number of benefits to a company. These benefits include focused marketing to help reduce marketing cost, effective ways in bringing in new customers, better forecasting methods, customer information collection, current and would-be customers needs and interest analysis, great customer satisfaction, productivity boosts, and sales improvement.

Many service call centers use CRM software to keep their customer's information. When a customer calls, the system can be used to retrieve and save information relevant to the customer. By serving the customer quickly and efficiently, and also keeping all information on a customer in one place, a company is able to answer customer's questions in an efficient and effective manner. For example, airlines use call centers to book tickets, track mileage program, check arrival and departure schedules, and look for luggage information.

CRM solutions also allow customers to perform their own service via a variety of communication channels. For example, the US post office provides a website for customers to check delivery status via the Internet for priority mails without ever having to talk to them. This practice saves money for the post office and saves time for the customer.

Gartner Group summarized three core components of CRM solutions; they are sales force automation, customer service and support, and enterprise marketing automation.

Sales force automation provides a sales force a tool to quote, forecast, check available inventory, and access customer's accounts while they are traveling. This feature highly improves the productivity of the field sales force.

Customer service and support handles customer service requests, product catalog, service information, product returns, complaints, and other customer needed information. Customer Interaction Center (CIC) applies multiple e-Solutions such as company website, call-center, kiosk, email, and direct contact to provide customer services.

Enterprise marketing automation provides information about the business environment such as industry and market trend, technology advancement, global competition, competitors, promotion, customer profiling, and database connectivity. This module improves the efficiency of marketing campaign.

10.3.2 CRM implementation

A survey of chief information officers conducted by CIO Magazine (CIO.com) indicated that CRM implementation projects generally took an average of 12 to 18 months to complete and the average investment in CRM systems was $3.2 million. Over half of the organizations invested in CRM reported that they implemented CRM system incrementally through small or pilot projects, instead of implementing the entire system all at once[3].

---

[3] *CIO Magazine*, retrieved from www.cio.com, July 2006.

A more innovative use of CRM is to regain market position through implementing CRM. By the end of 1980s, Circuit City was the top consumer electronics retailer. By 2001, Best Buy, also an electronic retailer raced past Circuit City, becoming the number one seller of consumer electronics. Since then, Circuit City has been trying to regain its top contender position in the consumer electronics retailing industry. The strategy Circuit City formulated in 2005 was to turn the company into a customer-focused business that provides all its customers with a personalized experience through retail stores, call centers and company website. The enabler to realize this strategy is high-profile technology, including point-of-sale (POS) system, enterprise information system, and customer relation management software. The top executives of Circuit City envisioned that the cutting-edge technology would enable store associates to recognize and greet their loyalty cards customers as soon as they enter the store, and assist the management team to develop effective promotion plans to determine which products should be displayed at the ends of aisles in stores. All this is fact-based, data-driven, and analytical work[3]. Will the right technology support Circuit City's customer focused innovation? We shall judge the result in a couple of years.

10.4 Other e-Business Solutions

10.4.1 Collaborative planning, forecasting, and replenishment (CPFR)

A supply chain is as strong as its weakest link. The notion here focuses on strong and effective collaboration. The fundamental point that distinguishes supply chain management and traditional materials management is how the collaboration of trading partners is managed.

The process of collaborative planning, forecasting, and replenishment was originally called C-FAR when Wal-Mart and Warner Lambert Company piloted a project focused on collaborative forecasting and replenishment (C-FAR) in 1995. The acronym evolved to CPFR after the planning function was integrated into the project. The predecessors of CPFR are: Electronic Data Interchange (EDI), bar coding, and vendor-managed inventory (VMI). The more current version of CPFR is in a format of e-solution utilizing XML technology and B2B exchanges in addition to EDI, bar-coding and VMI.

A 2002 report on CPFR on American Grocery Producers reports that about 70 percent of companies have engaged in some level of CPFR implementation[4]. Using CPFR as an e-solution, trading partners update real-time sales data based on shop floor on-going activities, share sales information, and benefit from total supply chain visibility. Nevertheless, integrating disconnected forecasting and planning activities in the entire supply chain is still a challenge. Many companies recognize the need to optimize internal processes and improve data accuracy.

Many grocery manufacturers consider CPFR solutions as a facilitator of efficient response system. Before investing in CPFR software, managers of Perdue Farms went by the gut feel of its suppliers and customers, as well as the seasonal demand history. It worked well in general. However, when holidays, such as Thanksgiving, were approaching, managers needed to observe the market trend more frequently.

In order to provide high quality products and incomparable service to their customers, Perdue Farm's CIO, Don Taylor, led Perdue's investment in technology to radically reshape the company's supply chain infrastructure to implement CPFR in the late 1990's. The $20 million investment in the cutting edge information systems such as Manugistics, a CPFR software solution, enables Perdue Farms to collaborate and share critical information on forecasting, point-of-sale data, promotion activities, inventory, and replenish plans with its trading partners. Using Manugistics forecasting software and supply chain planning tools, Perdue has become more adept at delivering the right amount of poultry product to the right customers at the right time[5].

The CPFR software solution, Manugistics, also enables Perdue Farms to collaborate with major food service and grocery companies such as

---

[4] Groceries Manufacturers of America, 2002. CPFR Baseline Study of Manufacturer Profile, by KJR Consulting.

[5] Manugistics Forum, http://www.manugistics.com/envision2005/speakers.html.

Chick-Fil-A restaurant, Wal-Mart and Sam's Club for production planning, demand forecasting, and inventory replenishment. Furthermore, CPFR implementation enables Perdue Farms to proactively assess its production capacity and make the necessary investments to satisfy the expected demand level. In 2004, Perdue Farms purchased a 500,000-square-foot plant near Perry, GA. from Cagle's for $45 million. The plant processes up to 350,000 birds per week to meet the demand from Chick-Fil-A restaurants, and an additional 450,000 birds per week for tray-pack products sold at Wal-Mart and Sam's Club[6].

10.4.2 e-Hub

e-Hub is an Internet-based business-to-business e-Market that provides a platform for buyer and sellers to conduct business in a virtual environment. There are many such trading hubs now. B2B e-Hubs can be classified into four categories: e-catalog hub, material exchange (such as MRO) e-Hub, yield managers e-Hub and exchanges e-Hub. e-Hubs in general are neutral, not favoring either buyers or sellers. Some of the well-known examples are Ariba, Covisint, Chemdex, and Commerce One. Each e-Hub has its own niche and serves a certain market segment.

For example, Covisint is an Internet-based Business-to-Business exchange hub connecting the Auto Industry in a virtual environment. It collaborates large powerful industry leaders such as GM to sponsor industry e-marketplaces. Suppliers of all sizes and original equipment manufacturers (OEMs) meet at the e-Hub, Covisint, to do business in a business environment using the same tools and the same user interface, with one user ID and password. Covisint has three major objectives: (i) to promote collaborative product development by harnessing the Internet's communications prowess; (ii) to streamline procurement process for the auto companies by setting up market mechanisms such as auctions; and (iii) to streamline the operations of the auto industry's supply chains. As networks of buyers and suppliers interact in virtual

---

[6] Charlie Lanter, (2004). Perdue Farms Executives Show Off Perry, Ga. Facility, *American Stock Exchange*, May 13, 2004, www.amex.com.

space, the founders of the e-Hub hope that the auto industry's work processes will become more efficient and customer-friendly through Covisint[7].

Covisint provides users with various features such as Covisint Fulfillment, which is a web-based direct material fulfillment service for auto industry suppliers. The fulfillment feature responds quickly to actual supply and demand problems with real time visibility. As such, cost savings are achieved through inventory reductions, premium freight cost reductions and administration cost reductions.

Ariba, another e-Hub, is an information technology and spend management solution. Spend Management is a relatively new term, meaning to take a comprehensive approach to assess how assets and inventory are managed, how sourcing and procurement are conducted, and how supplier relationships in a supply chain are optimized. The benefits Ariba offers include cutting operating and other costs associated with doing business. Some of Ariba's regular customers include Chevron, Cisco Systems, BMW, and Unilever, to name a few[8].

10.4.3 Electronic product code: radio frequency ID (RFID)

Commercialized radio frequency identification (RFID) technology began as early as 2003, when the U.S. Customs Service and the U.S. Department of Defense began asking their vendors and suppliers to adopt RFID technology. RFID is a general term referring to the application of radio frequency waves to identify objects. In supply chain, RFID uses a unique code stored in a RFID tag that contains a serial numbers linked to the product information that stored in a central database. Once the unique code is retrieved from the tag, it can be associated with dynamic data such as where an item is originated, the date of its production, and the physical location of the product.

Wal-Mart is one of the pioneers to popularize RFID in supply chain management. Since 2004, Wal-Mart and its top 100 suppliers have

---

[7] e-biz Chronicle.com.
[8] www.Ariba.com.

engaged in shifting to RFID-tagging of all cartons and pallets bound for Wal-Mart distribution centers. In October 2005, the University of Arkansas reported some initial results having implemented RFID technology at Wal-Mart. The benefits include reduction in out-of-stock items by 16%, three-times faster to replenish out-of-stock items with RFID-tags than bar-coded items, 10% reduction in manual orders, 63% more effective of RFID enabled stores than regular stores in replenishing out-of-stock items. As a result, the customer service level has improved due to availability of customer-favored items[9]. At an RFID World panel discussion, Carolyn Walters, vice president of Information Systems at Wal-Mart talked about the objective of increasing RFID capability, "Sensor tags are around $20. That's a high cost, but we want to find a way to put bananas on shelves in our food department so they're at the perfect ripeness."

By 2006, Wal-Mart has 300 suppliers sending products to 500 RFID-enabled Wal-Mart and Sam's Club stores. Additionally, five distribution centers are equipped to take in RFID-tagged pallets and cases from suppliers.

The major downside of implementing RFID is the private issue. Customers are concerned about being watched without their awareness. Moreover, the unique product ID may be used to track a person's movement over a period of time and personal data stored in a database may be accessed due to the use of RFID technology.

10.4.4 Global available-to-promise (GATP)

Global available to promise (ATP) is a software application that automates the search for available production capacity, as well as inventory in multiple warehouses and factories to maximize the use of various resources. Global ATP allows a company to reallocate its inventory system-wide, based on changing customer needs or market dynamics. Companies can view the existing inventory and production in

---

[9] University of Arkansas Study Quantifies RFID-Initiated Improvement. *PRNewswire – FirstCall*, October 14, 2005.

progress. In case of shortage, available substitutable products will be identified to fill orders.

For example, Beer-Mart's warehouse has confirmed an order of 80,000 cases of beer for a large grocery store to be shipped in a week. Meanwhile, a large restaurant chain placed an order of 10,000 cases to be delivered in two days for a banquet. Beer-Mart's warehouse only had 5,000 cases available. Because the initial order of 80,000 cases is reserved two weeks ago for delivery, those cases are labeled as soft-pegged for shipment. Meanwhile, the Beer-Mart company's global ATP system shows that enough beer can be produced in five days. A reallocation schedule was planned and 5,000 cases of beer from the pallets waiting to be shipped are transferred to the new order from the restaurant. Eventually, both orders are filled.

Global ATP software can not only allow companies to allocate and reallocate available inventory and production, but also tell the customers when it will be able to fill the order, with single shipment or multiple shipments. Global ATP helps to improve customer satisfaction and optimally utilize inventory and production capacity.

10.4.5 Vendor managed inventory (VMI)

Vendor managed inventory (VMI) is a set of agreement on product specifications, proper payment, procedures, and other terms negotiated between the vendors and customers in advance. VMI enables suppliers to continually restock their customers' inventory based on the actual quantity of products or materials consumed. At the same time, the customer will notify the supplier the quantity of the product consumed and the vendor will automatically replenish inventory according to the agreement. This is also a form of outsourcing.

There are some potential obstacles to implementing VMI. Major issues include the employee at the consumer company who fears a reduction in workforce due to the outsourced function. Information security can be an issue to the consumer company since the supplier may serve a number of customers including the consumer company's competitors; and the supplier may not want to be held accountable for quality and other product related issues.

10.4.6 Cross docking

Cross Docking moves materials directly from receiving to shipping with minimum lag time in between. The key to improving Cross Docking efficiency is Advance Ship Notice (ASN). Wal-Mart is one of the first companies to implement Cross Docking solution. This solution reduces inventory, labor cost, and warehouse space. Cross Docking requires accurate information on in-coming products, outgoing product configuration, the transportation mode used for shipping products, quantity of products, product markings and identification, unloading location, interim and final destinations, and special handling requirement.

10.4.7 Geographic information systems (GIS)

Geographic information systems (GIS) were developed in the 1960s and were first used by government and military. The newer version of GIS is a very effective database that can be used by business to access an enormous amount of information such as target markets, demographic data of customers, distribution location, and zoning restrictions. Today, GIS can be employed to assist supply chain managers for planning, forecasting, inventory management, customer profile analysis, shortest travel routes, and distribution location selection. GIS software creates maps electronically, and can add layers to integrate more information. For example, the first layer of the map is distribution centers; the second layer of the map shows the transportation network, and the third layer illustrates customer demographic information.

Many retailers, such as Best Buy, Talbot's, and Sears ask their customers about their zip code and phone number starting with area code at the checkout point. This information reveals the percentage of market share by area or zip code. For example, Quaker Oats noticed that 80% of their ethnic customers lived in 18 of their 55 sales zones. Using geographic information technology, Quaker was able to visualize customer shopping data and formulate effective promotion strategy.

Walgreens, a retail drugstore, is engaged in the retail sale of prescription and nonprescription drugs, and other product lines such as cosmetics, toiletries, and household items. As such, it is very important for the company to identify customer density, customer size, and most importantly the customer age profile because prescription drug usage is highly correlated with age groups. In the past 20 years, Walgreens expanded rapidly. By 1984, Walgreens opened its 1,000th store in Chicago. In 2000, Walgreens reached the 3,000-store mark. As of August 31, 2003, the Company has 4,224 stores located in 44 states and Puerto Rico. To support this rapid expansion program, Walgreens uses GIS for retail area selection and distribution center location analysis. With the assistance of GIS, Walgreens opened a new distribution center in Perrysburg, Ohio in May 2003 to support its retailing expansion plan.

10.5 Technology Standardization of e-Business

In order to transfer business information easily and securely, commonly acceptable e-business standards have to be developed and implemented by businesses. Electronic Data Interchange (EDI) was a standard for the past 25 to 30 years. Since 1996, Extensible Markup Language (XML) was introduced to provide a simple and affordable solution for secure transactional exchanges between firms.

10.5.1 Electronic data interchange (EDI)

EDI is a technology that enables the transmission of routine business transactions such as order receiving, order shipment, accounts receivable and payables between companies. EDI has been widely used in retailing and other business transactions. The retailer use Universal Product Code (UPC) and point-of-sale (POS) to tract customer purchasing patterns. The benefits of EDI include:
- Increased productivity
- Creating paperless business transactions
- Reduction in business lead time
- Reduction in inventory

- Increased data accuracy
- Enabling electronic funds transfer

However, EDI is fairly complicated and expensive to use. It has high maintenance overhead cost and expensive leased lines. Using a compressed and cumbersome set of codes, an EDI message is difficult to program. It is reported that only 300,000 firms worldwide have ever adopted EDI and many of these firms are large corporations. Each industry has its own set of EDI. Some examples of industry EDI standards include:

- EDI standards of Grocery industry: Uniform Communication Standards (UCS);
- EDI standards of Automotive Industry: Automotive Industry Action Group (AIAG);
- EDI standards of Mass Merchandisers: Volunteer Inter-Industry Communication Standards Committee (VICS);
- EDI standards of Warehouse and Distribution Operators: Warehouse Information Network Standards (WINS);
- EDI standards of Transportation and Logistics Operators: Transportation Data Coordinating Committee (TDCC).

10.5.2 Extensible markup language (XML)

Extensible Markup Language (XML) is a subset of the Standard General Markup Language (SGML). It is not a programming language, but a markup language standard that provides a flexible and inexpensive way to create data. XML uses plain text to provide tags that describe the format of the data and content of the data. Regular text generated in a text editor can be displayed in the web browser.

An XML document is self defined and has its own Document Type Definition that provides an explanation of the data language used in the document. Any system that supports XML can read and understand the data inside the document.

The Data Interchange Standards Association (DISA) predicts that the XML may replace EDI as a business-to-business standard in the future. If this happens, buyers will have direct access to secure business data transfer to their suppliers and suppliers will have a less expensive way to communicate with their customers.

The future trends and issues of information technology in supply chain include:

- Best of breed versus single integrator
- Shifts in platform technology
  - o The browser-based Internet application
  - o The role of application service providers (ASP)
- The role of the Internet and B2B exchanges

10.6 Enhancing Value through e-Business Solutions

The rise of global supply chain is a result of the availability of the digital technology. E-solutions are not an option that a company can adopt or do without them. E-solutions are a must-have weapon for a company to compete in today's global market. E-Business solutions such as Enterprise Information System (EIS) integrate business functional areas and link suppliers and customers of the entire supply chain. The B2B e-solutions provide an enormous amount of information on what customers need, what is available in inventory and available in real time to all trading partners in a supply chain.

The Internet commerce and e-Business give rise to a new platform upon which supply chain management deploys new business models. The true value e-Solution adds to supply chain management is difficult to assess because the digital business has changed way organizations used to do business. Let us consider the textile industry. Li & Fung, supported by a comprehensive database, developed a dispersed manufacturing model. For example, when it receives an order, Li & Fung identifies the best fit supplier to fulfill the order. Best fit means to analyze all the information needed for the order, such as quality requirement, cost range, textile product quotas, and labor skills. The company then comes up with a dispersed plan to source yarn in Korea and have it dyed in Taiwan; purchase zippers in Japan because YKK makes high quality zippers, and split the order among five factories in Thailand to have the garments made to meet the delivery time. The value the digital solution adds to the dispersed manufacturing model is tremendous. Cycle time is reduced, cost is contained, and quality is assured.

10.7 Summary

In recent years, e-business has emerged as a new way of conducting business in a competitive global market. In this chapter, we give an overview of various e-Business solutions developed in recent years and their applications and implication in supply chain management. We have covered an array of emerging e-solutions in this chapter, including Enterprise Information Systems, Customer Relationship Management, GIS, RFID, VMI, CFPR and Global ATP. There are new e-solutions developed in conjunction with the existing ones as we mentioned here to tackle new problems facing the supply chain. E-Solution is a facilitator or a driver of the digital supply chain. We predict that e-solutions will be more sophisticated and tailored-made in the near future.

Questions for Pondering

1. Why should business process reengineering (BPR) precede enterprise information system (EIS) implementation? What is the relationship between BPR and EIS implementation?
2. What are the major challenges a firm should expect when it implements an integrated EIS system or other e-solutions?
3. Discuss the role of customer relationship management in enhancing a firm's market competitiveness and performance.
4. Discuss the value globalization adds to the supply chain. As jobs are outsourced to a global market, first it was the manufacturing industry, then IT software development, now service components, what strategy should traditional industrialized nations come up with to compete?

References

CIO Magazine, www.cio.com.

Churbuck, David (1992). "Geographic," Fortune, 149(1), January 6, 1992, 262-265.

Covisint, http://www.covisint.com/.

Curran, T.A. and Ladd, A. (2000). SAP R/3: Business Blueprint. Prentice Hall: New Jersey.

Heinrich, C. and Betts, B. (2002). Adapt or Die. John Wiley & Sons, Inc.: New York.

Levison, Meridith (2005). Circuit City Rewires, *CIO Magazine*, www.cio.com, July 2005.

Li and Fung Group, http://www.lifunggroup.com/.

Magretta, J. (1998). "Fast, global, and entrepreneurial: supply chain management, Hong Kong style, an interview with Victor Fung. *Harvard Business Review*, September-October, 1998.

Neff, D. (2001). e-Procurement: from strategy to implementation. Prentice Hall: New Jersey.

Wikipedia Encyclopedia, http://en.wikipedia.org.

Chapter 11

Business Intelligence in Supply Chain Management: Data, Information, and Knowledge

11.1 Business Intelligence

11.1.1 Business intelligence definition

War intelligence can be traced back to Sun Tzu's *The Art of War* written during the 6th century BC. Sun Tzu asserts that to succeed in war, one should have complete knowledge of one's own strengths and weaknesses as well as complete knowledge of one's enemy's strengths and weaknesses, which can simply be put as "know yourselves and know your enemy, one hundred battles one hundred victories." An analogy can be drawn between the war intelligence and business intelligence in a supply chain.

As technology advances at an exponential rate and market competition is getting fierce each day, business intelligence has moved to the center of supply chain management. Business intelligence is an umbrella term used to describe the application of data collection and organization, information analysis and extraction, and decision support insights about the markets, customers, suppliers, and products. Additionally, competitive business intelligence applications provide supply chain managers with tools for performance data analysis that helps to uncover potential problems and predict business trends. Most organizations have some sort of business intelligence function in house, some are a part of the IT department, some are a part of marketing research, and others are an independent department.

The tools used to realize business intelligence in supply chain include data warehouse, data mining, reporting and query tools, data visualization tools, and online analytical processing (OLAP). The application of these tools transforms data to valuable information, transforms information to competitive decisions, transforms decisions to forward-looking actions, and transforms actions to sustainable high performance.

11.1.2 Business intelligence value chain

To meet supply chain challenges, timely information about market, customers and competitors are crucial. Business intelligence value chain is an interrelated process of suppliers, manufacturers, distributors, and customers that uses data, information, and knowledge to pilot a company towards competitive success.

Business intelligence (BI) is grounded in various supply chain activities and processes that serve as the sources of BI data and information. Enhanced intelligence analysis and awareness of the latest developments in data collection and information analysis, as well as networking are vital components of value chain management. While some supply chain managers may attempt to cruise blindly through the local, national, or even the global marketplaces, it comes undoubtedly that informed decisions on alternative courses may avoid potential risks and lead to enhanced bottom-line success.

There are several levels of business intelligence application in a supply chain as indicated in Table 11.1. They are strategic, tactic, operational, and R&D and market research.

Strategic decisions are made at the top management level. Chief executives usually require long-term, historical data, integrated information on environmental changes and industry trends that are combined with business performance to drive decisions. Insightful business decisions can create unprecedented success through adjusting supply chain directions. For example, eBay bought Billpoint in May

1999 in the hope to beat the rival PayPal. Nevertheless, despite heavy promotion, Billpoint was not able to win electronic payment market share from PayPal. Comprehensive analysis of market data indicated that it was easier to acquire PayPal than to beat it because PayPal had some 20 million registered account holders; about $1.5 billion in payments sent to its customers in the second quarter of 2002. Merrill Lynch analyst Justin Baldauf commented market power of PayPal and eBay, "PayPal is the 'gorilla' in the online payment market and eBay is the 'gorilla' in the online auction market." On July 2, 2002 eBay purchased PayPal. Today, the implication of this strategic decision is obvious. eBay and PayPal together make online trading more compelling and have built a vibrant virtual market on the Internet.

At the tactic level, aggregate information is needed to provide visibility across multiple processes within a supply chain to facilitate actionable changes. Decision support systems are commonly used by the managers at this level. Aggregated data across business units assist managers to make informed decisions, analyze business trends, and deliver promised services or products with a consistent quality. For example, the vice president in charge of forecasting at Anheuser-Busch needs to determine correct amounts of beer arriving from the breweries and support centers to maintain satisfactory inventory levels. Given a maximum life of 110 days from brewery to consumption to ensure freshness, forecasts must be fairly accurate. Collecting data from various business units, the vice president aggregates information on the trend of past seasons, the cyclical pattern of beer consumption, and external factors on special promotion offered by grocery stores, the weather, holidays, special events such as the HarborFest and the Bayou Boogalo in downtown Norfolk. Based on the intelligence information, the vice president formulates forecasts that are six weeks in advance to decide on a trend pattern, as well as to cover last minute orders from their clients. The forecasts are then sent to its host brewery via Anheuser-Busch's computer information system "BudNET".

Operational level decision requires daily and real-time data to satisfy customer demand on time. The line manager is responsible for day-to-day business of a certain business processes. Line managers may use real-time monitoring tools to access data and make timely decisions. For example, Wal-Mart installed an information system called RetailLink, which connects all of its stores to corporate headquarters and to each other. Store managers frequently hold videoconferences to exchange information on what is happening in the field, such as which products are selling and which aren't, which promotions work and which do not. Feasible decisions are made right on the retail store floor.

At the R&D and data analysis level, professional staff members may not be directly involve in daily decision making, but they collect and organize data, analyze data through modeling and simulation to extract supply chain information, and uncover knowledge of customers and competitors that are embedded in the supply chain process. For example, a research scientist of a pharmaceutical company may use historical data of clinical trials to assimilate the effectiveness of a new medicine.

Table 11.1. Business Intelligence Value Chain

BI Decision Level	Data needed	Information	Knowledge
Strategic	Long term, historic	Integrated cross business & industry	Environment, supply chain wide, customers & competitors
Tactic	Periodic, historic	Aggregated across business units	Environment, supply chain wide, customers & competitors
Operational	Daily & real-time	Aggregated across departments	Environment, supply chain wide, customers & competitors
R&D and data analysis	Long-term, periodic, daily, & real-time	Supply chain information	Environment, supply chain wide, customers & competitors

11.2 The Value of Business Intelligence

Prior to the information age of the late 20th century, businesses usually collected data from non-automated sources and made decisions primarily based on intuition or expert experience. As computer power increases exponentially in recent years, more and more data on supply chain activities have become available through employing ERP and CRM. However, ERP and CRM collect too much data that is difficult for the supply chain manager to focus on decision support insights. Business intelligence provides a hope for managers to extract information embedded in ERP and CRM; it analyzes the information to bring out the most important aspects of the data. A recent report on benefits of BI and information management indicates that the types of benefits BI generates include faster and accurate reporting, improved decision making, improved customer service, increased revenue, savings on non-IT costs, and IT savings[1].

11.2.1 Bullwhip effects

The bullwhip effect is essentially the artificial distortion of consumer demand volumes as they are transmitted back to the suppliers from the retailer. Many suppliers and retailers have observed the phenomenon of demand fluctuation in the upstream of the supply chain. For instance, in examining the demand for Pampers disposal diapers, Proctor & Gamble noticed that retail sales of the product were fairly uniform; there is no particular day or month in which the demand is significantly higher or lower than any other. However, the distributor's orders placed to the factory fluctuated much more than retail sales. In addition, P&G's orders to its suppliers fluctuate even more. This phenomenon of increasing variability in demand in a supply chain is known as the bullwhip effect.

---

[1] Olin Thompson, "Business intelligence success, lesson learned," retrieved from www.technologyevaluation.com.

To understand the impact of increasing variability on the supply chain, consider the demand management of a wholesaler of window blinds. The wholesaler receives the order from the retailer and places the order to the manufacturer. To determine the order size for window blinds the wholesaler must predict the demand from the retailers and places order to the manufacturer. If the wholesaler does not have information about the demand from the retailer, he must estimate the demand and place order to the manufacturer. In this case, the wholesaler has to carry more safety stock to protect itself from stockout.

The following is some strategies that can be considered to reduce the bullwhip effects through applying business intelligence:

- Forging strategic partners within the supply chain to share demand, inventory, and production information to reduce inventory. This decision is at the strategic level and will use long-term, historical data, integrated information on environmental changes and industry trend.
- Reducing demand uncertainty through data-mining customer purchasing patterns. This decision is at the tactical level. Aggregated data across business units will be needed to make informed decision on demand patterns.
- Reducing demand variability through reducing the variability inherent in the customer demand process. Possible approaches include Everyday Low Price (EDLP), which can lead to stable customer demand pattern, and vendor managed inventory (VMI) which can reduce order variability to the upstream of the supply chain. This practice is at the tactical level.
- Shortening lead time through data analysis and information sharing along the supply chain. This decision is at the operational level. Application of real-time monitoring tools will be needed to make timely decisions

11.2.2 Effects of information flow on material flow

The customer eventually gets physical products from a supply chain. Therefore, managing material flow is an important task facing a supply chain manager. The new paradigm in supply chain management is to replace inventory with information through cutting non-value-added activities.

In the past, inventory was the result of a misinformed decision to produce large batches of an item in order to take advantage of economies of scale. The good side of inventory is that it allows organizations to satisfy customer demand from stock. The down side of inventory is that it represents a large investment. In supply chain, inventory can be found in many places. Raw materials, parts and components are held at various stages of the supply chain, so are finished goods inventories that can be found at suppliers, manufacturers, distributors, and retailers. Obviously, large investment in inventory makes supply chain less competitive.

With the assistance of the Internet, information sharing among members of the supply chain has increased dramatically. As such, the material management decision can be better made if accurate demand information is available. The ubiquity of new telecommunications and the Internet has made real-time, on-line communications throughout the supply chain a reality. Effective information enables supply chains to reduce paperwork, improve communication, and reduce lead time. Ultimately, better information flow reduces inventory held due to distorted demand projection and accelerates the delivery of physical goods to the customer.

11.3 Data, Information, and Knowledge in Supply Chain Management

In the Information Age, productivity is based on not only labor and material, but also information and knowledge. The rapid progress of Internet and data warehouse technology has helped supply chain quickly respond to customer demands.

11.3.1 Data collection and organization

Data is a representation of facts in a formalized manner suitable for interpretation or processing. In supply chain management, customer names, production lead time, inventory levels are useful data for customer services. Data can be stored in some sort of technology system which is called a database. Managers may not always have the data they need to make effective business decisions. In this case, data may be derived from existing information.

The backbone of effective business decision is data. Companies may have obtained data from different sources, but these data are often not in a ready-to-use format. It is fairly common for the data analyst to spend 70% of data analysis time on preparing data. Data have many categories. Most common types include categorical and continuous:

- Categorical data or nominal data: customer gender and race
- Binary data: female and male
- Ordinal data: such as ranks in survey, strongly agree or disagree
- Continuous data: customer income level, purchasing amount

Data warehouse is an extension of database management. Data warehouses make full use of historic data to provide valuable information on products, suppliers, and customers. The process of data organizing and data mining include the following phases:

- Data - collect data on demand, supply, inventory, lead time, cost, and many other supply chain aspects
- Database - create client database, define attributes, processing transactional data
- Data warehouse - reduce and transform data, and
- Select data mining technique - summarizing, classification, clustering, regression, etc.

11.3.2 Information extraction

In supply chain management, managers suffer from an over-abundance of data. What they really want to know is what makes customer more likely to purchase the product produced by their companies. To meet this objective, fragmented data need to be filtered and condensed, and to be transformed into relevant information.

Information is different from data. Information is data processed for a certain purpose. Information has meaning. The relationship between information and data can be classified as follows:

- Contextualization: the purpose of data gathered is known. For example, customer purchasing data are gathered.
- Categorization: the units of analysis or key components of the data are known. For example, customers' incomes have been categorized.
- Calculation: the data has been analyzed mathematically or statistically. For example, the correlation of customer incomes and their purchasing behavior has been studied. This correlation has become information.
- Correction: errors in the data have been removed. For example, the number 668 was keyed in as 688 and this error has been corrected.
- Condensation: the data has been summarized in a more concise form. For example, the mean and standard deviation of demand for low fat ice cream have been summarized. The mean and standard deviation of demand for a product has become information.

Figure 11.1 illustrates the forward and backward flow of data and information in a supply chain. Information extracted from data and knowledge derived from information. However, if there is too much information, information can be reduced to data. One of the important issues in applying information for decision-making is to know how your competitors are applying the same information that you are using. Armed with this business intelligence, your company is able to identify business applications that will lead to top performance and may have applicability elsewhere.

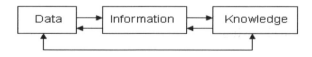

Figure 11.1. Three components of a knowledge system in supply chain[2]

---

[2] *Source*: adapted from Li, L and Xu, L (2001) "Knowledge-based problem solving," *Encyclopedia of Microcomputers,* Vol. 28, Supplement 7, 149-167.

11.3.3 Knowledge management

Knowledge is the fact or condition of knowing something with familiarity gained through experience or association[3]. According to Devenport and Prusak, "knowledge is a fluid mix of framed experience, values, contextual information, and expert insight that provides a framework for evaluating and incorporating new experiences and information. It originates and is applied in the minds of knowers." In a supply chain, knowledge becomes embedded not only in demand and inventory documents but also in the routines, processes, practices, and norms of the supply chain. Knowledge can be derived from information, just as information can be derived from data. Interestingly, a substantial amount of knowledge may be required to infer an essential set of data. These relationships are illustrated in Figure 11.1.

It has been recognized that supply chain management knowledge generation and application are at the core of existence for many organizations. It is obvious that the growing importance of knowledge of customer demand, inventory levels, supplier relations, and production scheduling helps strategic decision making.

Currently, information technology helps in the generation of business data, information, and knowledge. The usage of knowledge is moving from traditional knowledge-based problem solving to integrated knowledge-based problem solving in total enterprise integration (TEI) environment. Substantial efforts have been made in this direction including exploring and developing multi-dimensional knowledge structures.

11.4 Business Intelligence Methodology

11.4.1 Data warehousing

Data warehousing is an action that processes, constructs and uses data collected. The state-of-art technology in data warehousing has been the basis for applying collaborative planning, forecasting, and replenishment

---

[3] Merriam Webster's Collegiate Dictionary, 1996

(CPFR) in a supply chain. As early as 1966, Sam Walton, the founder of Wal-Mart, started to automate the Wal-Mart retail distribution system. Today, Wal-Mart possesses the largest commercial database in the world, which stores more than 7.5 terabytes of data including information such as inventory, forecasts, demographics, sale promotions, exchanges and returns, and market baskets (the items a shopper buys in a single trip). Wal-Mart's data warehouse is stocked with 65 weeks of data categorized by item, store, and day. Using data mining techniques, Wal-Mart develops accurate forecasts about customer demand. It keeps 65 weeks of point-of-sale data so that a full comparison between current year and past year for the same quarter can be made. The completeness of its data warehouse has been transformed to its competitive advantages through data mining solutions.

A data warehouse is a subject-oriented, integrated data mart in support of supply chain management decision-making. Data warehouse integrates various types of data. For example, it integrates multiple, heterogeneous data sources, such as relational databases, on-line transaction records, flat files, etc. It focuses on the modeling and analysis of data for decision makers. It provides a concise view around particular subject issues such as customer demographic information in a supply chain through extracting useful information and excluding data that are not useful in the decision support process.

Data warehouse is time-variant. The time horizon for the data warehouse is significantly longer than that of operational database that keeps transaction information. Data warehouse provides information from a historical perspective. For example, 65-week's point-of-sale information provides Wal-Mart historical information on sales.

11.4.2 Data mining

Data mining is a process of discovering knowledge in a warehouse of databases. Some people refer to this process as "knowledge discovery in databases" (KDD).

In supply chain management, data mining extracts previously unknown knowledge or patterns on demand, lead time, production, sales, etc. Data mining is an especially useful tool to profile customers and demand to a level not possible before. Some people refer to this as "one-to-one" marketing. Very soon, data mining will be a requirement of supply chain management rather than a competitive advantage as we see in today's market.

Data mining is a process of model building. Various models, such as clustering, decision tree, genetic algorithms, neural networks, statistics, hybrid models, etc., can be used to develop useful trends, patterns, correlation, as well as predictions based on historical data. In general, data mining extracts a portion of a data warehouse which is large enough to contain the significant information, yet small enough to manipulate quickly. It explores the data by searching for unknown or unanticipated trends to gain an understanding of market dynamics and generate new ideas. It modifies the data by creating, selecting, and transforming the variables to focus on decision formulation. It searches the database automatically to predict a desired outcome. It assesses the data by evaluating the usefulness of the findings from the data mining process.

11.5 Enhancing Value through Knowledge Management in Supply Chain

Distilling knowledge out of a supply chain data warehouse will be a major focus of managing the supply chain successfully today and for the years to come. The global network of supply and demand will depend increasingly on knowledge generation. This trend requires us to understand how to manage data, to transform data to relevant information, and to generate knowledge out of data and information. An ideal business intelligence system should permeate the entire supply chain, span all functions and members, and coordinate information flows.

Nevertheless, given good information and knowledge of the market will not automatically lead to competitive decisions. Managers need to absorb information and digest information to assist their decision-making. Better decisions may require different organizational governance, processes, and rules, such as collaboratively share data, information and knowledge on business with all the players in the same supply chain. Ultimately, managers are the ones who evaluate and control the business intelligence system rather than be controlled by it.

As part of the business intelligence strategy, a company needs to align the business intelligence environment with its business objectives, and develop a phased plan that is best suited to the current and evolving needs of its business. When a company decides to implement a business intelligence system, it should assess its staff's business intelligence awareness, the cultural fit of BI system, and the support from the top management. Upon completion the assessment, the company will have a better understanding of its information requirements and how the right BI system can help generate integrated, high quality information.

11.6 Summary

In this chapter, we have discussed the relationship among data, information, and knowledge. We have also discussed the latest development in data warehouse and data mining. As the next natural phase of data mining, Business Intelligence provides the supply chain with the technology foundation for building a complete knowledge system. The system allows the supply chain to rapidly develop and deploy data warehouses with an integrated array of query, reporting, analysis, alerting, data integration and BI application development capabilities.

Questions for Pondering

1. Discuss the possible benefits and risks of business intelligence facing supply chain players?
2. Supply chain controls extensive customer private information through customer purchasing history using data mining technology. What is the legal implication of this practice?
3. Will data mining and knowledge management improve forecasting accuracy of customer demand pattern and overall supply chain performance?

References

Devenport, T., and Prusak, L. (1998). *Working Knowledge: How Organizations Manage What They Know.* Boston, Mass.

Fernandez, G. (2002). *Data Mining Using SAS Application.* Chapman & Hall/CRC, New York.

Groth, R. (1998). *Data Mining.* Prentice Hall PTR, Upper Saddle River, New Jersey.

Li, L and Xu, L (2001). "Knowledge-based problem solving," *Encyclopedia of Microcomputers,* Vol. 28, Supplement 7, 149-167.

Manglik, Anupam (2006). "Increasing BI adoption: An enterprise approach." *Business Intelligence Journal*, 11(2), 44-52.

Appendix 3

Data Mining and Warehousing Tools and Vendors

There are a number of data mining tools available now on the market. The following list gives the names of a few representative data mining vendors.

- **BusinessMiner** by Business Objects: an integrated client-sided data mining solution with Business object's query, reporting, and OLAP solutions.
- **BI Suite** by Oracle: designed to provide enhanced reporting and analysis across firms' heterogeneous IT environments
- **Cognos 8 BI** platform by Cognos: including a search service that taps back-end ERP and CRM systems.
- **DataMind Professional Edition**, **DataMind DataCruncher** by DataMind Corporation: integrating relational database and data mining to provide business solution.
- **Enterprise Miner** by SAS Institute Inc.: This data mining solution is considered a process rather than a set of analytical tools. The process includes sampling data, exploring trends, modifying data, modeling data, and assessing data.
- **Falcon, Eagle, Colleague, AREAS, SkuPLAN, DataBase Mining Workstation** by HNC Software Inc.: a number of software applications based on neural network predictive models.
- **Intelligent Miner** by IBM: provide a high-end data mining solution.
- **KnowledgeSEEKER** by Angoss International Limited: performs data mining using decision tree techniques.
- **Scenario** by Cognos Sofware: a data mining solution for integration based on decision tree.
- **SPSS CHAID** by SPSS Inc.: a decision tree based data mining software tool for analysts that develops predictive models and produces tree diagrams.
- **XpertRule** by Attar Software USA: a development package, with in-built resource optimization for building knowledge based systems.

PART SIX

Supply Chain Performance and Evaluation

Chapter 12
Performance Measures: From Order Winning to Order Fulfillment

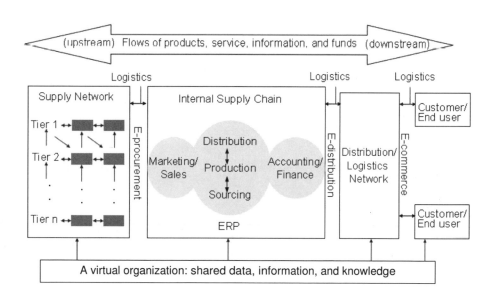

Chapter 12

Performance Measures: From Order Winning to Order Fulfillment

12.1 Introduction

Performance measure is a gauge typically applied to supply chain, as businesses search the crossover appeal of sustaining a competitive position in the market place. The front-runners, Dell Inc., Wal-Mart, and many other best practices are eager to capture and retain the right customers. Consequently, performance measures become crucial yardsticks for business to improve its market image and revenue. The well-known saying states, "You can't improve what you can't measure." As such, a few supply chain measurement models have been introduced recently. Among them, order winning, order fulfillment, financial measurement, the Supply Chain Operations Reference Model (SCOR), and the balanced scorecard are well accepted.

12.2 Order Winning in Supply Chain

12.2.1 Identify and capture the right customers

A good supply chain model wins orders in the market place. As such, the supply chain model begins with the careful selection of customers and the company's identity in the market place. Scholastic, the world's leading publisher and distributor of children's books serves as a good example of capturing the right customers. By applying a unique marketing strategy to attract the right customers, Scholastic has won orders by combining a diverse portfolio of titles, such as <u>Clifford the Big</u>

325

Red Dog, the Babysitters, and Harry Potter. This approach has led the direct-sale-to-classroom book club model in the United States. Scholastic treats each teacher as an individual customer and promotes its new titles to the teachers. Meanwhile, Scholastic's direct-sale-to-classroom book clubs provide students with a defined set of books and other media from which they can choose. Scholastic offers what it has in stock with a fixed period of time, responds to predictable order patterns, and manages prices relative to a given offer. Moreover, Scholastic works to enhance school-channel loyalty by providing credits for free books, classroom technology support, and syllabus-support materials. The direct-sale-to-classroom model has effectively created a barrier for Scholastic's competitors to enter the same market because the teachers are the point-of-order contact with students. Due to its effort to identify and capture the right customers, Scholastic has been able to double its revenue in the past years.

12.2.2 Create a customer-responsive supply chain

Linking supply chain operational processes directly to the customer order process serves to increase sensitivity to the ever-changing customer demands. Technology greatly enables supply chain responsiveness. As such, Dell Computer has completely automated its process to take hundreds and thousands of orders, translate them into millions of component requirements, and work directly with its suppliers to build and deliver products to meet individual customer requirements. Today, even if a company's operating model differs from that of Dell's, responding more efficiently to customer demands can be achieved through connecting to online devices.

Operating within the customer's operations is a more recent quick response strategy. This strategy has been the key to Dell's effort to dominate the corporate PC channel. By creating custom-tailored account pages for each corporate customer, Dell provides "in-customer" services, which includes customer-specific asset tagging, software image support that integrates Dell with customer operations. Similarly, Hewlett-

Packard has designed electronic appliances specifically for Wal-Mart to meet the customer profile of Wal-Mart.

Creating a customer-responsive supply chain through integrating the supplier's process with customer's order process has dramatically enhanced both Dell Inc. and Wal-Mart responsiveness. This level of response has provided both companies the cutting-edge competitiveness that is difficult for their competitors to replicate in a short time.

12.3 Fulfilling Orders in Supply Chain

12.3.1 Creating a collaborative, flexible and cost-efficient order fulfilling process

Order fulfillment comes close to an order winning business model. Leading companies employ a variety of strategies to reduce the cost of operations and maintain agility during order fulfillment process.

The collaborative planning, forecasting, and replenishment (CPFR) model that we discussed in chapters 1, 5 and 6 enables supply chain members to work together to design products that offer the greatest potential return across the supply chain and across the complete product lifecycle. Collaboration brings tremendous gains to companies seeking to reduce development costs and time-to-market cycle time.

Since acquired McDonnell Douglas Corporation and Rockwell International Corporation's A&D businesses, Boeing has collaborated with Dassault Systems. The Dassault's Catia computer-aided-design environment enables Boeing engineers worldwide to share design ideas among themselves and with its suppliers, which increases the flow of innovative ideas. This design collaboration process contributes significantly to supply chain performance in terms of faster time-to-market, increased revenue, reduction in the cost of goods sold, reduction in service and support expenses, and cut in research and development costs.

Flexible and cost-efficient supply chains have a strong focus on supply network consolidation. Dell consolidated its supply base, invested in make-to-order manufacturing capability, and implemented a demand-fulfillment system. All these moves make Dell extremely agile to schedule assembly production with real-time order data and fulfill customer orders in a JIT fashion. In a similar manner, Wal-Mart consolidated its supply base and invested heavily in demand management analysis. The result is better estimates on market demand and reduction in the order fulfillment cycle time.

To be more cost efficient and flexible, supply chain managers combine regional order fulfillment functions with centralized manufacturing and sourcing. It becomes increasingly common to centralize product design and development, and decentralize the order fulfillment task to the local markets. Sport-Obermeyer is a high-end fashion ski-wear designer and merchandise company, headquartered in Aspen, Colorado, USA. Although the company has a global supply network, it keeps its critical ski-wear design at its headquarters and outsources production to its joint venture partner, Obersport, a Hong Kong-based company. With this order fulfillment process, Sport-Obermeyer is able to introduce high-quality design products and maintain low manufacturing cost. Sport-Obermeyer's experience well depicts the importance of partnership selection strategy in order fulfillment that we discussed in Chapter 3.

12.3.2 Choosing the right technology to support supply chain operations

Technology is a core component in the order winning and order fulfillment process. E-auction, event management software, ERP, and private exchanges network, to name a few, are a handful of the technology innovations that are changing the way supply chains do business today. The Internet brings immediacy to supply chain event by enabling business partners to capture real-time customer demands and maximize visibility into the inventory positions, the location of in-transit inventory, and the supplier's production schedule. Wal-Mart's Retail Link system has been considered one of the best practices in technology management. This system provides vendors with up-to-date access to point-of-sale price, inventory positions, as well as estimated demands.

Furthermore, the system helps the vendors to position the right inventories and to talk with Wal-Mart about movement and promotions for their products.

However, simply investing in technology is not the whole story. By investing in a combination of technology and supply chain capabilities, companies like Dell and Wal-Mart have successfully leveraged their business models and created market differentiation. When integrated properly with supply chain infrastructure, technology can support a supply chain's market competitiveness, improve collaboration, increase production flexibility, and achieve cost-efficient results.

12.3.3 Fulfilling customer orders in supply chain

A successful order fulfilling process connects back-office information to front office operations. The fulfillment-focused processes focus on tight, synergistic relationships in areas such as warehousing, transportation, customer service, and the transaction flow. Working together, these innovations are helping companies reduce order-entry-cycle times, respond to order-fulfillment needs more effectively, and manage customers' expectations more reliably.

Amazon.com, Gap, and Toys "R" Us are a few good examples of "e-tailers". These retailers show online customers precisely what is available in the warehouse. Integrating order winning in the front-end office and order fulfillment in the back-end office makes it possible for these companies to formulate better and timely decisions about transportation, distribution, manufacturing, and marketing. A more sophisticated function lies in integrating event management and supply chain visibility systems. This innovation validates customer-requested shipping dates, notifies a customer when an out-of-stock item replenishes.

12.4 Financial Measurement

Supply chain involves managing the flow of material, information, and funds. Consequently, financial measures are the most commonly used yardstick to evaluate performance. Good performance on cost, revenue and profit gives a company a solid market presence and attracts investors to make investment decisions.

12.4.1 Inventory measures

Inventory is considered an investment because it is an asset created for future use. Additionally, inventory ties up funds that might be used for operations that are more profitable.

Usually, companies want to have just enough inventories to cover demand. Excess inventory is a cost. Typical inventory performance measures include average annual aggregate inventory value, weeks of supply, and inventory turns.

Average aggregate inventory value is the total value of all inventory including raw material, work-in-process inventory and finished good inventory. Average aggregate inventory is expressed in dollar values. The methods used to estimate aggregate inventory value, weeks of supply, and inventory turns are discussed in Section 7.2.6.

12.4.2 Relationship of supply chain variables to income statement

The outcomes of business models and supply chain activities affect a company's financial performance as shown in its income statement. An income statement indicates the company's financial performance, estimates its cash flow, and assesses its future growth. Table 12.1 shows the correlation between income statement items, supply chain activities, and performances.

Net sales are related to demand management and customer relations management, which is a key indicator of a firm's order winning and fulfilling capability and revenue.

Cost of goods sold is determined through the financial arrangements with suppliers, production costs, and other overhead costs. Quality problems in the supply chain can also increase the cost of goods produced, so as the cost of goods sold. On the other hand, increasing the percent of on-time delivery from suppliers has the effect of reducing amount of safety inventory, which leads to reduced inventory cost, and cost of goods sold.

Selling and administrative expenses represent expenses needed to sell products or deliver services. These expenses include salaries, commissions, advertising, freight, shipping, warehouse management, and depreciation of sales equipment. The effect on selling and administrative activities is order fulfillment rate and speed, logistics, transportation, and overhead costs.

Inventory expenses relate to inventory control policies, supply network, and demand prediction. Better demand estimation and reliable suppliers can reduce the level of safety stock. Both reorder point inventory control system (discussed in Chapter 7) and risk-pooling method (discussed in Supplement 7.2) contribute to less cycle inventory and safety stock.

Other well-accepted financial measures include cash-to-cash cycle time, working capitals, return-on-investment, and return-on-assets.

Cash-to-cash cycle time measures the number of days between the date a company pays its suppliers for material to the date it gets paid by its customers. The shorter the cash-to-cash cycle time the better. A long the cash-to-cash cycle may indicate that the company has a large volume of accounts receivable.

Accounts receivable may be large due to sales promotions such as "no pay for 6 months," or customers with bad credit history. The cash tied up in the accounts receivable costs the company other profitable investment opportunities.

Return-on-assets (ROA) is an important financial measure, which indicates how effective a supply chain capitalizes its resource. ROA is achieved through dividing the net income by total assets. Reducing the aggregate inventory investment reduces a company's total assets. Consequently, reduction in aggregate inventory increases return-on-assets if the net sales remain the same. The appropriate asset management strategy is not to have the least amount of inventory, but to have proper amount of the right products in stock.

Working capital, which is money used to finance ongoing operations, is a surrogate indicator for inventory turns and weeks of supply. Increase in inventory investment requires increased payments to suppliers. As such, decreasing weeks of inventory supply or increase inventory turns helps reduce the pressure on working capital and improves cost performance.

Table 12.1. Income statement and performance measures

Income Statement Items	Supply Chain Management Variables	Performance Measures
Net sales	Demand management CRM Order winning	Number of orders, revenue
Cost of goods sold	Purchasing Supply network Production planning & control	Cost & profit
Selling & administrative expenses	Order processing Transportation Warehousing Inventory costs Packaging Other support activities	Order fulfillment costs, Transportation & logistics costs, & overhead costs
Inventory expenses	Inventory control Inventory carrying cost	Costs, ROA, ROI
Income before taxes	Orders Revenue	Profit contribution

12.4.3 The shortcomings of financial performance

Financial measures are very important indicators of supply chain performance, but it sometimes cannot reflect a firm's true performance. For example, when gas price goes up, trucking companies will experience higher fuel cost and that results in lower profit. Therefore, in recent years, more comprehensive performance measurement models have been introduced to measure supply chain performance. The Supply Chain Operations Reference Model (SCOR) and the balanced scorecard model are two commonly applied supply chain measurement approaches. We are going to introduce these two models in the following sections.

12.5 The Supply Chain Operations Reference Model (SCOR)

The Supply Chain Operations Reference Model (SCOR) is introduced by the Supply-Chain Council (SCC), an independent, not-for-profit, global corporation with membership open to all companies and organizations interested in applying and advancing the state-of-the-art in supply-chain management systems and practices. The SCC was organized in 1996 by Pittiglio Rabin Todd & McGrath (PRTM) and AMR Research, and initially included 69 voluntary member companies. Now, the Council has approximately 750 members worldwide and has established international chapters in Europe, Japan, Korea, Latin America, Australia, New Zealand and Southeast Asia.

The SCC's members represent manufacturers, distributors, and retailers. Other important contributors to the advancement of the SCOR-model are the technology suppliers and implementers, the academicians, and the government organizations. The SCOR-model presented in Table 12.2 is the fifth version. In this version, e-Business best practices are introduced. Currently, a major revision of the metrics is planned and will be available in future versions.

The SCOR model integrates business operations with performance measures. For example, customer service (that includes fill rate, on-time delivery, and product returns) is related to plan (that includes demand forecast, product pricing and inventory management) as shown by an "X" in the cell. The performance categories in the SCOR model include customer service, internal efficiency, demand flexibility, and product development. The first column of Table 12.2 illustrates business operations, which include plan, source, make, and deliver.

At the request of the Supply Chain Council, all companies that use the SCOR-model should share their implementation experience with the Supply-Chain Council members. Consequently, the wide-spread use of the SCOR model results in better customer-supplier relationships, better system integration, and better knowledge dissemination of best supply chain practices.

Table 12.2. SCOR-model Version 5.0[1]

Performance Categories		Customer Service	Internal Efficiency	Demand Flexibility	Product Development
Business Operations		. Fill rate . On-time delivery . Product returns	.Inventory turns .Return on sales .Cash-to-cash	.Cycle times .Upside flexibility .Outside flexibility	.New product sales % revenue .Cycle time
Plan	Demand forecast	X	X	X	
	Product pricing	X	X		
	Inventory management	X	X	X	
Source	Procurement		X	X	
	Credit & collection	X	X		
Make	Product design	X			X
	Production scheduling		X	X	
	Facility management	X	X		
Delivery	Order management	X	X		X
	Delivery scheduling	X	X		

---

[1] Supply Chain Council's SCOR model, www.supply-chain.org.

12.6 The Balanced Scorecard

Using the balanced scorecard to measure business performance was initiated by Kaplan and Norton in 1992. The balanced scorecard aligns an organization's performance measures with its strategic plan and goals. By 1998, 60 percent of the Fortune 1000 companies had experimented with the balanced scorecard[2]. Companies such as Mobil Oil, Tenneco, AT&T, Intel, and Ernest & Young reported noticeable success using the balanced scorecard approach.

The balanced scorecard takes account of both financial and non-financial indices for measuring short-term and long-term performance. The balanced scorecard approach includes four areas: customer, financial, learning and growth, and internal business processes. Figure 12.1 provides the framework of the balanced scorecard.

Customer perspective focuses on customer requirements and satisfaction including customer satisfaction ratings, customer retention, new customer acquisition, customer valued attributes, and market share.

Financial perspective addresses revenue growth, product mix, cost reduction, productivity, asset utilization and investment strategy.

Learning and growth focuses on the organization's people, systems, and procedures including intellectual assets, re-training employees, enhancing information technology and systems, and employee satisfaction.

Internal business process addresses the critical business process issues such as quality, flexibility, innovation, and time-based measures.

The four measurement areas reflect the strategic goal of an organization or a supply chain, and are linked together to measure both the long-term and short-term performance. The process of developing a balanced scorecard begins with defining the company's strategy, then translates company's strategy to operational activities, and finally translates the scorecard to a system of performance measures.

---

[2] Silk, S, (1998) "Automating the balanced scorecard," *Management Accounting*, May 1998, 38-44.

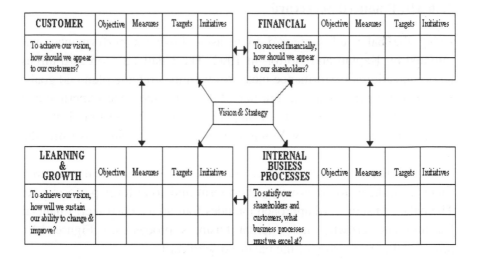

Figure 12.1. Balanced scorecard[3]

12.7 The Future of Supply Chain Management

Supply chain is facing a paradigm change in e-Biz environment as shown in Table 12.3. Four noticeable paradigm changes are summarized as follows.

(i)   Supply chain operations are moving from cost management to revenue management, thus emphasizing on customer relationship management and order winning;

(ii) Supply chain operations are moving from functional focus to order fulfillment process focus, thus emphasizing on the integrated goods and service delivery flow;

(iii) Supply chain operations are moving from inventory management to information management, thus emphasize on quick response systems and knowledge management; and

---

[3] R.S. Kaplan and D.P. Norton, (1996) "Linking the balanced scorecard to strategy." *California Management Review*, 39(1), 53-79.

(iv) Supply chain operations are moving from arm's length transactional relationship to strategic alliances, thus emphasizing on win-win strategic collaborative relationship.

Table 12.3. The new paradigm

Existing Paradigm	New Paradigm	Indicators
Cost management	Revenue management	CRM and order winning
Functional	Order fulfillment process	Integrated goods and service delivery flow
Inventory management	Information management	Quick response and knowledge management
Arm's length transactional relationship	strategic alliances	win-win strategic collaborative relationship

The term, "collaboration" has become today's hottest buzzword. To be competitive, a supply chain will have to be cost-efficient, responsive, flexible, and agile. Consequently, it will be able to provide the right product, in the right quantity, at the right place and time, and in right quality.

Today, many companies see global expansion of markets and use of foreign suppliers as strategies for enhanced profitability and competitiveness. Dell, Sport Obermeyer, and many other market leaders are profiting greatly from its use of global supply chain. Global expansion of the supply chain has also increased the need for third party and fourth-party supply chain service providers. UPS has acquired over twenty-five transportation and logistics companies in recent years to create a global logistics footprint network. At the same time, UPS has been building up a technology infrastructure to help customers control the global supply chain and enhance e-commerce capabilities.

The future of supply chain management lies in globalization, collaboration, technology application, and process re-engineering.

Questions for Pondering

1. In building supply chain competencies, what are the trade-offs that must be considered?
2. Explain why cost-based performance measures are important to a company?
3. What is the realistic way to measure a supply chain that has many companies?
4. What makes a performance measurement system "world class"?

References

Christopher, M. (1998). "Logistics and Supply Chain Management," 2nd edition, Great Britain: Prentice Hall.

Gable, R. (1997). "The history of consumer goods: How supply-chain management is driving the next consumer goods revolution," *Manufacturing Systems*, 15(10), 70-84.

Kaplan, R.S. and Norton, D.P. (1992). "The balanced scorecard – Measures that drive performance." *Harvard Business Review*, 70(1), 71-79.

Silk, S. (1998). "Automating the balanced scorecard," *Management Accounting*, May 1998, 38-44.

Subject Index

Company Index